HOLT McDOUGAL

Ancient World History

PATTERNS OF INTERACTION

Guided Reading Workbook

HOLT McDOUGAL
a division of Houghton Mifflin Harcourt

Contents

How to Use This Book

The purpose of this *Guided Reading Workbook* is to help you read and understand your history textbook, *Ancient World History: Patterns of Interaction*. You can use this *Guided Reading Workbook* in two ways.

1. **Use the *Guided Reading Workbook* side-by-side with your history book.**

- Turn to the section that you are going to read in the textbook. Then, next to the book, put the pages from the *Guided Reading Workbook* that accompany that section. All of the heads in the *Guided Reading Workbook* match the heads in the textbook.

- Use the *Guided Reading Workbook* to help you read and organize the information in the textbook.

2. **Use the *Guided Reading Workbook* to study the material that will appear in the chapter tests.**

- Reread the summary of every chapter.

- Review the definitions of the **Terms and Names** in the *Guided Reading Workbook*.

- Review the graphic organizer that you created as you read the summaries.

- Review your answers to questions.

Strategy: Read the **Terms and Names** and the definition of each. The **Terms and Names** are in dark type in the section.

Name _____ Class _____ Date _____

European Renaissance and Reformation

Section 1

Italy: Birthplace of the Renaissance

Terms and Names

Renaissance Period of rebirth of art and learning in Europe lasting from about 1300 to 1600

humanism Focus on human potential and achievements

secular Concerned with worldly rather than spiritual matters

patrons People who financially supported artists

perspective Art technique that re-creates three dimensions

vernacular Use of native language instead of classical Latin

Before You Read

In the last section, you read about the development of the Incan Empire.

In this section, you will learn about the beginning of the Renaissance.

As You Read

Use an outline to organize each summary's main ideas and details.

ITALY'S ADVANTAGES
(Pages 471–472)
Why did the Renaissance begin in Italy?

The years 1300 to 1600 saw a rebirth of learning and culture in Europe called the **Renaissance.** This rebirth spread north from Italy. It began there for three reasons. First, Italy had several important cities. Cities were places where people exchanged ideas. Second, these cities included a class of merchants and bankers who were becoming wealthy and powerful. This class strongly believed in the idea of individual achievement. Third, Italian artists and scholars were inspired by the ruined buildings and other reminders of classical Rome.

1. What are three reasons why the Renaissance began in Italy?

_____

_____

CLASSICAL AND WORLDLY VALUES (Pages 472–473)
What new values did people hold?

Interest in the classical past led to an important value in Renaissance culture—**humanism.** This was a deep interest in what people have already achieved as well as what they could achieve in the future. Scholars did not try to connect classical writings to Christian teaching. Instead, they tried to understand them on their own terms.

Original content © Houghton Mifflin Harcourt Publishing Company. Additions and changes to the original content are the responsibility of the instructor.

181   Guided Reading Workbook

Strategy: Use a graphic organizer to help you organize information in the section.

Strategy: Read the summary. It contains the main ideas and the key information under the head.

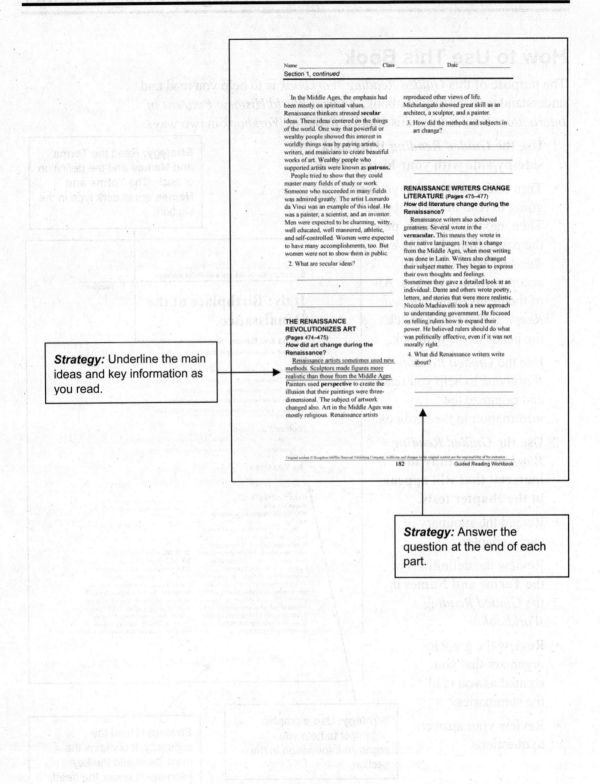

Name _____ Class _____ Date _____

Section 1, *continued*

In the Middle Ages, the emphasis had been mostly on spiritual values. Renaissance thinkers stressed **secular** ideas. These ideas centered on the things of the world. One way that powerful or wealthy people showed this interest in worldly things was by paying artists, writers, and musicians to create beautiful works of art. Wealthy people who supported artists were known as **patrons.**

People tried to show that they could master many fields of study or work. Someone who succeeded in many fields was admired greatly. The artist Leonardo da Vinci was an example of this ideal. He was a painter, a scientist, and an inventor. Men were expected to be charming, witty, well educated, well mannered, athletic, and self-controlled. Women were expected to have many accomplishments, too. But women were not to show them in public.

2. What are secular ideas?

_____
_____

THE RENAISSANCE REVOLUTIONIZES ART
(Pages 474–475)
How **did art change during the Renaissance?**
    Renaissance artists sometimes used new methods. Sculptors made figures more realistic than those from the Middle Ages. Painters used **perspective** to create the illusion that their paintings were three-dimensional. The subject of artwork changed also. Art in the Middle Ages was mostly religious. Renaissance artists

reproduced other views of life. Michelangelo showed great skill as an architect, a sculptor, and a painter.

3. How did the methods and subjects in art change?

_____
_____

RENAISSANCE WRITERS CHANGE LITERATURE (Pages 475–477)
How **did literature change during the Renaissance?**
    Renaissance writers also achieved greatness. Several wrote in the **vernacular.** This means they wrote in their native languages. It was a change from the Middle Ages, when most writing was done in Latin. Writers also changed their subject matter. They began to express their own thoughts and feelings. Sometimes they gave a detailed look at an individual. Dante and others wrote poetry, letters, and stories that were more realistic. Niccolò Machiavelli took a new approach to understanding government. He focused on telling rulers how to expand their power. He believed rulers should do what was politically effective, even if it was not morally right.

4. What did Renaissance writers write about?

_____
_____

182   Guided Reading Workbook

Strategy: Underline the main ideas and key information as you read.

Strategy: Answer the question at the end of each part.

The last page of each section of the *Guided Reading Workbook* ends with a graphic organizer that will help you better understand the information in the section. Use the graphic organizer to take notes as you read. The notes can help you to prepare for the section quiz and chapter tests.

Name _____ Class _____ Date _____

Section 1, *continued*

As you read about the rebirth of learning and the arts in Italy, write notes to answer the questions.

In Italy, thriving urban centers, a wealthy merchant class, and the classical heritage of Greece and Rome encouraged the development of new ideas and values.

1. How did humanism influence the growth of learning?	
2. How did ideas about piety and a simple life change?	
3. What role did patrons of the arts play in the development of Renaissance ideas?	

Styles in art and literature changed as artists and writers emphasized the individual.

4. What effects did the emphasis on individuals have on painters and sculptors?	
5. How did writers reflect Renaissance values in their work?	
6. How did the writing of Petrarch, Boccaccio, and Machiavelli demonstrate the values of humanism?	

183   Guided Reading Workbook

The first page of each section of the Guided Reading Workbook provides an organizer that will help you better understand the information in the section. Use the graphic organizer to take notes as you read. The notes can help you to prepare for the section quiz and chapter test.

The Peopling of the World

Section 1

Human Origins in Africa

Terms and Names

artifact Remains, such as tools, jewelry, and other human-made objects

culture People's way of life

hominid Human or other creature that walks upright

Paleolithic Age Old Stone Age

Neolithic Age New Stone Age

technology Ways of applying knowledge, tools, and inventions to meet needs

Homo sapiens Species name for modern humans

Before You Read

In this section, you will read about the earliest humans.

As You Read

Use a diagram to list the advances of the hominids discussed in the section.

SCIENTISTS SEARCH FOR HUMAN ORIGINS (Pages 5–7)
How do scientists learn about early humans?

People can learn about the past by using written records. But these records cover only the last 5,000 years or so of human life. To learn about the time before written records, scientists called archaeologists use special skills and tools.

Archaeologists work at places called digs. They uncover **artifacts:** tools, jewelry, or other things made by people. Archaeologists also dig up bones—the bones of ancient humans and of the animals that lived with them. Some of these bones have become fossils, meaning they have survived over time because they were preserved in stone. By studying bones and artifacts, scientists learn about the **culture,** or way of life, of early humans.

In the early 1970s, archaeologists in East Africa found the footprints of humanlike beings, called australopithecines. Humans and other creatures that walk upright, such as australopithecines, are called **hominids.** These footprints were made about 3.5 million years ago.

Because these early beings walked upright, they could travel long distances more easily than four-footed ones. They could also use their free arms to carry food, tools, and children. They also had an opposable thumb that could move across the palms of their hands and touch their other fingers. The opposable thumb allowed them to pick up and hold objects.

1. What were the first humanlike beings, and where were they found?

_____

THE OLD STONE AGE BEGINS
(Pages 7–8)
What advances did hominids make during the Stone Age?

Humans made important advances during a period called the Stone Age, when people used tools made of stone. At this time, they also began to use fire and learned to speak.

Scientists divide the Stone Age into two parts. The **Paleolithic Age,** or Old Stone Age, began about 2.5 million years ago and lasted until about 8000 B.C. The **Neolithic Age,** or New Stone Age, went from about 8000 B.C. to around 3000 B.C.

Much of the Old Stone Age overlapped the Ice Age, when the earth was colder than it is now. Huge sheets of ice—glaciers—covered much of the land. About 10,000 years ago, the earth's temperature increased. The ice sheets grew smaller. People began to roam wider stretches of land.

In East Africa, archaeologists found a hominid fossil they named *Homo habilis*. It means "man of skill." The fossil was given this name because the site also held tools made of lava rock. *Homo habilis* lived about 2.5 million years ago.

About 1.6 million years ago, another kind of hominid lived. This one was *Homo erectus*. *Homo erectus* began to use tools for special purposes. That is when **technology** began. *Homo erectus* dug for food in the ground, cut meat from animal bones, and scraped animal skins. *Homo erectus* also used fire and may have had spoken language.

2. Who were *Homo habilis* and *Homo erectus*?

_____

_____

_____

_____

_____

THE DAWN OF MODERN HUMANS; NEW FINDINGS ADD TO KNOWLEDGE (Pages 8–13)
Who were the Neanderthals and Cro-Magnons?

Many scientists believe that *Homo erectus* eventually developed into humans, or ***Homo sapiens.***

Scientists once thought that Neanderthals were ancestors of modern humans but no longer do. These hominids appeared 200,000 years ago. They lived in caves or built shelters of wood or animal skins. At one time, they were thought to be rough and wild people. Now scientists think that they may have held religious beliefs. These people found ways to survive the freezing cold of the Ice Age. About 30,000 years ago, though, the Neanderthals strangely disappeared.

About 10,000 years before these people vanished, the Cro-Magnons appeared. Their bodies were just like those of modern people. Scientists think that these people worked with one another in planning large-scale hunts of animals. They may have also had more skill at speaking than did the Neanderthals. Because they had these skills, the Cro-Magnons were better at finding food. That may explain why Cro-Magnons survived and Neanderthals did not.

Scientists are continuing to work on many sites in Africa. New discoveries continually add to what we know about human origins.

3. How is the species *Homo sapiens* different from earlier hominids?

_____

_____

_____

_____

_____

Section 1, *continued*

As you read about early humans, fill in the chart below by describing the
physical traits and achievements of each species of hominid listed.

Name	Traits	Achievements
1. Australopithecines		
2. *Homo habilis*		
3. *Homo erectus*		
4. Neanderthals		
5. Cro-Magnons		

Fill in the chart below to compare the Old Stone Age and the New Stone
Age.

Stone Age	Began	Ended	Achievements
Paleolithic Age			
Neolithic Age			

The Peopling of the World

Section 2

Humans Try to Control Nature

Terms and Names

nomad Person who wanders from place to place

hunter-gatherer Person whose food supply depends on hunting animals and collecting plant foods

Neolithic Revolution Agricultural revolution that occurred during the Neolithic period

slash-and-burn farming Early farming method that some groups used to clear fields

domestication Taming of animals

Before You Read

In the last section, you read about the earliest humans.

In this section, you will read about the development of agriculture and a settled way of life.

As You Read

Use an outline to organize the section's main ideas and details.

EARLY ADVANCES IN TECHNOLOGY AND ART

(Pages 14–15)

What advances occurred in technology and art?

The first humans had faced a struggle for survival. For thousands and thousands of years, they had two concerns: finding food and protecting themselves. They used fire, built shelters, made clothes, and developed spoken language. These areas of life are all part of culture. Human culture changed over time as new tools replaced old and people tested new ideas. Later some modern humans increased the pace of change.

The people who had lived in the early part of the Old Stone Age were **nomads.** They moved from place to place. They were **hunter-gatherers.**

They found food by hunting and gathering nuts, berries, and roots. The

Cro-Magnon people, who came later, made tools to help them in their search.

These early modern humans used many tools—more than 100 different ones. They used stone, bone, and wood. They made knives, hooks, and bone needles.

Cro-Magnon people also created works of art, including paintings. Thousands of years ago, Stone Age artists mixed charcoal, mud, and animal blood to make paint. They used this paint to draw pictures of animals on cave walls and rocks.

1. In what ways did Cro-Magnon people change human culture?

_____

_____

THE BEGINNINGS OF AGRICULTURE (Pages 15–16)
What was the Neolithic Revolution?

For centuries, humans lived by hunting and gathering. Humans lived in small groups of 25 to 70 people. They often returned to a certain area in the same season each year because they knew it would be rich in food at that time.

Over the years, some humans realized that they could leave plant seeds in an area one year and find plants growing there the next year. This was the beginning of a new part of human life: farming.

Scientists think that the climate became warmer all around the world at about the same time. Humans' new knowledge about planting seeds combined with this warmer climate to create the **Neolithic Revolution**—the agricultural revolution that occurred during the Neolithic period.

Instead of relying on gathering food, people began to produce food. One early farming method was **slash-and-burn farming.** That meant cutting trees and burning them to clear a field. The ashes were used to fertilize the soil.

Along with growing food, they also began to raise animals. They tamed horses, dogs, goats, and pigs. **Domestication** is the taming of animals.

Archaeologists have studied a site in the northeastern part of modern Iraq. It is called Jarmo. The people who lived in this region began farming and raising animals about 9,000 years ago.

2. How did life change during the Neolithic Revolution?

_____

_____

VILLAGES GROW AND PROSPER (Pages 16–18)
How did the growth of farming villages change life?

People began to farm in many spots all over the world. The study of one village in modern-day Turkey shows what early farming communities were like.

The village called Catal Huyuk grew on the good land near a river. Some workers grew wheat, barley, and peas. Others raised sheep and cattle. Because these workers produced enough food for all the people, others could begin developing other kinds of skills. Some made pots out of clay that they baked. Others worked as weavers. Some artists decorated the village. Archaeologists have found wall paintings that show animals and hunting scenes. They have found evidence that the people had a religion, too.

Early farming villagers had problems, too. If the farm crop failed or the lack of rain caused a drought, people starved. Floods and fires caused damage and death. With more people living near each other than before, diseases spread easily. Still, some of these early villages grew into great cities.

3. What problems did early farming villages face?

_____

_____

As you read this section, take notes to answer questions about the development of agriculture.

People of the Old Stone Age were nomads who wandered from place to place in search of food.

1. How did hunter-gatherers use technology to improve their chances of survival?	2. What types of art did Paleolithic people create?

About 10,000 years ago, an agricultural revolution began.

3. What factors led to the agricultural revolution?	4. How did farming develop and spread worldwide?

Farming led to a settled way of life.

5. What were some of the cultural achievements of Neolithic villagers?	6. What problems did early villagers face?

Guided Reading Workbook

Section 3

Civilization Case Study: Ur in Sumer

Terms and Names

civilization Culture with advanced cities, specialized workers, complex institutions, record keeping, and improved technology

specialization Development of skills in a specific kind of work

artisan Skilled worker that makes goods by hand

institution Long-lasting pattern of organization in a community

scribe Professional record keeper

cuneiform Wedge-shaped writing developed in Sumer

Bronze Age Time when people began using bronze

barter Trading goods and services without money

ziggurat Pyramid-shaped monument; part of a temple in Sumer

Before You Read

In the last section, you read about the development of agriculture and a settled way of life.

In this section, you will read about factors leading to the rise of civilizations.

As You Read

Use a chart to summarize characteristics of the civilization at Sumer.

VILLAGES GROW INTO CITIES
(Pages 19–20)
What changed as villages grew into cities?

Over time, farmers developed new tools—hoes, sickles, and plow sticks. These helped them grow even more food. They decided to plant larger areas of land. The people in some villages began to irrigate the land, bringing water to new areas. People invented the wheel for carts and the sail for boats. These new inventions made it easier to travel between distant villages and to trade.

Life became more complex as the villages began to grow. People were divided into social classes. Some people had more wealth and power than others. People began to worship gods and goddesses that they felt would protect their crops and make their harvests large.

1. How did life become more complex?

_____

_____

_____

_____

HOW CIVILIZATION DEVELOPS
(Pages 20–21)
What makes a civilization?

One of the first civilizations arose in Sumer. It was in Mesopotamia, between the Tigris and Euphrates rivers of modern Iraq. A **civilization** has five features.

First, a civilization has advanced cities that contain many people and serve as centers for trade.

Second, civilizations have specialized workers. **Specialization** is the development of skills needed for one specific kind of work. Skilled workers who make goods by hand are called **artisans.**

Third, civilizations have complex institutions. Government, organized religion, and an economy are examples of complex **institutions.**

A fourth feature of civilizations is record keeping, which is needed to keep track of laws, debts, and payments. It also creates the need for writing. **Scribes** were people who used writing to keep records. **Cuneiform,** which means "wedge shaped," was a form of writing invented in Sumer.

Fifth, civilizations have improved technology that can provide new tools and methods to solve problems.

Sumer had all the features of a civilization. One of the new technologies in Sumer was making a metal called bronze. The term **Bronze Age** refers to the time when people began using bronze to make tools and weapons.

2. Name the five features of a civilization.

_____

_____

_____

_____

_____

CIVILIZATION EMERGES IN UR
(Pages 22–23)
What was civilization like in Ur?

One of the early cities of Sumer was named Ur. The city was surrounded by walls built of mud dried into bricks. Ur held about 30,000 people. Social classes included rulers and priests, traders, craft workers, and artists.

Farmers outside the city walls raised the food for them all. Some workers dug ditches to carry water to the fields. Officials of the city government planned all this activity.

Inside the city, metalworkers made bronze points for spears. Potters made clay pots. Traders met people from other areas. They traded the spear points and pots for goods that Ur could not produce. This way of trading goods and services without money is called **barter.** Sometimes their deals were written down by scribes.

Ur's most important building was the temple. Part of the temple was a **ziggurat,** a pyramid-shaped structure. Priests there led the city's religious life.

3. What social classes existed in Ur?

_____

_____

_____

_____

_____

As you read this section, fill in the boxes below. List the social and economic changes that led to the development of cities and the rise of civilizations.

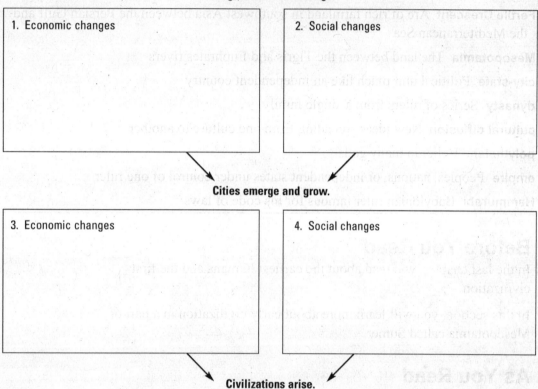

Village and town life begin.

1. Economic changes

2. Social changes

Cities emerge and grow.

3. Economic changes

4. Social changes

Civilizations arise.

Section 1

City-States in Mesopotamia

Terms and Names

Fertile Crescent Arc of rich farmland in southwest Asia between the Persian Gulf and the Mediterranean Sea

Mesopotamia The land between the Tigris and Euphrates rivers

city-state Political unit much like an independent country

dynasty Series of rulers from a single family

cultural diffusion New ideas spreading from one culture to another

polytheism Belief in many gods

empire Peoples, nations, or independent states under control of one ruler

Hammurabi Babylonian ruler famous for his code of laws

Before You Read

In the last chapter, you read about the earliest humans and the first civilization.

In this section, you will learn more about early civilization in a part of Mesopotamia called Sumer.

As You Read

Use a chart to identify Sumer's environmental problems and solutions.

GEOGRAPHY OF THE FERTILE CRESCENT (Pages 29–30)
What problems did the Sumerians face?

There is an arc of rich land in Southwest Asia that is called the **Fertile Crescent.** Two of its rivers, the Tigris and the Euphrates, flood in the spring. This flooding leaves rich mud, called silt, in the plain between the rivers. Because of this, many thousands of years ago humans began to settle in that plain, known as Mesopotamia. They grew wheat and barley. It was here that the first civilization began.

About 3300 B.C., the Sumerians moved into this region and settled. They faced three problems. First, the floods were not regular, and once they passed, the hot sun

quickly baked the land into clay. Second, the small farming villages had no protection against enemies. Third, the area lacked stone, wood, and metal to use for tools.

The Sumerians solved these problems. They dug irrigation ditches from the river to their fields so they could bring water to their crops. They built walls of baked mud around their villages for defense. Because they could grow more food than they needed, they traded the extra for stone, wood, and metal from other lands.

1. How did the Sumerians solve the problems they faced?

_____

_____

SUMERIANS CREATE CITY-STATES (Page 30)
How did the Sumerians govern?

Several large city-states were at the center of the Sumerian world. These **city-states** had control over a surrounding area. They could act independently, much like a country does today. Slowly, some people rose to power in a number of the city-states. They became rulers, as did their children after them. Rule of an area by the same family is called a **dynasty.**

As population and trade grew, Sumerians came into contact with other peoples. Their own ideas affected others. The Sumerians also got ideas from other cultures. This process of spreading ideas or products is called **cultural diffusion.**

2. Who governed the city-states?

_____

_____

SUMERIAN CULTURE (Pages 31–32)
What did the Sumerians believe and accomplish?

The Sumerians believed in **polytheism,** or many gods. Each god had power over different forces of nature or parts of their lives. Sumerians believed that people were just the servants of the gods. Souls of the dead went to a joyless place under the earth's crust. These views spread to other areas and shaped the ideas of other peoples.

Society was divided into social classes. At the top were the priests and kings, after whom came wealthy merchants. Next were workers in fields and workshops. Slaves made up the lowest level. Women could enter most careers and could own

property. But there were some limits on them.

The people of Sumer invented the sail, the wheel, and the plow. They were the first to use bronze. They also developed the first writing system—on clay tablets. They invented arithmetic and geometry, which they used to help build large structures.

3. How was Sumerian society organized?

_____

_____

THE FIRST EMPIRE BUILDERS (Pages 32–34)
Who built the world's first empire?

Centuries of fighting between the city-states made the Sumerians weak. In 2350 B.C., the conqueror Sargon defeated Sumer and captured other cities to the north. He built the world's first **empire.** An empire brings together several peoples, nations, or previously independent states. It puts them under the control of one ruler.

A few hundred years later, a different group of people conquered the Sumerians. These people built a capital at Babylon, establishing the Babylonian Empire. They were led by a king named **Hammurabi.** He is famous for his code of laws. It was a harsh code that punished people for wrong doing. However, it also made it clear that the government had some responsibility for taking care of its people.

4. Why was Hammurabi's Code important?

_____

_____

As you read about the Sumerians, fill in the chart below to explain how they solved problems they faced.

The Problems		The Solutions
1. With flooding of the rivers unpredictable, how could farmers water their fields during the dry summer months?	→	
2. With no natural barriers, how could villagers protect themselves?	→	
3. With limited natural resources, how could Sumerians get the materials for tools and buildings?	→	
4. How should the Sumerian city-states be ruled?	→	
5. What could be done to please the gods and earn their protection in life?	→	

List examples of Sumerian culture in the boxes below.

Religion	Literature	Architecture	Inventions

Section 2

Pyramids on the Nile

Terms and Names

delta Marshy area at the mouth of a river

Narmer King of Upper Egypt who united Upper and Lower Egypt

pharaoh Egyptian ruler thought of as a god

theocracy Government in which the ruler is considered to be a divine figure

pyramid Resting place for Egyptian kings after death

mummification Process by which a body is preserved after death

hieroglyphics Egyptian writing system

papyrus Plant used to make a paper-like material

Before You Read

In the last section, you read about the city-states that arose in Mesopotamia.

In this section, you will learn about early civilization along the Nile.

As You Read

Use a web diagram to summarize Egyptian achievements.

THE GEOGRAPHY OF EGYPT
(Pages 35–37)
What was the key feature of early Egypt's geography?

Another civilization arose along the banks of the Nile River of East Africa. The Nile flows to the North, toward the Mediterranean Sea. It, too, floods each year. The waters leave rich soil on the river banks. There the people of ancient Egypt grew food and began to build their own culture. They worshiped the Nile as a life-giving god.

For many centuries, the people of Egypt lived in two kingdoms, Upper Egypt and Lower Egypt. Upper Egypt extended north from the Nile's first area of rapids, or cataracts, to the Nile **delta.** The delta is a broad, marshy, triangular area of rich land. Lower Egypt began here and continued

north to the Mediterranean, just 100 miles away.

1. How did the Nile create boundaries?

_____

_____

EGYPT UNITES INTO A KINGDOM
(Pages 37–38)
Who ruled the kingdom?

About 3000 B.C., the king of Upper Egypt, **Narmer,** united the two kingdoms. In the years between 2660 and 2180 B.C., the basic marks of the culture of Egypt arose. Ruling over the land was the **pharaoh.** He was not only a king but was also seen as a god. A government in which a ruler is seen as a divine figure is a **theocracy.**

Pharaohs believed they would rule the land after their death. So these kings built themselves magnificent tombs. The tombs were huge **pyramids** made out of massive limestone blocks.

2. Why did pharaohs build pyramids?

_____

_____

_____

EGYPTIAN CULTURE; INVADERS CONTROL EGYPT

(Pages 38–41)

What were the features of Egyptian culture?

Egyptians believed in many gods and in an after-life. One god, they thought, weighed the hearts of each dead person. Hearts judged heavy with sin were eaten by a beast. Good people, with featherweight hearts, would live forever in a beautiful Other World. To prepare for this, Egyptians preserved a dead person's body by **mummification.** This kept the body from decaying.

The pharaoh and his family were at the top of Egyptian society. Below them were people of wealth who owned large amounts of land, the priests, and members of the government and army. Then came the middle class—merchants and people who worked in crafts. At the bottom were the peasants. In later times, the Egyptians had slaves. People could move from one rank of society to another. Those who could read and write held important positions.

The Egyptians, like the Sumerians, developed a way of writing. In their writing system, **hieroglyphics,** pictures stood for sounds or ideas. The pictures could be put together to make words and sentences. At first they wrote on stone. Later they began to make a kind of paper from the **papyrus** plant. The Egyptians invented a system of written numbers and a calendar. Their calendar had 12 months, each of which had 30 days. They were famous in the ancient world for their ideas in medicine.

After 2180 B.C., the pharaohs lost power. Egypt went through a time of troubles. Then strong rulers once again took control. They ruled for four centuries until a group of Asians called the Hyksos arrived in horse-drawn chariots. The land fell to these invaders in 1640 B.C.

3. How was Egyptian society organized?

_____

_____

_____

Name _____ Class _____ Date _____

As you read about ancient Egyptian civilization, fill out the chart below by writing notes to answer the questions.

Government	
1. Why is Narmer a legendary hero in ancient Egyptian history?	
2. How did the role of Egyptian pharaohs differ from the role of Mesopotamian rulers?	
3. Why did the Egyptians build great pyramids for their kings?	

Culture	
4. How did Egyptian religious beliefs compare with those of the Mesopotamians?	
5. What social classes made up Egyptian society?	
6. What were significant achievements of the ancient Egyptians in science and technology?	
7. How did the Egyptian writing system compare with the Mesopotamian system?	

Early River Valley Civilizations

Section 3

Planned Cities on the Indus

Terms and Names

subcontinent Land mass that is a distinct part of a continent

monsoon Seasonal wind

Harappan civilization Ancient settlements in the Indus River Valley

Before You Read

In the last section, you read about the development of culture along the Nile.

In this section, you will learn about the first civilization in India.

As You Read

Use a chart to draw conclusions about Indus valley civilizations.

THE GEOGRAPHY OF THE INDIAN SUBCONTINENT (Pages 44–45)
What is a subcontinent?

South Asia—modern India, Pakistan, and Bangladesh—is a **sub continent.** It is separated from the rest of Asia by tall mountains. Just below the mountains are two large plains that hold the Ganges and Indus rivers. The high mountains gave the people safety from invaders. Because they lived close to the sea, the people could travel over the water to trade with other peoples.

The people along the Indus River faced many of the same challenges that the people in Mesopotamia did. Their river flooded each year and left soil good for farming. But the floods did not occur at the same time each year. Also, the river sometimes changed course. The region's weather caused problems, too. Each winter, strong winds blew dry air across the area. Each spring, the winds brought heavy rains. These seasonal winds are called **monsoons.**

1. What challenges did the people along the Indus River face?

_____

_____

CIVILIZATION EMERGES ON THE INDUS; HARAPPAN CULTURE (Pages 46–48)
What were cities like on the Indus?

Historians cannot understand the writings of the people who settled in the Indus Valley. So, they have not learned much about these people. They do know that they were farming along the river by about 3200 B.C. The culture is called **Harappan civilization** because many discoveries were made near the city of Harappa. They also know that the culture of these people covered an area larger than either Mesopotamia or Egypt.

About 2500 B.C., these people began building their first cities. In Mesopotamia, cities were a jumble of winding streets.

In the Indus Valley, however, the builders carefully planned their cities. They made a grid of streets. They built an area called a citadel that was easy to defend. All the important buildings were here. They also had systems for carrying water and sewage.

Because the houses were mostly alike, scholars think that the Indus culture did not have big differences between social classes.

These early people left an important mark on the region. Some religious objects include symbols that became part of later Indian culture. Historians also think that the people of the area had extensive trade with people in the region and with the people of Mesopotamia.

2. Name two conclusions that have been drawn about Harappan civilization.

_____

_____

MYSTERIOUS END TO INDUS VALLEY CULTURE (Page 49)
How did Indus Valley culture end?

Around 1750 B.C., the cities began to show signs of decline. The Indus Valley civilization collapsed around 1500 B.C. Satellite images suggest a shift in the earth's crust that caused earthquakes. Because of the quakes the Indus River may have changed its course. This would stop the good effects of the yearly floods. The people may have overworked the land. This would have left the soil too poor to produce crops.

3. Name two reasons why Indus Valley civilization may have ended.

_____

_____

As you read this section, list the key characteristics of the first Indian civilization in the web diagram below.

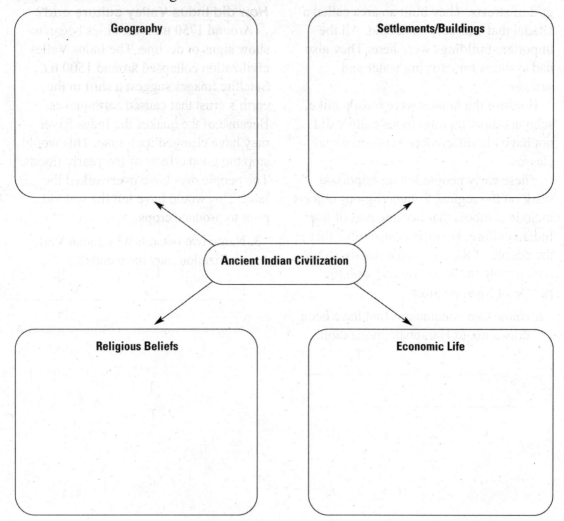

Geography

Settlements/Buildings

Ancient Indian Civilization

Religious Beliefs

Economic Life

River Dynasties in China

Terms and Names

loess Fertile soil

oracle bone Animal bone used by ancient Chinese priests to communicate with the gods

Mandate of Heaven Divine approval of the ruler

dynastic cycle Pattern of rise, fall, and replacement of dynasties

feudalism Political system in which nobles or lords are granted the use of lands that belong to the king

Before You Read

In the last section, you read about Indus Valley culture.

In this section, you will learn about the earliest cultures in China.

As You Read

Use a time line to identify major events in early Chinese dynasties.

THE GEOGRAPHY OF CHINA
(Pages 50–51)
How **did geography affect China's past?**

China's geography caused it to develop apart from other cultures. A great ocean, huge deserts, and high mountains isolate China from other areas. The mountains did not protect China totally, however. People living to the north and west invaded the land many times during Chinese history.

There are two rich rivers within China—the Huang He and the Yangtze. Almost all the good farmland in China lies between these rivers. The Huang He deposited huge amounts of silt when it overflowed. This silt is fertile soil called **loess.** The Chinese people also made use of the flood waters of these rivers.

1. Why did China develop apart from other cultures?

CIVILIZATION EMERGES IN SHANG TIMES (Pages 51–52)]
What **was the Shang Dynasty?**

A few thousand years ago, some people began to farm along China's rivers. About 2000 B.C., the first dynasty of rulers brought government to China.

Around 1500 B.C., a new dynasty, the Shang, began to rule. This dynasty left the first written records in China. Objects found in their palaces and tombs also tell us much about their society. Chinese people built their buildings of wood, not mud-dried brick as the other early cultures did. Huge walls made of earth surrounded these buildings to protect them. The walls were needed because it was a time of constant war.

The king and the nobles who helped him fight these wars were at the top of Shang society. At the bottom was the mass of peasants who lived in simple huts outside the city walls. They worked hard on the farms, using wooden tools because the Shang believed that bronze was too good to be used for farming.

2. What were three features of Shang culture?

_____

THE DEVELOPMENT OF CHINESE CULTURE (Pages 52–54)
What beliefs shaped Shang society?

Shang society was held together by a strong belief in the importance of the group—all the people—and not any single person. The most important part of society was the family. Children grew up learning to respect their parents.

The family played a central role in Chinese religion, too. The Chinese thought that family members who had died could still influence the lives of family members who were alive. They gave respect to dead members of the family, hoping to keep them happy. The Shang also asked for advice from the gods. They used **oracle bones** to do this. These were animal bones and shells.

The Chinese system of writing differed from those of other groups. Symbols stood for ideas, not sounds. This allowed the many different groups in China to understand the same writing even though each had a special spoken language. The written language had thousands of symbols, however. Only specially trained people learned to read and write.

3. Name three important values of Shang culture.

ZHOU AND THE DYNASTIC CYCLE (Pages 54–55)
What is the Mandate of Heaven?

About 1027 B.C., a new group, the Zhou, took control of China. They adopted Shang culture. They also started an idea of royalty that was new to China. Good rulers, they said, got authority to rule from heaven. This was known as the **Mandate of Heaven.** They claimed the Shang rulers were not just and had lost the favor of the gods. That is why they had to be replaced. From then on, the Chinese believed in divine rule. However, it also meant that disasters such as floods or war pointed to a ruler that had lost the support of the gods and needed to be replaced. Until the early 1900s, the Chinese had one dynasty after another. This pattern of rise, fall, and replacement of dynasties is known as the **dynastic cycle.**

The Zhou gave members of the royal family and other nobles the rights to large areas of land. They established **feudalism.** Feudalism is a political system in which the nobles owe loyalty to the king. The nobles promise to fight for the rulers and to protect the peasants who live on the land.

Eventually the Zhou rulers lost all power. The nobles fought each other for control of China in a period called the "time of the warring states." It lasted many hundred years. The Chinese people suffered during this time.

4. Name two important changes brought about by the Zhou.

_____

As you read this section, fill out the chart below by describing key features of ancient China under the Shang Dynasty.

1. Geographic features	2. Environmental challenges	3. Settlements
4. Social classes	5. Role of family	6. Religious beliefs
7. Writing system	8. Technological advances	9. Artistry

People and Ideas on the Move

Section 1

The Indo-Europeans

Terms and Names

Indo-Europeans Group of Asian peoples who migrated to many different places

steppes Dry grasslands

migration Movement of people from one place to another

Hittites Group of Indo-European peoples who occupied Anatolia

Anatolia Large peninsula in modern-day Turkey

Aryans Group of Indo-Europeans

Vedas Sacred literature of the Aryans

Brahmin Priest

caste Class

Mahabharata Poem that tells the story of a great war

Before You Read

In the last chapter, you read about peoples who built civilizations in the great river valleys.

In this section, you will learn about the movements of two groups of people who lived on the grasslands of Asia.

As You Read

Use a web diagram to record some of the languages that stem from Indo-European.

INDO-EUROPEANS MIGRATE
(**Pages** 61–62)
Who **were the Indo-Europeans?**

   The Indo-Europeans were a group of peoples who came from the **steppes**—the dry grasslands of western Asia. The Indo-Europeans rode horses and tended cattle, sheep, and goats. They spoke many different languages, but all of them came from the same original language.

   For some reason, starting about 1700 B.C., the Indo-Europeans began to leave their homeland. They moved into some of the settled areas and began to conquer them. These **migrations,**

movements of people from one region to another, took place over a long period of time.

   1. What happened to the Indo-Europeans?

   _____

   _____

THE HITTITE EMPIRE (**Pages** 62–63)
Who **were the Hittites?**

   The **Hittites** were Indo-European peoples. They rode two-wheeled chariots and used iron weapons to conquer **Anatolia.**

Guided Reading Workbook

Anatolia is also called Asia Minor. It is a huge peninsula in modern-day Turkey. The Hittites moved farther and took the ancient lands of Mesopotamia. When they moved to the south, they ran into the Egyptians. Neither side was able to defeat the other. So, they decided to make peace.

The Hittites adopted many features of the culture that had grown in Mesopotamia before they arrived. They changed others to suit their own ideas. Their laws, for instance, were less harsh than the code of Hammurabi. The Hittites ruled their Southwest Asian empire from about 2000 to 1190 B.C. Then they fell to a new wave of invaders.

2. How did the Hittites react to the culture they found in Mesopotamia?

_____

_____

_____

ARYANS TRANSFORM INDIA
(Pages 63–65)
Who **were the Aryans?**

The **Aryans** were another group of Indo-European people. They moved into what is now India and transformed it. They first captured the land of the people of the Indus Valley. Archaeology tells almost nothing about the Aryans. But their sacred literature, the **Vedas,** tells a lot about them.

The Aryans were divided into three classes of people. There were priests (**Brahmins**), warriors, and peasants or traders. They viewed the non-Aryans living in the area as a fourth class. Over time, they made many rules for how people in these classes, or **castes,** could interact with one another. People were born into their caste for life. Some "impure" people lived in a group outside this class system. They were butchers, grave diggers, and trash collectors. Because they did work that was thought unclean, they were called "untouchables."

Over many centuries, the Aryans took more and more of what is now India. Eventually many powerful people tried to create their own kingdoms. They fought each other until one kingdom, Magadha, won control over almost all of India. Around this time, an epic poem, the **Mahabharata,** was written. It tells of the blending of cultures at the time. It also sets down ideals that were to become important in Hindu life.

3. What is the caste system?

_____

_____

_____

_____

Guided Reading Workbook

As you read about the migration of Indo-European peoples, fill in the blanks in the following summary.

From about 1700 to 1200 B.C., waves of Indo-European nomads

migrated from their homelands in the (1) _____, the dry

grasslands north of the Caucasus Mountains. One group, the Hittites,

settled in (2) _____, a rugged peninsula in a region today

called Turkey. They conquered (3) _____, the chief city in the

Tigris-Euphrates valley, signed a peace treaty with Egypt, and blended

many of their traditions with the more advanced Mesopotamian culture.

With their superior two-wheeled (4) _____ and their war

weapons made of (5) _____, the Hittites created an empire that

dominated Southwest Asia for over 450 years.

About 1500 B.C., another Indo-European group, the (6) _____,

entered India through the mountain passes of the Hindu Kush. Unlike the

people they conquered, they were light skinned and had not developed a

writing system. The invaders were divided into social classes, later called

(7) _____. Over time four major social classes developed, the

highest being the (8) _____, or priests, and the lowest, the

(9) _____, or laborers. Beginning around 1000 B.C., chiefs

began to set up kingdoms in the Indian subcontinent; the most important of

these kingdoms was (10) _____.

Many modern languages trace their origins to languages spoken by the

Indo-Europeans. Among the Indo-European family of languages spoken in

Europe and Asia today are (11) _____ and (12) _____.

People and Ideas on the Move

Hinduism and Buddhism Develop

Terms and Names

reincarnation Belief that the soul is reborn

karma Good or bad deeds

Jainism Religion that teaches that every living creature has a soul and no living creature can be harmed

Siddhartha Gautama Founder of Buddhism

enlightenment Wisdom

nirvana Buddha's word for release from selfishness and pain

Before You Read

In the last section, you read about the Hittites and the Aryans.

In this section, you will learn about the roots of Hinduism and Buddhism.

As You Read

Use a Venn diagram to compare the beliefs and practices of Buddhism and Hinduism.

HINDUISM EVOLVES OVER CENTURIES (Pages 66–68)
What is Hinduism?

Hinduism is a collection of religious beliefs that forms no one system. Unlike many religions, it was not founded by only one person. It is a religion that allows great variety for its followers. Certain ideas became common to the beliefs of all Hindus.

Hindus believe that each person has a soul. However, there is also a larger soul, called Brahman, that brings together all the individual souls. A person's goal is to become free of desire and not bothered by suffering. When that takes place, the person's soul wins escape from life on Earth. Hindus believe in **reincarnation.** They believe the soul is born again into another body after death. In the next life, the soul has another chance to learn its lessons. According to Hindus, how a person behaves in one life has an effect on the person's next life. This is the soul's **karma**—good or bad deeds.

Another religion that arose in India was **Jainism.** It was started by Mahavira, a man who lived from about 599 to 527 B.C. He believed that every creature in the world—even an animal—has a soul. Because of that, people must be sure not to harm any creature. Today, Jains take jobs that are certain not to hurt living things.

1. Name three Hindu beliefs.

_____

_____

_____

THE BUDDHA SEEKS ENLIGHTENMENT (Pages 68–71)
What is Buddhism?

Another new religion, Buddhism, arose about the same time as Hinduism and Jainism. Buddhism has millions of followers all around the world. It was started around 528 B.C. by **Siddhartha Gautama.**

Siddhartha searched for a way that would allow him to escape the suffering of human life. He spent many years searching for this answer. He was looking for **enlightenment,** or wisdom. Finally, he sat down and meditated under a tree. After 49 days, he had his answer. He was now called the Buddha, which means the "enlightened one."

The Buddha began to teach others how to attain enlightenment. They were to follow a plan of behavior called the Eightfold Path—right views, right resolve, right speech, right conduct, right livelihood, right effort, right mindfulness, and right concentration. This would lead to **nirvana,** or a release from selfishness and pain.

As with Hinduism, the Buddha taught that the soul would be reborn into a new life. This chain of new lives would continue until the soul, like Buddha, reached understanding.

These ideas attracted many followers. Many people who lived in the lower classes of Indian society saw these ideas as a chance to escape from the limits placed on them. This teaching also spread in southern India. There the Aryans did not have much influence. Some followers took the ideas to other lands.

In the centuries after Buddha's death in 483 B.C., Buddhism appeared in Southeast Asia. Later it was carried to China and then to Korea and Japan. Merchants and traders played an important role in spreading the religion. Strangely, in India where Buddhism was founded, the religion faded. Many places that are important to Buddhism remain in India, however. Buddhists from around the world come there to visit locations connected to the life of Buddha.

2. Name four basic beliefs of Buddhism.

_____

_____

_____

As you read about Hinduism and Buddhism, take notes to fill in the comparison chart below.

	Hinduism	Buddhism
1. Founder/origins		
2. Key beliefs		
3. Gods		
4. Sacred literature		
5. Effect on society		
6. Modern-day traditions		

People and Ideas on the Move

Seafaring Traders

Terms and Names

Minoans Group of powerful seafaring people

Aegean Sea Sea between modern-day Greece and Turkey

Knossos Minoan capital city

King Minos King of Knossos

Phoenicians Most powerful traders along the Mediterranean

Before You Read

In the last section, you read about major religions that developed in India.

In this section, you will learn about traders whose influence spread throughout the Mediterranean.

As You Read

Use a chart to identify Minoan and Phoenician accomplishments.

MINOANS TRADE IN THE MEDITERRANEAN (Pages 72–73)
Who were the Minoans?

In the Mediterranean area, a new culture arose on the island of Crete. The **Minoans** were peaceful people who lived in rich cities that were safe from invaders. They controlled trade in their area, Crete. Crete is a large island on the southern edge of the **Aegean Sea.** The Minoans sent their fine pottery, swords, and metal drinking cups to other lands. They also sent other countries their style of art and architecture. This style later had influence on the art of Greece.

Archaeologists have explored the ruins of **Knossos,** the capital city of the Minoans. It was the archaeologists that first called the culture Minoan, after its famous ruler, **King Minos.** They found beautiful wall paintings that offer views of Minoan culture. One interesting feature of Minoan life was the high position that women appear to have held. An earth goddess seems to have headed all the gods of Crete, and women ruled over some important religious places. Women did not play such important roles among other peoples who lived nearby.

Minoan cities were damaged in 1470 B.C. by a series of disasters. First, a number of earthquakes rocked the island, destroying buildings. Then a volcano exploded on a nearby island. That was followed by huge waves and clouds of white ash from the volcano's fire. These shocks seem to have been too much for the Minoans. The Minoan civilization ended about 1200 B.C.

1. What were three important features of Minoan culture?

_____

_____

_____

_____

PHOENICIANS SPREAD TRADE AND CIVILIZATION (Pages 73–76)
Who were the Phoenicians?

Another group of people arose in the Mediterranean. They lived in several city-states in what is today Lebanon. They traded far and wide. Some may have even sailed as far as Britain—and perhaps around Africa. They were the **Phoenicians.**

The Phoenicians put colonies all along the Mediterranean coast. Colonies were 30 miles apart. This was the distance that one of their ships could travel in a day. One of those colonies, Carthage, in North Africa, later became a major power in the Mediterranean world. Phoenicians traded such goods as wine, weapons, metals, ivory, slaves, and objects made of wood and glass. They also made a purple dye that was highly valued.

The important achievement of the Phoenicians was their alphabet. They used symbols to stand for the sounds of consonants. They brought their system of writing to other lands such as Greece, where Greeks changed the form of some

letters. The alphabet that we use today, however, had its beginnings in Phoenician writing.

2. How did the Phoenicians spread their culture?

_____

_____

_____

_____

ANCIENT TRADE ROUTES (Page 76)
What were the major trading networks?

Trading networks also connected the Mediterranean Sea with other centers of world commerce in South and East Asia. Some routes went across Central Asia by land. Some sea routes went across the Arabian Sea. These networks helped people exchange products and information. Traders carried ideas, religious beliefs, art, and ways of living. They did not just trade goods. They also helped "trade" culture.

3. Why were trade networks so important?

_____

_____

_____

_____

As you read about the Minoan and Phoenician civilizations, write notes to explain what each statement listed below suggests about these seafaring traders.

1. Minoan cities had no fortifications. →	
2. Archaeologists excavating the Minoan capital city found the remains of wall paintings, seals, and fine painted pottery. →	
3. Many works of Minoan art depict women as major goddesses and priestesses. →	
4. Minoans sacrificed bulls to their gods and enjoyed the sport of bull-leaping. →	
5. The Phoenicians were the first Mediterranean people to sail beyond the Straits of Gibraltar, possibly even around Africa by way of the Red Sea. →	
6. The Phoenicians worked in wood, metal, glass, and ivory and produced red-purple dye from snails in the waters off the city-states of Sidon and Tyre. →	
7. There are some similarities among Phoenician, Greek, and modern-day alphabets. →	

People and Ideas on the Move

The Origins of Judaism

Terms and Names

Canaan Ancient home of the Israelites

Torah First five books of the Hebrew Bible

Abraham "Father," or the first, of the Jewish people

monotheism Belief in a single God

covenant Mutual promise between God and the Jewish people

Moses According to the Torah, the man who led the Israelites out of slavery

Israel Kingdom on the eastern end of the Mediterranean Sea

Judah Israelite kingdom in Canaan

tribute Payment made by a weaker power to a stronger power

Before You Read

In the last section, you read about the spread of culture through trade.

In this section, you will learn about the origins of Judaism.

As You Read

Use a time line to show major Hebrew, Israelite, and Jewish leaders and one fact about each.

THE SEARCH FOR A PROMISED LAND (Pages 77–78)
Where did the Israelites claim land?

The Israelites made a claim to an important piece of land that was called **Canaan.** They believed the land had been promised to them by God. This region sat on the eastern edge of the Mediterranean Sea and on the Red Sea, which leads to the Indian Ocean. It was open to the trade of many lands. Most of what we know about the early history of the Israelites comes from the **Torah,** the sacred writings of the Jewish people.

The story of the Israelites began in Mesopotamia. There, according to the Torah, God chose a man named **Abraham** to be the "father," or the first, of the Jewish people. God told Abraham to move his family to Canaan. Abraham promised that he and his people would always obey God. (The Israelites were among the world's earliest peoples to believe in one God, or **monotheism.**) God, in turn, promised to always protect them from their enemies. This was the first of many **covenants**—promises between God and the Jewish people.

1. What role did Abraham play in early Jewish history?

_____

_____

MOSES AND THE EXODUS (Pages 78–80)
Who was Moses?

When their crops failed, the Israelites moved to Egypt around 1650 B.C. Over time, they were forced to become slaves.

Guided Reading Workbook

After many years, they fled. Jews call this mass departure "the Exodus."

According to the Torah, a man named **Moses** led them out of Egypt between 1300 and 1200 B.C. They traveled 40 years in a wilderness. During that time, the Torah says, God gave Moses the Ten Commandments, a part of a code of laws that the Israelites were to follow. They regulated social and religious life and emphasized mercy. God again promised to protect them in return for their obedience to his laws.

After Moses died, the Israelites finally reached Canaan and settled. There they began to adopt new ways of life. They often fought with other peoples living in the area, as each group tried to control the best land and other resources.

The Israelites were organized into twelve groups, called tribes. Each tribe was distinct, but in times of danger they would unite under leaders called judges. One of those judges was a woman named Deborah. It was unusual for women in ancient society to hold such a position. Women usually were expected to stay home and raise children.

The Jews had other leaders called prophets. They said that they were messengers sent by God to tell the people how he wanted them to act. These prophets told the people that they had two duties: to worship God and to deal in just and fair ways with one another. The goal of Jewish religion was that each person should live a moral life in accordance with God's laws.

2. What are the Ten Commandments?

_____

_____

THE KINGDOM OF ISRAEL
(Pages 81–82)
How was Israel formed?

From about 1020 to 922 B.C., the Israelites were united into one kingdom,

Israel. Three kings helped unite them. The first, Saul, drove off their enemies. The second, David, made Jerusalem the capital. The third, Solomon, built a magnificent temple to be used to worship God.

After Solomon's death, though, the kingdom split in two, with Israel in the north and **Judah** in the south. For the next two centuries, each kingdom had times of prosperity, followed by low periods.

3. How was Israel split?

_____

_____

THE BABYLONIAN CAPTIVITY
(Page 82)
Who conquered Israel and Judah?

Disaster came when both kingdoms lost their independence. Israel and Judah began to pay tribute to Assyria. **Tribute** is money paid by a weaker power to a stronger power to make sure it does not attack.

Eventually, the northern kingdom fell to the Assyrians. Later, the southern kingdom fell to the Babylonians. Many Jews were forced into exile in Babylon. They lived there for many years during what was known as the Babylonian Captivity. Then the Babylonians themselves were conquered by the Persian king Cyrus the Great. The new ruler let 40,000 Jews return home.

After the exile, the only large tribe left was the tribe of Judah. As a result, the Israelites came to be known as the Jews. Their religion is called Judaism.

4. What was the Babylonian Captivity?

_____

_____

As you read this section, take notes to answer the questions about the time line.

2000 B.C.	God commands Abraham to take his people to Canaan.	→ 1. What sacred writings describe the early history of the Israelites?
1650 B.C.	Descendants of Abraham move to Egypt.	2. How were the Israelites treated in Egypt?
		3. Why is Moses an important figure in Jewish history?
1300-1200 B.C.	Israelites begin their "exodus" from Egypt.	
		4. What were the achievements of Saul and David?
1020 B.C.	The Israelites unite and form the kingdom of Israel.	
962 B.C.	King David is succeeded by his son Solomon.	5. Why did King Solomon build a great temple in Jerusalem?
922 B.C.	Kingdom splits into two, Israel and Judah.	
		6. What were the reasons for the division?
722 B.C.	Assyrians conquer Israel.	
		7. Who was Nebuchadnezzar?
586 B.C.	Chaldeans attack Jerusalem and destroy Solomon's Temple.	
515 B.C.	Second Temple is completed.	8. What ruler allowed the Jewish people to return to Jerusalem?

Guided Reading Workbook

The Egyptian and Nubian Empires

Terms and Names

Hyksos Invaders that ruled Egypt from 1640 to 1570 B.C.

New Kingdom Period after the Hyksos rulers

Hatshepsut New Kingdom ruler who encouraged trade

Thutmose III Warlike ruler; stepson of Hatshepsut

Nubia Region of Africa bordering Egypt

Ramses II Pharaoh and great builder of Egypt

Kush Nubian kingdom

Piankhi Kushite king who forced the Libyans out of Egypt

Meroë Home and trading center of the Kush kingdom

Before You Read
In the last section, you read about the religion of the ancient Israelites.

In this section, you will read about the interaction of Egypt and Nubia.

As You Read
Use a time line to identify important events in the history of Egypt and Nubia.

NOMADIC INVADERS RULE EGYPT
(**Page** 89)
Who were the Hyksos?
At the end of its second period of glory, power struggles weakened Egypt. New invaders, the **Hyksos,** arrived. They had the chariot. Egyptians had never seen this war machine before. The Hyksos ruled Egypt for many years. Some historians believe that the Hyksos encouraged the Israelites to settle there.

Around 1600 B.C., a series of warlike rulers began to restore Egypt's power. Eventually, the Hyksos were driven completely out of Egypt. The pharaohs began some conquests of their own.

1. How did Egypt fall to the Hyksos?

_____

_____

THE NEW KINGDOM OF EGYPT
(**Pages** 90–91)
The time from 1570 to 1075 B.C. is called the **New Kingdom.** In this third period, Egypt was richer and more powerful than ever.

Hatshepsut was one of the rulers of the New Kingdom. She encouraged trade. Her stepson, **Thutmose III,** was more warlike.

He and other New Kingdom pharaohs brought Egyptian rule to Syria and Canaan in the east. They also moved south into **Nubia.** This was a part of Africa near where the Nile began. Egypt had traded with Nubia and influenced the region since the time of the Middle Kingdom.

The pharaohs of the New Kingdom did not build pyramids, like those who had come before. Instead, they built great tombs in a secret place called the Valley of the Kings. Some pharaohs also built huge palaces for themselves or temples to the Egyptian gods.

Ramses II stood out among the great builders of the New Kingdom. He reigned from about 1290 to 1244 B.C.

2. What was the relationship between Nubia and Egypt during the New Kingdom?

_____

_____

_____

THE EMPIRE DECLINES (Pages 91–92)
How did Egypt lose power?

Around 1200 B.C., invaders attacked the eastern Mediterranean. They brought trouble with them.

Some of these invaders were called the "Sea Peoples." They attacked the Egyptian empire. They attacked the Hittite kingdom, too.

As the power of Egypt fell, the land broke into many small kingdoms. People from Libya began to invade Egypt. They took control of the land. They followed the Egyptian way of life.

3. Who invaded Egypt?

_____

_____

_____

THE KUSHITES CONQUER THE NILE REGION (Pages 92–93)
How did the Kushites rule?

As Egypt grew weaker, the Nubian kingdom of **Kush** became more powerful. Under Egyptian rule, the people of Kush accepted many Egyptian traditions and customs. They felt that they had to protect Egyptian values.

A Kushite king named **Piankhi** moved into Egypt to force out the Libyans. He united the Nile Valley. He wanted to bring back Egypt's glory. The Kushites ruled Egypt for a few decades. Then the Assyrians invaded. They forced the Kushites back to their home.

4. How did the Kushites view Egyptian culture?

_____

_____

_____

THE GOLDEN AGE OF MEROË (Page 94)
What was Meroë?

The Kushite kings settled in the city of Meroë, south of Egypt. Their kingdom entered a golden age. The city played an important role in trade. Meroë also became an important center for making iron weapons and tools.

Traders in the city brought their iron to the ports of the Red Sea. These goods were taken on ships to Arabia and India. The traders from Meroë, in the meantime, brought back jewelry, cloth, silver lamps, and glass bottles. The city thrived from about 250 B.C. to about A.D. 150. By A.D. 350 Meroë had fallen to rival Aksum, a seaport farther south.

5. Why was Meroë important?

_____

_____

_____

As you read about the Egyptian empire, fill in the chart below with the dates and achievements of the rulers listed.

Name of Ruler	Time of Reign	Achievements
Queen Ahhotep		
Hatshepsut		
Thutmose III		
Ramses II		
Libyan pharaohs		
Piankhi		

Guided Reading Workbook

Section 2

The Assyrian Empire

Terms and Names

Assyria Powerful empire in northern Mesopotamia

Sennacherib Assyrian king and empire builder

Nineveh Assyria's capital on the Tigris River

Ashurbanipal Assyrian king who gathered writing tablets from many lands

Medes People who helped to destroy the Assyrian empire

Chaldeans People who helped to destroy the Assyrian empire

Nebuchadnezzar Chaldean king who rebuilt Babylon

Before You Read

In the last section, you read about Egypt and Nubia.

In this section, you will read about the Assyrians, the people who took over Egypt.

As You Read

Use a chart to identify the causes of the rise and decline of the Assyrian power.

A MIGHTY MILITARY MACHINE
(**Pages** 95–96)
Who were the Assyrians?

For a time, **Assyria** was the greatest power in Southwest Asia. The Assyrians began as a farming people in the northern part of Mesopotamia. Because their homes were open to attack, they formed a strong fighting force. Soon they turned to conquest. Assyrian kings, including the fierce **Sennacherib,** built an empire that stretched from east and north of the Tigris River all the way to central Egypt.

The Assyrians used many different methods to win their battles. Their soldiers carried strong iron-tipped spears and iron swords. They used large numbers of men with bows. They dug tunnels under city walls to weaken them. They used heavy battering rams to knock down the wooden gates of the city.

The Assyrians conquered almost everything in their path. They usually killed or enslaved those they defeated. Some Assyrian kings bragged about their cruelty toward people they captured.

Sometimes conquered peoples would revolt. Assyrians wanted to stop these rebellions and dominate the peoples. They forced groups of captives to leave their homelands. Then the captives were too far away to cause trouble.

1. What made the Assyrians such a strong fighting force?

_____

_____

THE EMPIRE EXPANDS
(Page 96)
Whom did the Assyrians conquer?

Between 850 and 650 B.C., the Assyrians conquered all of Mesopotamia along with Syria and Canaan. Then they took modern Turkey and Egypt. They ruled by putting in power kings who would support them. They also collected taxes and tribute—yearly payments from peoples who were weaker. If a city did not pay, the Assyrian army moved in and destroyed it.

The Assyrian kings were builders, too. One built the city of **Nineveh** on the north branch of the Tigris River. It was the largest city of its day. The city was surrounded with walls.

Another king, **Ashurbanipal,** gathered thousands of writing tablets from the lands that had been taken. Some of these tablets were dictionaries. The collection provided historians with much information about the earliest civilizations in Southwest Asia. The library was also the first to have many of the features of a modern library, including a cataloging system.

2. Besides conquering other people, what did the Assyrians accomplish?

_____

_____

_____

THE EMPIRE CRUMBLES
(Pages 97–98)
Why did the Assyrians fall?

The Assyrians had also made many enemies over the years. After a while, those enemies banded together. An army made up of **Medes, Chaldeans,** and others struck back. In 612 B.C., they destroyed the city of Nineveh. Many people in the area were glad that the city was in ruins.

The Chaldeans, who had ruled the area earlier, took control of Mesopotamia again. A Chaldean king named **Nebuchadnezzar** rebuilt the city of Babylon. Once more it was one of the greatest cities of the world. The city included famous hanging gardens with many different plants from the cool mountain regions, Slaves watered the plants with hidden pumps.

Babylon also featured a ziggurat. This step-shaped pyramid soared 300 feet into the air. It was the tallest building in Babylon. At night, priests would study the stars and the planets. They recorded what they saw. This was the beginning of the science of astronomy.

3. Who were the Chaldeans?

_____

_____

_____

_____

Section 2, *continued*

As you read about the rise and fall of the Assyrian Empire, fill in the diagram below.

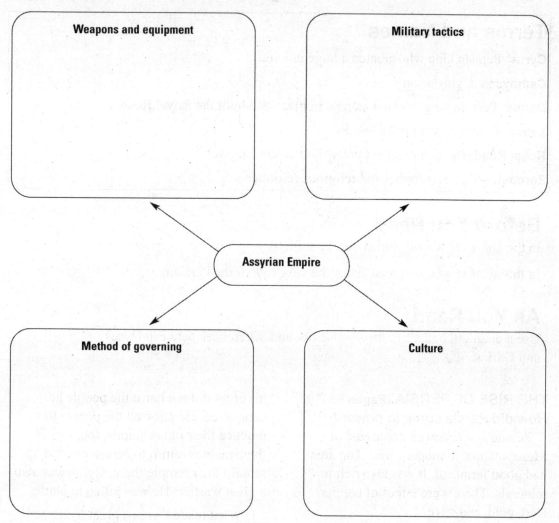

Weapons and equipment

Military tactics

Assyrian Empire

Method of governing

Culture

Guided Reading Workbook

First Age of Empires

The Persian Empire

Terms and Names

Cyrus Persian king who created a huge empire

Cambyses Cyrus's son

Darius Persian king who put satraps in place and built the Royal Road

satrap Governor who ruled locally

Royal Road Road that helped unify the Persian Empire

Zoroaster Persian prophet and religious reformer

Before You Read

In the last section, you read about the military might of the Assyrians.

In this section, you will read about the wise rule of the Persians.

As You Read

Use a diagram to identify the similarities and differences between Cyrus and Darius.

THE RISE OF PERSIA (Pages 99–100)
How did Persia come to power?

Persia, a new power, arose east of Mesopotamia, in modern Iran. The area had good farmland. It was also rich in minerals. There were mines of copper, lead, gold, and silver.

The Persians joined with other forces to help defeat the Assyrians. About 550 B.C., the Persians began their own conquests.

Their king was **Cyrus,** an excellent general. Cyrus led his army to conquer a huge empire. It stretched from the Indus River in India all the way to Anatolia. The empire covered about 2,000 miles. Cyrus took all this land in just over 10 years.

Cyrus won this vast land in part because of the wise way he treated the people there. Cyrus did not follow the examples of the Assyrians. They destroyed towns and cities. Cyrus, however, made sure that his army did not harm the people he conquered. He allowed the people to practice their old religions, too. Cyrus let the Israelites return to Jerusalem and rebuild their temple there. Cyrus was also a great warrior. He was killed in battle.

1. What made Cyrus a great leader?

_____

_____

PERSIAN RULE (Pages 100–101)
Who was Darius?

Cyrus died in 530 B.C. The kings who followed him had to decide how to run the vast new empire. His son, **Cambyses,** conquered Egypt. Cambyses was not like his father. He was not wise or understanding. He did not respect the Egyptians and their way of life.

Guided Reading Workbook

The next king, **Darius,** proved as able as Cyrus. Darius put down several revolts. He won more land for the empire and created a government for the empire. Only Greece escaped Persian control.

Darius divided the land into 20 provinces, each holding a certain group of people. He allowed each group to practice its own religion, speak its own language, and obey many of its own laws. He also put royal governors—**satraps**—in place to make sure that the people obeyed his laws.

Darius built the **Royal Road** to unite his large empire. This excellent road system ran 1,677 miles. Royal messengers on horses could travel this distance in about seven days. The Royal Road made communication better within the empire. Transportation became easier too.

Darius also had metal coins made that could be used for business anywhere in the empire. The coins had a standard value. This money system, along with the Royal Road, helped increase trade.

2. How did Darius change Persia?

_____

_____

_____

_____

THE PERSIAN LEGACY (Page 103)
What is the legacy of the Persian Empire?

During the Persian Empire, a new religion arose in Southwest Asia. A prophet named **Zoroaster** said there were two powerful spirits. One stood for truth and light. The other represented evil and darkness. The two spirits were in a constant struggle. People needed to take part in the struggle. They would be judged on how well they fought. These ideas influenced later religions.

The Persians left their mark in history. They were fair and understanding. The Persians showed respect for other cultures. Their government brought order to Southwest Asia.

3. What mark did the Persians leave on history?

_____

_____

_____

As you read about the Persian Empire, take notes to fill in the Venn diagram below to compare the reign of King Cyrus with that of King Darius.

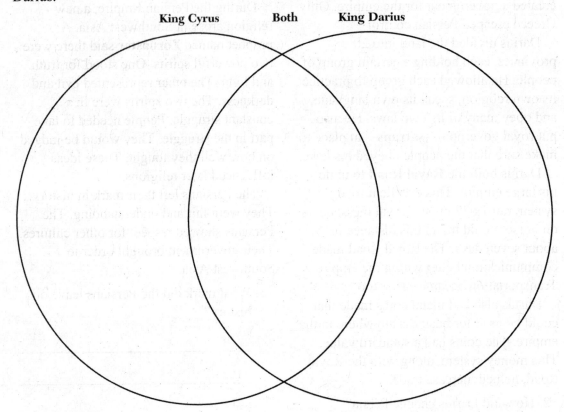

King Cyrus   **Both**   **King Darius**

Section 4

The Unification of China

Terms and Names

Confucius China's most influential scholar

filial piety Children's respect for their parents and elders

bureaucracy Organization of government into agencies and departments

Daoism Philosophy of Laozi that puts people in touch with the forces of nature

Legalism Chinese idea that a highly efficient and powerful government is the key to social order

I Ching Chinese book that gave advice on practical and everyday problems

yin and yang Powers that govern the natural rhythms of life and must be balanced

Qin Dynasty Dynasty that unified China

Shi Huangdi First emperor of China; leader of the Qin Dynasty

autocracy Government in which the ruler has unlimited power

Before You Read

In the last section, you read about the Persian empire.

In this section, you will learn how China was restored to order.

As You Read

Use a web to indicate how the chaos of the warring states affected the philosophy, politics, and cities of China.

CONFUCIUS AND THE SOCIAL ORDER (Pages 104–105)
***How* did Confucius try to restore order in China?**

After the fall of the Zhou Dynasty, China became a land of troubles. Ancient Chinese values were forgotten. Civilization seemed doomed. Yet some thinkers tried to find ways to restore these values.

One of the most important thinkers was **Confucius.** He was born in 551 B.C. Confucius believed that order could return. But first, the people would have to work at five basic relationships. These were ruler and subject, father and son, husband and

wife, older and younger brothers, and friend. The family relationships, he thought, were the most important. Confucius stressed that children should practice **filial piety.** This is respect for parents and elders.

Confucius also tried to make government better. He helped create the basis of a **bureaucracy.** This is a system of departments and agencies for running the government. Education was important for the people who held jobs in this kind of government. Over time, the ideas of Confucius spread to other countries of East Asia.

1. How did Confucius try to restore ancient Chinese values?

_____

_____

OTHER ETHICAL SYSTEMS
(Pages 105–107)
What **other ethical systems developed?**

Another thinker of this period was Laozi. He said nature follows a universal force called the Dao, or "the Way." His beliefs are called **Daoism.**

Other thinkers formed a set of beliefs called **Legalism.** They said the government should use the law to restore order in China.

Some Chinese people looked for practical advice in solving problems. They might refer to a book called *I Ching.* Other people turned to the idea of **yin and yang.** These two powers represented the harmony between opposite forces in the universe.

2. What was the basic purpose of all these ethical systems?

_____

_____

THE QIN DYNASTY UNIFIES CHINA
(Pages 107–109)
What **happened during the Qin Dynasty?**

A 13-year-old ruler became ruler of the **Qin Dynasty.** He ended the troubles of the warring states. This young ruler used the ideas of Legalism to unite China. After ruling for 20 years, he took a new name— **Shi Huangdi.** This means "First Emperor."

Shi Huangdi doubled the size of China. He established an **autocracy.** In this kind of government, a ruler has unlimited power. Shi Huangdi forced wealthy nobles to give up their land in the country and move to his capital city. He destroyed his enemies. The emperor wanted to control ideas, too. He ordered his government to burn books.

Shi Huangdi also had peasants build a network of roads that linked one corner of the empire to another. He set standards for writing, law, money, and weights and measures to be followed throughout the empire.

In the past, some Chinese rulers had built sections of wall to try to block attacks from northern nomads. Shi Huangdi had hundreds of thousands of poor people connect these sections of wall and make a huge barrier. When finished, the Great Wall of China stretched for thousands of miles.

These steps won the emperor little support. When he died, his son took the throne. Just three years into his reign, peasants revolted and managed to overthrow the emperor. By 202 B.C., the Qin Dynasty had given way to the Han Dynasty.

3. Name two changes that Shi Huangdi made.

_____

_____

As you read this section, take notes summarizing the basic ideas of the following Chinese philosophies.

1. Confucianism	Ideas about social order:	Ideas about government:
Founder:		

2. Daoism	Ideas about order and harmony:	Ideas about a universal force:
Founder:		

3. Legalists	Ideas about social order:	Ideas about government:
Founder:		

Classical Greece

Cultures of the Mountains and the Sea

Terms and Names

Mycenaean Member of a group who settled on the Greek mainland around 2000 B.C.

Trojan War War in which the Mycenaeans attacked the city of Troy

Dorian Member of a group of people who migrated into the Greek mainland

Homer Greek poet who composed the *Iliad* and the *Odyssey*

epic Heroic story told in the form of a long poem

myth Traditional story that explains why the world is the way it is

Before You Read

In the last section, you read about belief systems in ancient China and the Qin Dynasty.

In this section, you will read about the development of culture in ancient Greece.

As You Read

Use a chart to organize information about the roots of Greek culture.

GEOGRAPHY SHAPES GREEK LIFE
(Pages 123–124)
How did geography influence the Greeks?

The lives of the ancient Greeks were shaped by the geography of their land. Greece is a rocky land with high mountains and deep valleys. These land forms were like barriers. Moving over the land was difficult. For these reasons, Greeks living in different areas could not be easily united.

Good farmland covered only about one-fourth of Greece and could not support many people. The need for more living space and the lack of good farmland may have influenced the Greeks to find new colonies.

The Greeks had easy access to the sea, however. They became excellent sailors. Trade became important because Greece had few natural resources.

The climate is mild. As a result, Greek people spent much time outdoors. They attended public events and even conducted government outside.

1. Why was sea trade important for the Greeks?

_____

_____

_____

_____

MYCENAEAN CIVILIZATION DEVELOPS (Pages 124–125)
Who were the Mycenaeans?

A large wave of people moved from Europe, India, and Southwest Asia. Some of these people settled on the Greek mainland around 2000 B.C. They were later called **Mycenaeans.** They were ruled by powerful warrior-kings.

The Mycenaeans developed a strong culture. They borrowed from the Minoan culture of Crete. They adapted the Minoan form of writing and artistic design. The Mycenaeans also became interested in trade.

According to legend, Mycenaeans fought a long war with the people of Troy, a city in Turkey. This conflict was called the **Trojan War.**

The war was said to have started because a Trojan youth kidnapped a Greek woman. Her name was Helen. She was the beautiful wife of a Greek king. The Greek army later destroyed Troy.

2. How were the Mycenaeans influenced by the Minoans?

_____

_____

_____

_____

GREEK CULTURE DECLINES UNDER THE DORIANS
(Pages 125–126)
What was Greece like under the Dorians?

The culture of the Mycenaeans fell about 1200 B.C. Sea raiders destroyed their palaces. A less advanced people called the **Dorians** occupied the land. For the next 400 years, Greece went into decline. No written records exist from this period. Little is known about this era.

The spoken word lived on, however. A great storyteller named **Homer** made up **epics,** long poems, based on tales he heard. Epics are about heroes and their deeds. One of Homer's great epics was the *Iliad*. It centers on the heroes of the Trojan War. The heroes of the *Iliad* are warriors. Homer tells about their courage and noble actions in battle.

The Greeks also created a rich set of **myths.** These stories explain the actions of gods and events in nature. In Greek myths, gods often act like humans. For example, they show feelings, such as love, hate, and jealousy. Unlike humans, though, the Greek gods lived forever.

3. How did Homer keep Greek culture alive under the Dorians?

_____

_____

_____

_____

As you read this section, make notes in the chart to explain how each geographic characteristic or historical event influenced the history and culture of early Greek civilization.

History and Culture	
1. Location "around" a sea	
2. Rugged mountains	
3. Little fertile farmland	
4. Moderate climate	
5. Mycenaean adaptation of Minoan culture	
6. The Trojan War	
7. The collapse of Mycenaean civilization	

Section 2

Warring City-States

Terms and Names

polis City-state of ancient Greece

acropolis Fortified hilltop in an ancient Greek city

monarchy Government ruled by a king or queen

aristocracy Government ruled by a small group of noble families

oligarchy Government ruled by a few powerful people

tyrant Powerful ruler who gained control of a city-state's government by asking the common people for support

democracy Rule by the people

helot Peasant forced to stay on the land

phalanx Side-by-side fighting formation of Greek foot soldiers

Persian Wars Wars between Greece and the Persian Empire

Before You Read

In the last section, you read about the rise of early cultures in Greece.

In this section, you will read about city-states and their governments.

As You Read

On a double time line, note the important events in the development of Athens and Sparta.

RULE AND ORDER IN GREEK CITY-STATES (Page 127)
How were city-states governed?

The center of Greek life was the **polis,** or city-state. A polis was made up of a city and the countryside villages surrounding it. Men would gather in the marketplace or on a fortified hilltop in the polis, called an **acropolis,** to conduct business.

The city-states had different kinds of government. Some had a **monarchy,** a government ruled by a king or queen. Some had an **aristocracy,** a government ruled by a small group of noble families. Later, some merchants and craft workers formed an **oligarchy,** a government ruled by a few powerful people.

Sometimes, the common people clashed with the rulers of the city-states. Powerful individuals called **tyrants** sometimes appealed to the common people for support. Tyrants would then rule the city-state. Unlike today, tyrants generally were not considered harsh or cruel. Rather, they were looked upon as leaders who did things for the ordinary people.

1. What types of government existed in the city-states?

_____

_____

_____

ATHENS BUILDS A LIMITED DEMOCRACY (Pages 128–129)
How was Athens governed?

In some city-states, most notably Athens, the idea of representative government took hold. In Athens, as in other city-states, wealthy nobles and poor people clashed. The people of Athens avoided major political problems, however, by making reforms. Reformers in Athens tried to build a **democracy,** or government by the people.

In 594 B.C., a trusted statesman named Solon came to power. He introduced far-reaching changes to the government of Athens. He gave citizens a greater voice. He made it possible for any citizen of Athens to join discussions in the assembly, which approved laws. About 90 years later a leader named Cleisthenes took power and introduced further democratic reforms.

Athenian citizens, then, were able to participate in a limited democracy. Not everyone was involved in making political decisions, though. Only free adult men were citizens. Women and slaves had few rights. They played little or no role in political life.

2. Why was Athens not a full democracy?

_____

_____

SPARTA BUILDS A MILITARY STATE (Pages 129, 131)
How was Sparta governed?

Sparta was a very strong city-state in the south of Greece. It conquered its neighbor Messenia. The people of Messenia became **helots.** They were peasants forced to stay on the land they worked. They had to give the Spartans half their crops.

An assembly, the Council of Elders, and elected officials governed Sparta. Two kings ruled over Sparta's military. Sparta prized military skills. Boys joined the army at the age of seven and went through a long period of training as soldiers. Spartan women ran the family estates, freeing their husbands to serve in the army.

3. What was Sparta's focus as a city-state?

_____

_____

_____

THE PERSIAN WARS (Pages 131–133)
Who fought the Persian Wars?

Over the years, the Greeks developed the ability to make iron weapons. Because these cost less than weapons made of bronze, more people could afford them. Soon each city-state had its own army. In this army, soldiers stood side by side. They had a spear in one hand and a shield in the other. Together they formed a **phalanx.**

The Persian Wars were fought between Greece and the Persian Empire. In 490 B.C., Persian ships landed 25,000 soldiers on the coast of Greece. At the Battle of Marathon, the Greeks won a tremendous victory that saved Athens.

Ten years later, the Persians returned. The Greeks lost a battle on land, despite the heroic efforts of a small band of Spartans. The Persians also burned Athens. However, the ships of Athens won a great sea battle. The Greeks followed it with another victory on land. The threat from Persia was over.

4. What was the outcome of the Persian Wars?

_____

_____

Guided Reading Workbook

As you read about the growth of Greek city-states, answer the questions about events in the time line. (Some dates are approximate.)

725 B.C.	Sparta conquers Messenia.	1. How did Sparta treat the Messenians?
650 B.C.	Spartans put down a revolt by Messenians.	2. What type of society did Sparta create in response to the revolt?
621 B.C.	Draco writes the first legal code.	3. How did Athenians avoid major political upheavals?
594 B.C.	Athenian aristocrats choose Solon to govern.	4. What economic and political reforms did Solon initiate?
500 B.C.	Cleisthenes introduces political reforms in Athens.	5. What steps did Cleisthenes take to create a limited democracy in Athens?
490 B.C.	Athenians defeat Persians in battle at Marathon.	6. What advantages did the Greek soldiers have over the Persians?
479 B.C.	Greeks defeat remaining Persian army.	7. What were the consequences of the Persian Wars?

Democracy and Greece's Golden Age

Terms and Names

direct democracy Form of government in which citizens rule directly

classical art Art in which harmony, order, and balance were emphasized

tragedy Serious drama dealing with such themes as love, hate, war, or betrayal

comedy Light and amusing play that may poke fun at serious subjects

Peloponnesian War War in which Athens and its allies were defeated by Sparta and its allies

philosopher Thinker who uses logic and reason to explore life's important questions

Socrates Greek thinker who explored truth and justice and developed a method of questioning and answering

Plato Socrates's student who wrote *The Republic*, a view of the ideal society

Aristotle Plato's student who developed a method for testing and organizing ideas.

Before You Read

In the last section, you read about the government of the city-states.

In this section, you will read about democracy and the Golden Age of Greece.

As You Read

Use a web diagram to organize information about Pericles' goals for Athens.

PERICLES' PLAN FOR ATHENS
(Pages 134–135)
How did Pericles change Athens?

Pericles led Athens during its golden age. He served in this role from 461 to 429 B.C. Greek culture reached new heights under his leadership.

Pericles set three goals. One goal was to make Athens much more democratic through **direct democracy.** This meant that citizens ruled directly and not through representatives.

Another goal was to make Athens stronger. Pericles helped build up Athens' navy. It became the strongest in the Mediterranean.

Another goal was to make Athens beautiful. Pericles used money from the empire to buy gold, ivory, and marble. He helped fund great works of art.

1. What were Pericles' three main goals for Athens?

_____

_____

_____

GLORIOUS ART AND ARCHITECTURE (Pages 135–136)
How was Greek art unique?

One of the glories of Athens was the Parthenon. This temple was built to honor the goddess Athena. It is a masterpiece of art. Like other buildings and sculptures in Greece, it is an example of **classical art.** It reflects order, balance, and proportion.

2. Why was the Parthenon built?

_____

_____

DRAMA AND HISTORY (Page 136)
What kinds of drama did Greeks produce?

Athens also became home to a group of very skilled playwrights. Some wrote **tragedies.** These plays were about the pain and suffering of human life.

Other playwrights wrote **comedies.** These plays made audiences laugh about important ideas. Some plays were critical of customs, politics, and people. Such performances showed that Athens was a free and open society.

Also, such writers as Herodotus and Thucydides pioneered the accurate reporting of events. Their works led to the development of the subject of history.

3. What was the purpose of Greek comedies?

_____

_____

ATHENIANS AND SPARTANS GO TO WAR (Pages 137–138)
What was the Peloponnesian War?

After being rivals for many years, Sparta and Athens finally went to war. The

Peloponnesian War began in 431 B.C. The conflict ended badly for Athens. In 430 B.C. a horrible plague killed a great many people in Athens. After several battles, the two sides signed a truce. However, they were soon back at war. Finally, Athens gave up in 404 B.C. Athens had lost its empire.

4. What was the result of the Peloponnesian War?

_____

_____

PHILOSOPHERS SEARCH FOR TRUTH (Pages 138–139)
What did philosophers contribute to Greek culture?

After Athens' defeat, this city-state became home to several **philosophers.** They were thinkers who tried to understand human life. One of these great thinkers was **Socrates.** He believed deeply in truth and justice. Yet many people did not trust him. They thought his teachings were dangerous. Socrates was brought to trial and condemned to death.

His pupil, **Plato,** recorded many of Socrates's ideas. Plato became an important thinker in his own right. Plato's student, **Aristotle,** wrote books that summarized the knowledge of the Greeks. His system of logic became the foundation of scientific thought used today.

5. Who were three important Greek philosophers?

_____

_____

_____

Guided Reading Workbook

As you read this section, take notes to answer questions about Athens' golden age.

Pericles had three goals for Athens.

1. How did Pericles strengthen democracy?	2. What steps did Pericles take to strengthen the empire and glorify Athens?

The Greeks invented drama.

3. What themes were common in Greek tragedy?	4. What do the themes of Greek comedies suggest about the men and women of Athens?

Greek philosophers search for truth.

5. What was Plato's vision of the ideal society?	6. What is the philosophic legacy of Aristotle?

Section 4

Alexander's Empire

Terms and Names

Philip II King of Macedonia who conquered Greece

Macedonia Kingdom located just north of Greece

Alexander the Great Philip II's son who established a huge empire

Darius III Persian king

Before You Read

In the last section, you read about the Golden Age of Greece and the fall of Athens.

In this section, you will learn about Alexander the Great and his empire.

As You Read

Use an outline to organize main ideas about the growth of Alexander's empire.

PHILIP BUILDS MACEDONIAN POWER (Pages 142–143)
Who were the Macedonians?

In 359 B.C., **Philip II** became king of **Macedonia,** a kingdom located just to the north of Greece. He was a strong leader and trained his troops to be tough fighters. Philip prepared his army to invade Greece.

The Athenian orator Demosthenes tried to warn the Greeks. He told them about Philip's plans. But they united too late to save themselves. The Macedonians won. Greek independence was now over.

Philip planned to invade Persia next. He never got the chance. He was killed. His son Alexander became king at age 20. He became known as **Alexander the Great.**

1. How did Greek independence end?

_____

_____

_____

ALEXANDER DEFEATS PERSIA (Pages 143–144)
How did Alexander defeat Persia?

Alexander was a brilliant general, just like his father. He was prepared to carry out his father's dream of world conquest. In 334 B.C., Alexander invaded Persia. After Alexander's first victory, the king of Persia, **Darius III,** raised a huge army to face him. Alexander then used a surprise attack. Darius III had to retreat.

Alexander then moved south to enter Egypt. He was crowned pharaoh and founded a city that he named for himself—Alexandria. He then turned back to Persia and won another great battle. It ended all Persian resistance. The empire was his.

2. What two kingdoms did Alexander defeat?

_____

_____

_____

ALEXANDER'S OTHER CONQUESTS (Pages 144–145)

How far east did Alexander push?

Alexander pushed east, taking his army as far as India. He moved deep into that country. After many years of marching and fighting, however, his soldiers wanted to return home. Alexander agreed and turned back. On the way home, he began to make plans for how to govern his new empire. Then he suddenly fell ill and died. He was not yet 33 years old.

Three of Alexander's generals divided his empire. One ruled Macedonia and Greece. Another took control of Egypt. The third became ruler of the lands that used to be in the Persian Empire. Alexander's empire was not long lasting. Yet it had important effects. After Alexander, the people of Greece and Persia and all the lands between mixed together and shared ideas and culture.

3. How did Alexander's power come to an end?

_____

_____

As you read about the empire-building of Alexander, note the goals and
results of some of his actions.

Action(s)	Goal(s)	Result(s)
1. Led soldiers across Hellespont into Anatolia		
2. Launched surprise attack against Persians near Issus		
3. Rejected Darius' peace settlement of all lands west of Euphrates River		
4. Launched a phalanx attack followed by a cavalry charge at Gaugamela		
5. Led army into Indus Valley		

Section 5

The Spread of Hellenistic Culture

Terms and Names

Hellenistic Relating to the culture that blended Greek with Egyptian, Persian, and Indian influences

Alexandria Egyptian city that was the center of Hellenistic culture

Euclid Greek mathematician and pioneer in geometry

Archimedes Greek scientist, inventor, and mathematician

Colossus of Rhodes Huge bronze statue created on the island of Rhodes

Before You Read

In the last section, you read about the military conquests of Alexander the Great.

In this section, you will learn about the spread of Hellenistic culture.

As You Read

Use a chart to list Hellenistic achievements in various categories.

HELLENISTIC CULTURE IN ALEXANDRIA (Pages 146–147)
What was Hellenistic culture?

A new culture arose—the **Hellenistic** culture. It blended Greek with Egyptian, Persian, and Indian influences. The center of this culture was **Alexandria,** Egypt. This city was located near the mouth of the Nile River on the Mediterranean Sea. Alexandria had a ship harbor. Trade was lively. Alexandria had a large population. These people were from many different countries.

Alexandria was also a beautiful city. Its huge lighthouse towered over the harbor. Its famous museum had works of art, a zoo, and a garden. Alexandria had the first true research library. It held half a million papyrus scrolls. These contained everything known in the Hellenistic world.

1. Give two reasons why Alexandria became a center of Hellenistic culture.

_____

_____

_____

_____

SCIENCE AND TECHNOLOGY (Pages 147–148)
What new ideas arose in science, technology, and mathematics?

While scholars kept what was known about science alive, others learned new ideas. Some used an observatory to look at the stars and planets. One of these astronomers developed the idea that the sun was actually larger than Earth. No one had believed this before.

　Guided Reading Workbook

The thinkers in Alexandria also made advances in mathematics. **Euclid** wrote a book with the basic ideas of geometry. His approach is still used today. **Archimedes** invented many clever machines. One was the pulley. Another is called the Archimedes screw. Its purpose was to bring water from a lower level to a higher one.

2. What two inventions did Archimedes make?

_____

_____

_____

_____

PHILOSOPHY AND ART
(**Pages** 148–149)
What **new developments occurred in philosophy and the arts?**

Two new schools of philosophy arose in these times. The Stoics argued that people should live a good life to keep themselves in harmony with natural laws. Desire, power, and wealth led people down the wrong path. The Epicureans said that people could rely only on what they learned from their five senses. They urged everyone to live moral lives.

The arts were also important in Hellenistic times. Great achievements occurred in sculpture. Sculpture in the earlier Greek style aimed at showing perfect forms. In the Hellenistic age, sculpted figures were more realistic and emotional. The largest known Hellenistic statue is the **Colossus of Rhodes.** It stood over 100 feet high.

3. How were Hellenistic sculptures different from earlier Greek sculptures?

_____

_____

_____

_____

Name _____ Class _____ Date _____

Section 5, *continued*

As you read this section, fill in the diagram by listing the achievements of Hellenistic scholars and philosophers.

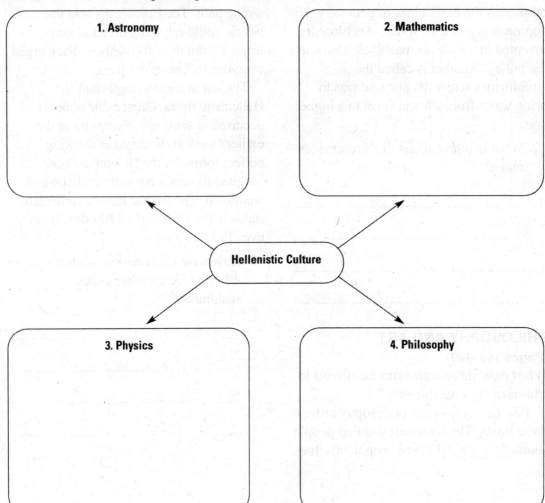

Guided Reading Workbook

Ancient Rome and Early Christianity

Section 1

The Roman Republic

Terms and Names

republic Government in which citizens have the right to select their own leader

patrician Aristocratic landowner

plebeian Farmer, artisan, or merchant; commoner

tribune Official who helped the plebeians protect their rights

consul Official who was like a king.

senate Aristocratic branch of Rome's government

dictator Roman leader who had absolute power to make laws and command the army for a brief period

legion Military unit of the ancient Roman army

Punic Wars Series of wars between Rome and Carthage

Hannibal Carthaginian general who invaded northern Italy

Before You Read

In the last section, you read about Hellenistic culture. In this section, you will read about the Roman Republic.

As You Read

Use an outline to take notes on the section's main ideas and details.

THE ORIGINS OF ROME
(Pages 155–156)
Where was Rome founded?

The city of Rome was founded by the Latin people on a river in the center of Italy. It was a good location, which gave them a chance to control all of Italy. It put them near to the midpoint of the Mediterranean Sea. Two other groups lived in what is now Italy: the Greeks in the south, and the Etruscans in the north. The Romans borrowed some ideas from both peoples.

1. What were the advantages of Rome's location?

_____

_____

THE EARLY REPUBLIC
(Pages 156–157)
How was Rome governed?

In 509 B.C., Romans overthrew the Etruscan king who had ruled over his people and over Rome. The Romans said Rome was now a **republic**. The people had the power to vote and choose leaders.

Two groups struggled for power in the new republic. One was the **patricians.** They were the aristocratic landowners who held most of the power. The other group was the **plebeians.** They were the common farmers, artisans, and merchants who made up most of the population. At first, the patricians had the most power.

Over time, the plebeians got the right to form their own assembly. They could elect representatives called **tribunes.**

The basis for Roman law was the Twelve Tables. This set of rules said that all free citizens were protected by law.

The government had three parts. Two **consuls,** or officials, were elected each year. They led the government and the army.

The second part of the government was the **senate.** It usually had 300 members chosen from the upper classes. The senate passed laws.

The third and most democratic part of government was the assemblies. The assemblies included members from different parts of society, such as citizen-soldiers or plebeians. The assemblies could also make laws.

If there were a crisis, the republic could appoint a **dictator.** This was a leader with absolute power. The dictator made laws and commanded the army. But his power lasted for only six months.

Any citizen who owned property had to serve in the army. Roman soldiers were organized into military units called legions. The Roman **legion** was made up of some 5,000 heavily armed foot soldiers.

2. What were the three main parts of Roman government?

_____

_____

_____

_____

_____

ROME SPREADS ITS POWER
(Pages 158–159)
How did Rome spread its power?

In the fourth century B.C., Rome began to get larger. Within 150 years, it had captured almost all of Italy. Rome allowed some of the conquered peoples to enjoy the benefits of citizenship. With its good location, Rome saw a growth in trade. This brought it into conflict with Carthage, a trading city in North Africa.

From 264 to 146 B.C., Rome and Carthage fought three bitter wars called the **Punic Wars.** In the first, Rome won control of the island of Sicily. In the second, **Hannibal,** a brilliant Carthaginian general invaded northern Italy. He and his soldiers did much damage. But he was unable to take Rome. It took an equally brilliant Roman general, Scipio, to defeat him. By the time of the third war, Carthage was no longer a threat to Rome. Even so, Rome destroyed the city and made its people slaves. Carthage became a new Roman province.

3. What happened as a result of the wars with Carthage?

_____

_____

_____

_____

_____

As you read about the growth of Rome into a powerful republic, answer the questions about events in the time line. (Some dates in the time line are approximate.)

753 B.C.	Rome is founded, according to legend.	1. How did geography affect the development of Rome?
		2. How did the Etruscans influence the development of Rome?
600 B.C.	Etruscan becomes king of Rome.	
		3. Which were the main groups that competed for power in the early Roman republic?
509 B.C.	Roman aristocrats overthrow monarchy and establish a republic.	4. What is the significance of the Twelve Tables in Roman law?
451 B.C.	Officials begin writing the Twelve Tables.	
		5. What were the causes of the first Punic War?
264 B.C.	Rome and Carthage go to war, and Punic Wars begin.	6. What tactic did Scipio use to defeat Hannibal?
218 B.C.	Second Punic War begins.	
202 B.C.	Romans defeat Hannibal's army.	7. What was the significance of the Punic Wars for Rome?
149 B.C. **146 B.C.**	Third Punic War begins when Rome lays siege to Carthage. Rome destroys Carthage.	

Ancient Rome and Early Christianity

The Roman Empire

Terms and Names

civil war Conflict between two groups in the same country

Julius Caesar Ambitious leader who brought order to Rome

triumvirate Group of three rulers

Augustus First ruler of imperial Rome

Pax Romana Period of Roman peace and prosperity

Before You Read

In the last section, you read about the creation of the Roman Republic.

In this section, you will read about the transformation of Rome from a republic to an empire.

As You Read

Use a chart to show how Rome changed as it became an empire.

THE REPUBLIC COLLAPSES
(Pages 160–162)
What **conflicts existed in Rome?**

Rome's victory in Carthage brought conflict between the rich and poor in Rome. **Civil war,** or fighting between groups in the same country, broke out. Leading generals fought for power.

Julius Caesar tried to take control. First he joined with two others—Crassus, a wealthy man, and Pompey, a successful general. They formed a **triumvirate,** a group of three leaders. For the next ten years, the triumvirate ruled Rome.

Caesar gained fame with several victories in battle. Pompey feared Caesar as a result. The two fought another civil war that lasted several years. Caesar won the civil war and then governed as an absolute ruler, or a leader who holds all power.

Caesar made some reforms that increased his popularity. But some members of the senate distrusted him.

They killed him because they feared he wanted to become king.

Once again, Rome suffered civil war. Caesar's nephew was the winner. He took the title **Augustus,** meaning "exalted one." The Roman Empire was now ruled by one man.

1. How did Caesar's rule lead to the end of the republic?

_____

_____

A VAST AND POWERFUL EMPIRE
(Pages 162–163)
What **was the** *Pax Romana?*

For about 200 years, the Roman Empire was a great power. Its population of between 60 and 80 million enjoyed peace and prosperity. This period is known as the *Pax Romana*—Roman peace.

Guided Reading Workbook

The empire stretched around the Mediterranean, from modern Syria and Turkey west and north to England and Germany. It relied on farming, which employed 90 percent of all workers.

Trade was also important. Traders used common coins to buy and sell goods. Coins made trading easier.

Rome had a vast trading network. Goods traveled throughout the empire by ship and along the Roman roads. The Roman navy protected trading ships.

The army defended all the people and Roman territories from attack. Many of the army's troops came from the conquered peoples. Once they finished their time in the army, they became Roman citizens.

Augustus was Rome's ablest emperor. He brought peace to the frontier, built many public buildings, and created a lasting government. He also set up a civil service. That is, he paid workers to manage the affairs of government.

Between A.D. 96 and A.D. 180, the Five Good Emperors ruled Rome. The death of Marcus Aurelius in A.D. 180 marked the beginning of the decline of the Roman Empire and the end of *Pax Romana*.

2. How were the people of the empire employed?

_____

_____

_____

_____

_____

THE ROMAN WORLD (Pages 163–165)
How did the quality of Roman life vary?

Throughout its history, Romans valued discipline, strength, and loyalty. The family was the center of Roman society. The oldest man in the family had complete authority in the household. He controlled all the property, too.

The Romans made more use of slaves than any civilization before. About one third of the people were slaves. Most slaves came from conquered lands. Slaves worked in the city and on farms. Some slaves were forced to become gladiators. Gladiators were professional fighters who fought to the death in public contests. Slaves did revolt from time to time. None of these revolts succeeded.

Quality of life in imperial Rome depended on social position. The wealthy ate well and enjoyed luxuries. The poor— including many people in Rome itself— had no jobs and received food from the government. Housing was poor. People lived in constant danger of fire. To distract people from their problems, the government gave many celebrations and spectacles.

3. Who were the slaves, and what work did they do?

_____

_____

_____

_____

_____

As you read about the creation of the Roman Empire, make notes in the
diagram to describe Roman government, society, economy, and culture.

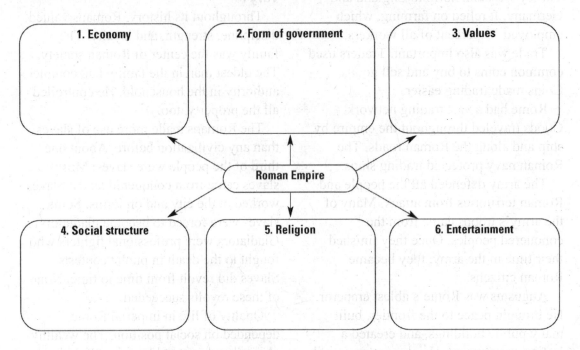

Explain how the following terms and names relate to Julius Caesar.

1. Civil war	
2. Triumvirate	
3. Gaul	
4. Absolute rule	
5. Marcus Brutus and Gaius Cassius	

The Rise of Christianity

Terms and Names

Jesus Jewish teacher whose followers came to call Christ, the Messiah or savior

apostle Close follower of Jesus.

Peter First apostle who helped spread Christianity through Judea and Syria

Paul Apostle who played a key role in the spread of Christianity throughout the Roman Empire

Diaspora Moving away of Jews from their homeland in Judea

bishop Head of all churches in one area

pope Head of the Roman Catholic Church

Constantine Roman emperor who ended persecution of Christians

Before You Read

In the last section, you read about the *Pax Romana*.

In this section, you will read about the development of Christianity.

As You Read

Use a chart to show the events that led to the spread of Christianity.

THE LIFE AND TEACHINGS OF JESUS (Pages 168–169)

Why **did people believe Jesus was the savior?**

One group of people that lost its land to the Romans was the Jews. Many Jews wanted the Romans to leave their land.

Others hoped for the coming of the Messiah—the savior. According to Jewish tradition, God promised that the Messiah would restore the kingdom of the Jews.

Jesus was born in Judea. At about age 30, Jesus began to preach. His message included many ideas from Jewish traditions, such as the principles of the Ten Commandments and the belief in one God. According to close followers, who were later called **apostles,** Jesus

performed many miracles. His fame grew. Some believed him to be the long-awaited Messiah. Roman leaders feared he would incite the people. The Romans arrested Jesus and put him to death.

After his death, Jesus' followers said that he appeared to them alive again and then went up into heaven. They said this proved he was the Messiah. They called him Christ, from the Greek word for savior. His followers came to be called Christians. Led by **Peter,** the first apostle, they spread his teachings throughout Judea and Syria.

1. Why was Jesus put to death?

_____

_____

_____

_____

_____

CHRISTIANITY SPREADS THROUGH THE EMPIRE
(Pages 169–170)
How did Christianity spread through the empire?

At first Jesus' followers were all Jewish. Later, under one apostle, **Paul,** Christians began to look to all people, even non-Jews, to join the church. The leaders of the early church traveled throughout the empire spreading the teachings of Jesus.

During this time, Jews made attempts to break free of the Romans. These movements did not succeed. Most Jews were driven from their homeland into exile. This scattering of the Jews is called the **Diaspora.**

At the same time, Roman leaders tried to punish the Christians. Some were put to death or killed by wild animals in the arena. But Christianity continued to spread.

2. What did the Romans do to the Jews?

_____

_____

_____

_____

A WORLD RELIGION (Pages 170–172)
Why did Christianity spread?

After almost 200 years, millions of people across the empire had become Christians. Christianity spread for several reasons. First, it accepted all believers, rich or poor, male or female. Second, it gave hope to the powerless. Third, it appealed to those who were bothered by the lack of morality in Rome. Fourth, it offered a personal relationship with God. Fifth, it offered the promise of life after death.

As the church grew, it became more organized. Priests were in charge of small churches. **Bishops** were in charge of all the churches in one area. The bishop of Rome was called the **pope**. The pope was later viewed as the head of the Roman Catholic Church.

In A.D. 313, Christianity entered a new era. The Roman emperor **Constantine** said that Christians would no longer be persecuted. He gave his official approval to Christianity. A few decades later, Christianity became the empire's official religion.

While Christianity grew in power, it went through changes. Church leaders sometimes disagreed over basic beliefs and argued about them. Church leaders called any belief that appeared to contradict the basic teachings a heresy. From time to time, councils met to end disagreements and define beliefs.

3. How was the church organized?

_____

_____

_____

_____

As you read about the rise of Christianity, fill in the charts below.

How did each of the following people influence the development of Christianity as a new religion?	
1. Jesus of Nazareth	
2. The Jews	
3. Pontius Pilate	
4. Peter	

How did each of the following help to promote the spread of Christianity?	
5. *Pax Romana*	
6. Paul	
7. Constantine	
8. Theodosius	

Section 4

The Fall of the Roman Empire

Terms and Names

inflation Large drop in the value of money and rise in the prices of goods

mercenary Foreign soldiers who fought for money

Diocletian Strong-willed army leader and Roman emperor

Constantinople New name for Byzantium under Constantine

Attila Powerful chieftain of Huns

Before You Read

In the last section, you read about the spread of Christianity.

.In this section, you will learn how the Roman Empire collapsed.

As You Read

Use a chart to identify what caused the problems facing the Roman Empire.

A CENTURY OF CRISIS (Page 173)
What problems did Rome face?

Rome entered a period of decline after the reign of Marcus Aurelius ended in A.D. 180. Rome suffered economic problems. Trade slowed as raiders threatened ships and caravans on sea and land. The economy suffered from **inflation,** a drastic drop in the value of money and a rise in prices. Food supplies also dropped as tired soil, warfare, and high taxes cut the amount of grain and other foods produced on farms.

The empire also had military problems. German tribes caused trouble on the frontiers. Persians defeated the Romans in A.D. 260 and captured the emperor. Roman soldiers could no longer be counted on. Instead, **mercenaries**—soldiers who fight for money—had to be hired. At the same time, Roman generals fought one another for control of the empire.

1. What economic problems did Rome face?

_____

_____

EMPERORS ATTEMPT REFORM
(Pages 174–175)
What changes did the emperors make?

Diocletian took the throne as emperor in 284. He passed many new laws to try to fix the economy. He tried to restore the status of the emperor by naming himself a son of the chief Roman god. He even divided the empire into eastern and western halves to make it easier to govern.

Constantine continued many of these changes. He became emperor of both halves of the empire in 324. A few years later, Constantine moved the capital of the empire to a new city in northwestern Turkey where Europe and Asia meet.

The city was Byzantium. In time, it was given a new name—**Constantinople,** the city of Constantine.

2. Who was Constantine?

_____

_____

THE WESTERN EMPIRE CRUMBLES (Pages 175–176)
Who overran Rome?

Reforms delayed the end of the Roman Empire but could not prevent its fall. The eastern part of the empire remained strong and unified. But troubles continued in the west. Germanic tribes moved into the empire. They were trying to escape from the Huns, fierce nomadic people from central Asia, who were moving into their land.

The Roman armies in the west collapsed. German armies twice entered Rome itself. In 408, Visigoths led by their king, Alaric, put the city under siege. In 444, the Huns united under a powerful chieftain named **Attila.** Attila and his armies terrorized both halves of the empire.

The invasions continued after Attila's death. The Germans had arrived for good. By 476, German peoples controlled many areas of Europe. That year a German general removed the last western Roman emperor from the throne.

3. What role did Attila play in the collapse of Rome?

_____

_____

As you read about the decline and fall of the Roman Empire, take notes to
answer the questions.

1. What were the causes of each condition that led to the fall of the Roman Empire?	
a. Disruption of trade	
b. Gold and silver drain	
c. Inflation	
d. Decline of loyalty and discipline in military	
e. Citizen indifference and loss of patriotism	

2. What steps did Diocletian take to restore order and reform the empire?

3. What did Constantine do to reform the empire?

4. What caused the final collapse of the Western Roman Empire?

Ancient Rome and Early Christianity

Section 5

Rome and the Roots of Western Civilization

Terms and Names

Greco-Roman culture Culture developed from the blending of Greek, Hellenistic, and Roman cultures

Pompeii Roman town destroyed by the eruption of Mount Vesuvius

Virgil Roman poet who wrote the *Aeneid*

Tacitus Roman historian who recorded the good and bad of imperial Rome

aqueduct Pipeline or channel built to carry water

Before You Read

In the last section, you read about the fall of Rome. In this section, you will learn about the contributions of Rome to Western civilization.

As You Read

Use a chart to list the accomplishments of the Roman Empire.

THE LEGACY OF GRECO-ROMAN CIVILIZATION
(Pages 178–181)
***What* is Greco-Roman culture?**

Rome took aspects of Greek and Hellenistic culture and added ideas of its own. The mixing of Greek, Hellenistic, and Roman culture produced a new culture called **Greco-Roman culture.** This is also often called classical civilization.

Roman artists, philosophers, and writers did not just copy Greek works. They created a style of their own for their own purposes. Much of Roman art had practical purposes. It was aimed at educating the public.

One example of the mixing of cultures occurred in sculpture. Romans borrowed Greek ideas but made their sculptures more realistic. The Romans also

developed a kind of sculpture in which images stood out from a flat background.

Romans were skilled at creating pictures made from tiny tiles, a process called mosaic. But Romans were perhaps most skilled at painting. The best examples of Roman painting are found in the Roman town of **Pompeii.** Pompeii was covered with ash after a volcanic eruption. The ash preserved many works of art and culture.

In both literature and philosophy, Romans were inspired by the Greeks. The poet **Virgil** wrote the most famous work of Latin literature, the *Aeneid*. It was modeled on the Greek epics of Homer.

The Romans also produced some important histories. **Tacitus** is an important Roman ancient historian.

Among ancient historians, he is known for presenting accurate facts. He described the good and bad parts of imperial Rome in his *Annals* and *Histories*.

1. Name three Roman cultural achievements.

   _____

   _____

   _____

   _____

THE LEGACY OF ROME
(**Pages** 181–183)
What **were Rome's most major contributions to Western culture?**

   The Roman language, Latin, was important in European history. It was the official language of the Roman Catholic Church into the 20th century. Many European languages developed from Latin, including French, Spanish, Portuguese, Italian, and Romanian. And many Latin words are used in other languages, including English.

   Romans also became famous for their skill at engineering. They used arches and domes to build large, impressive

buildings. Many of these forms are still used today. They also built an excellent system of roads and several **aqueducts.** Aqueducts carried water from distant lakes or rivers to large cities.

   But Rome's most lasting influence was in the field of law. The Roman government set standards of law that still influence people today. Some of the most important principles of Roman law were:

- All persons had the right to equal treatment under the law.

- A person was considered innocent until proven guilty.

- The burden of proof rested with the accuser rather than the accused.

- A person should be punished only for actions, not for thoughts.

- Any law that seemed unreasonable or unfair could be set aside.

2. What important standards of law were set by the Romans?

   _____

   _____

   _____

As you read about the roots of classical civilization, fill in the chart to identify elements of the Greco-Roman culture.

Cultural Element	Greek Contributions	Roman Contributions
1. Sculpture		
2. Philosophy		
3. Literature		

Identify Roman achievements in the boxes below.

4. Language	5. Architecture	6. Engineering

Section 1

India's First Empires

Terms and Names

Mauryan Empire First empire in India, founded by Chandragupta Maurya

Asoka Grandson of Chandragupta; leader who brought the Mauryan Empire to its greatest height

religious toleration Acceptance of the right of people to have differing religious beliefs

Tamil Language of southern India; also the people who speak that language

Gupta Empire Second empire in India, founded by Chandra Gupta

patriarchal Relating to a social system in which the father is the head of the family

matriarchal Relating to a social system in which the mother is the head of the family

Before You Read

In the last section, you read about the influence of ancient Rome.

In this section, you will read about the Mauryan and Gupta empires in India.

As You Read

Use a chart to compare the Mauryan and Gupta empires.

THE MAURYAN EMPIRE IS ESTABLISHED (Pages 189–192)
How did the Mauryan Empire begin?

In 321 B.C., Chandragupta Maurya used his army to defeat a powerful king in eastern India. He became king, and this started the **Mauryan Empire.**

Chandragupta then moved northwest. In 305 B.C., he began to challenge Seleucus, one of Alexander the Great's generals. The two armies fought for several years. Eventually Chandragupta won. For the first time, northeastern and northwestern India were joined under the rule of one person.

Chandragupta was a harsh ruler. He charged a heavy tax on farmers—one-half of the crop they grew each year. He used this wealth to build a huge army. He controlled his government by carefully choosing officials and watching them closely. He split his empire into four provinces, each ruled by a prince. These areas, in turn, were divided into smaller pieces that were run by members of the government. Life in Chandragupta's court was rich. The palace and capital city were beautiful.

Chandragupta's grandson, **Asoka,** took the throne in 269 B.C. He brought the Mauryan Empire to its greatest height. At first he was a warlike king and fought many fierce battles with an enemy to the south. Then he decided to accept the teachings of the Buddha.

Asoka promised to rule in a fair way. He issued laws that urged his subjects to avoid violence. He urged **religious toleration.** This is acceptance of people's rights to differing religious beliefs.

Guided Reading Workbook

He made great roads so that people could travel easily. Soon after Asoka died, however, his empire collapsed.

1. What changes did Asoka make in the Mauryan Empire?

_____

_____

_____

A PERIOD OF TURMOIL (Page 191)
What troubles did India face?

For 500 years after Asoka, India was a land of troubles. In the center of India, a new dynasty—the Andhra Dynasty—dominated the region. In the northwest, many Greeks, Persians, and Central Asians entered the land. They were fleeing the invasions of others. These peoples added new ideas and languages to India's rich mix of culture. In the south, three different kingdoms fought each other off and on. The people who lived in this region spoke the **Tamil** language. They are called the Tamil people.

2. Who are the Tamils?

_____

_____

_____

THE GUPTA EMPIRE IS ESTABLISHED (Pages 191–192)
What was life like in the Gupta Empire?

Around A.D. 320, Chandra Gupta I came to power in the north. He was not related to the first emperor. He took the title of king and began to conquer other areas.

His son, Samudra Gupta, followed the same policy. For 40 years, he fought to win new lands for the **Gupta Empire.** Samudra's son, Chandra Gupta II, brought the empire to its largest size. He added parts of western India, including some important ports on the Indian Ocean, to his empire. With these, the Guptas were able to take part in the rich trade that connected India, Southwest Asia, and the world of the Mediterranean Sea. The Gupta empire stretched all across northern India.

Most Indians lived in villages and were farmers. Part of each crop that they grew had to be paid to the king each year. Farmers also had to set aside part of each month to work on community resources, such as wells or dams. Craft workers and those who worked in trade lived in special sections of each village, town, or city.

Most families in northern India were **patriarchal.** They were headed by the oldest male. But in southern India, some Tamil families were **matriarchal.** This meant the mother was head of the family. Property, and sometimes the throne, were passed through the female side of the family.

The Gupta kings were patrons of the arts. Artists flourished during the Gupta rule. However, after the death of Chandra Gupta II, another wave of invaders moved into India. Over the next hundred years, the great Gupta Empire broke up into several smaller kingdoms. The empire ended about 535.

3. How did the Gupta Empire end?

_____

_____

_____

Guided Reading Workbook

As you read about the Mauryan and Gupta empires in India, take notes to answer the questions about the time line. (Some dates on the time line are approximate.)

321 B.C.	**Chandragupta Maurya claims the throne and the Mauryan Dynasty begins.**	1. How did Chandragupta support his successful war efforts?
301 B.C.	**Chandragupta's son assumes the throne.**	2. How did Chandragupta hold his vast empire together?
		3. Why did Asoka wage war early in his reign?
269 B.C.	**Asoka, Chandragupta's grandson, becomes king of the Mauryan Empire.**	
232 B.C.	**Asoka dies and the empire begins to break up.**	4. How did Asoka show concern for his subjects' well-being?
		5. What did Chandra Gupta I accomplish during his reign?
A.D. 320	**Chandra Gupta I becomes first Gupta emperor.**	
A.D. 335	**Chandra Gupta's son Samudra becomes ruler.**	6. What did Samudra accomplish during his reign?
		7. What was the significance of Chandra Gupta II's military victories?
A.D. 375	**Chandra Gupta II becomes king.**	8. What peaceful means did he use to strengthen his empire?

Guided Reading Workbook

Section 2

Trade Spreads Indian Religions and Culture

Terms and Names

Mahayana Sect of Buddhism that offers salvation to all and allows popular worship

Theravada Sect of Buddhism focusing on strict spiritual discipline

Brahma Creator of the world, in Hinduism

Vishnu Preserver of the world, in Hinduism

Shiva Destroyer of the world, in Hinduism

Kalidasa One of India's greatest poets and playwrights

Silk Roads Caravan routes that crisscrossed central Asia

Before You Read

In the last section, you read about the Mauryan and Gupta empires of India.

In this section, you will learn how trade caused changes in Indian religion and culture.

As You Read

Use a chart to list one or more specific developments of Indian culture.

BUDDHISM AND HINDUISM CHANGE (Pages 193–194)
What were the changes in religious thought?

Over time, the religions of Hinduism and Buddhism became more and more distant from the common people. Priests dominated Hinduism. Followers of the Buddha found it difficult to find the promised goal of release from this world. As new peoples moved into India, they brought new ideas. These ideas had an impact on these religions.

The Buddha had taught that a tough spiritual life was the way to escape from the suffering of the world. But self-denial was difficult for most people. Many people came to worship the Buddha

himself as a god, even though he had forbidden it. Some came to believe that other people could become Buddhas themselves. They could do this through good works and sacrifice.

These ideas created a new kind of Buddhism, the **Mahayana** sect. Those who held on to the stricter beliefs belonged to the **Theravada** sect. The new Mahayana approach helped Buddhism become a popular religion. All believers had the chance to be saved. This change caused an increase in art. Buddhists with money built temples and shrines and then paid artists to decorate them with sculptures and paintings.

Hinduism changed, too. By the time of the Mauryan Empire, only priests were involved in many rituals of the faith. For centuries, Hinduism had been a religion of many gods. Now other religions based on only one god were becoming more important. Many Hindus began to emphasize three gods in particular. One was **Brahma,** creator of the world. Another was **Vishnu,** preserver of the world. The third was **Shiva,** destroyer of the world. By devoting themselves to these gods, people began to feel the religion more directly in their lives.

1. What changes did the split in Buddhism bring?

   _____

   _____

   _____

ACHIEVEMENTS OF INDIAN CULTURE (Pages 194–195)
What advances occurred in the arts and sciences?

The amount and quality of Indian art increased. Poets and playwrights, such as **Kalidasa,** wrote beautiful works of literature. Other artists laid the foundations for the classical form of dance in India.

The scientists of India proved that Earth was indeed round 1,000 years before Columbus. They made great advances in mathematics, too. They invented the idea of zero and of decimal numbers. The doctors of India became highly skilled. They knew more than 1,000 diseases and used hundreds of medicines from plants to help their patients.

2. What advances did scientists and mathematicians make?

   _____

   _____

   _____

THE SPREAD OF INDIAN TRADE (Pages 195–197)
How did India's trade increase?

Soon Indians learned about the **Silk Roads.** These were caravan routes that crisscrossed central Asia. Indian traders joined in the trade along these routes. Indians traded cotton cloth and animals to China for silk. Traders brought spices from Southeast Asia to India and then sold them to Rome and other western peoples.

This trade was so busy that large numbers of Roman coins have been found in India. The Indians also traded their own cotton cloth in Africa for ivory and gold. They sent rice and wheat to Arabia for dates and horses. They carried out this trade by land and sea.

India's culture spread beyond India. The art and architecture of many lands in Southeast Asia show the influence of Indian art. Some people adopted Hinduism, and many began to follow Buddhism.

3. In addition to goods, what did India send to different parts of the world?

   _____

   _____

   _____

Guided Reading Workbook

As you read about the ways that Indian culture changed and expanded between about 200 B.C. and A.D. 300, fill out the chart by writing notes in the appropriate spaces.

Changes in Religious Thought	
1. Note how Buddhism changed and identify two effects of this change.	
2. Note how Hinduism changed and identify two effects of this change.	

Expansion of Culture	
3. Note at least two examples of the flowering of literature and performing arts.	
4. Note at least two examples of the flowering of science and mathematics.	

Expansion of Trade and Commerce	
5. Note how development of the Silk Roads and increased sea trade contributed to the expansion of Indian commerce.	
6. Note two effects of the expansion of Indian trade.	

India and China Establish Empires

Section 3

Han Emperors in China

Terms and Names

Han Dynasty Chinese dynasty that ruled for most of the period from 202 B.C. to A.D. 220

centralized government Government that concentrates power in a central authority

civil service Administrative departments of a government; also, word describing government jobs and employees

monopoly One group's complete control over the production and distribution of certain goods

assimilation Policy of encouraging conquered peoples to adopt the institutions and customs of the conquering nation

Before You Read

In the last section, you read about the spread of Indian religions and culture.

In this section, you will read about the Han Dynasty in China.

As You Read

Use an outline to organize main ideas and details on the Han Dynasty.

THE HAN RESTORE UNITY TO CHINA (Pages 200–202)
What changes did Han leaders make?

A strong empire also arose in China. The Chinese had been united briefly under the Qin empire. But it fell apart in a period of civil war. In 202 B.C., Liu Bang named himself the first emperor of the **Han Dynasty.** The Han would rule parts of China for the next 400 years. They set many patterns for Chinese culture for centuries to come.

Liu Bang created a **centralized government.** Local officials reported to the emperor. The rule of the previous emperor had been very harsh. Liu Bang took a different approach. He lowered taxes. He gave lighter penalties for crimes. Life became easier for the Chinese people.

From 141 to 87 B.C., the emperor Wudi ruled Han China. He made his empire almost the size of modern China. He defeated nomads in the north. He moved troops and settlers to the west. He sent soldiers to the north into modern Korea and to the south to modern Vietnam.

1. What changes did Liu Bang make?

_____

_____

A HIGHLY STRUCTURED SOCIETY; HAN TECHNOLOGY, COMMERCE, AND CULTURE (Pages 202–205)
What advances took place?

Chinese society under the Han Dynasty was very structured. The emperor was at the top. He had a large number of officials.

These officials reached down to the smallest village. They filled **civil service** jobs. Those who wanted these jobs had to pass an exam. The exam tested them on their knowledge of the writings of the Chinese philosopher Confucius.

To support a large government, the emperor collected taxes. Farmers paid part of the crops they gathered. Merchants paid taxes on the goods they traded. Peasants also had to work one month a year on government projects, such as dams and roads.

Under Han rule, the Chinese created many new inventions. One was paper. Paper made books more available and increased learning.

The Chinese also improved farming by inventing a new two-bladed plow. This change was important because the number of Chinese people had grown greatly. As Han emperors told their people, farming was the most important work. At the same time, several industries became important. The government had a **monopoly** on, or took complete control of, the mining of salt and making of iron, coins, and alcohol. It also made silk, which was in great demand in other lands.

2. Why were changes in farming so important?

_____

_____

THE HAN UNIFIES CHINESE CULTURE; THE FALL OF THE HAN AND THEIR RETURN (Pages 205–207)
Why **did problems develop?**

China now included many different peoples. The Han rulers encouraged

assimilation—making sure that these people learned Chinese ways. They urged the Chinese to marry them.

One group that did not do well in Han China was women. According to Confucius, women were limited to meeting the needs of their husband and children. Some upper-class women, however, were able to become involved in other areas of life.

The Han empire began to have problems. Rich people got richer, while the poor were forced to pay heavy taxes. Members of the court were caught up in plots to gain power. Eventually, the peasants rebelled against their high taxes and poor lives.

A government official named Wang Mang took the throne. He tried to help the poor by taking land from the large landholders. But a terrible flood struck China and the peasants rebelled again. The Han Dynasty was restored when a member of the Han family was put on the throne. This was called the Later Han Dynasty.

For the next few decades, China enjoyed peace and wealth. But the same problems arose. The gap between rich and poor was too great. By A.D. 220, the Han Dynasty had fallen for good.

3. What caused the fall of the Han Dynasty?

_____

_____

As you read about the Han Dynasty, take notes to fill in the charts.

Ruler	Objectives	How objectives were accomplished
1. Liu Bang	• Destroy rivals' power • Win popular support	
2. Empress Lü	• Keep control of throne	
3. Wudi	• Expand Chinese Empire • Appoint qualified people to government jobs	
4. Wang Mang	• Restore order and bring the country under control	

Use information from Section 3 to identify some results of each situation or event.

Situation or Event	Result(s)
5. Paper is invented.	
6. Government makes techniques of silk production a closely guarded secret.	
7. Territorial expansion brings people of many cultures under Chinese rule.	
8. Gap between rich and poor increases.	

Guided Reading Workbook

Section 1

Diverse Societies in Africa

Terms and Names

Sahara Large desert in Africa

savanna Grassy plain

Sahel Land at the southern edge of the Sahara

animism Religion in which spirits play a role in daily life

Nok African people who lived in what is now Nigeria from 500 B.C. to A.D. 200

Djenné-Djeno Oldest known city in Africa south of the Sahara

Before You Read

In the last section, you read about empires in China.

In this section, you will learn how African people developed diverse societies.

As You Read

Use an outline to organize ideas and details about Africa.

A LAND OF GEOGRAPHIC CONTRASTS (Pages 213–215)
What are some of the geographic contrasts in Africa?

Africa is the second largest continent in the world. It stretches 4,600 miles from east to west and 5,000 miles from north to south. It has about one-fifth of the earth's land. Much of the land is a high plateau, with lower land near the coasts. The rivers that flow along this high land often form waterfalls or rapids. As a result, boats cannot use these rivers to travel either to or from the coast. Also, the coast has few harbors for so large a landmass.

Africa has many different environments. There are hot, dry deserts; steamy, wet rain forests; and high, cool mountains.

About a third of Africa's land is desert. Few people live there. Deserts form a barrier to people who want to move from one area to another. The **Sahara** Desert in the north of Africa is about one-third the size of the United States. Dense rain forests cover much of the central part of Africa.

The northern and southern regions of Africa have large numbers of people. Most Africans live on the **savannas,** grasslands that cover almost half of the continent. They grow grains, including rice and wheat, and tend cattle.

The land at the southern edge of the Sahara Desert is the **Sahel.** Each year, the Sahara Desert takes over a little more of this Sahel.

1. Name three contrasting features of African geography.

_____

_____

_____

EARLY HUMANS ADAPT TO THEIR ENVIRONMENTS (Pages 215–216)
When and where did people begin to farm?

The first humans in Africa got food by hunting animals and gathering plants. Even today, some African peoples still use this method to get food.

Over time, these people learned to tame animals and raise them for food. Like the hunters and gatherers, these herders were nomadic people. As they moved, they looked for grass and for water for their animals. When food or water was used up in one area, they moved to another.

About 10,000 B.C., some people in Africa began to farm. People used to farm in the area of the Sahara before it became a desert. They also farmed in the Nile Valley and West Africa or on the grass-lands. Some moved to the rain forest.

2. Where did African people settle and begin farming?

   _____

   _____

EARLY SOCIETIES IN WEST AFRICA (Pages 216–217)
How did early societies live?

The diverse environments of Africa created much variety in the way different African peoples lived, The people who lived south of the Sahara, though, had these features in common:

- The family was the most important unit of society. The family was an extended family that included grandparents, aunts, uncles, and cousins. In some groups, family included all the people who came from common ancestors. This is called a clan.

- They believed that one god created the world. Their beliefs included **animism.** They felt that plants, animals, and other natural forces all have spirits that play an important role in life.

- They relied on oral storytelling, rather than writing, to pass on the traditions of their people. In West Africa, for example, storytellers, or **griots,** kept history alive.

3. What features did people living south of the Sahara have in common?

   _____

   _____

WEST AFRICAN IRON AGE (Pages 217–219)
Who were the Iron Age societies?

The West African **Nok** culture existed from about 500 B.C, to A.D. 200. The Nok people made pottery figures and were the first people in Africa who knew how to make iron. Some styles of Nok pottery are still found in Africa today.

Djenné-Djeno is the oldest known African city south of the Sahara. It is located on the banks of the Niger River. It dates from about 250 B.C. About 50,000 people lived there at its height. At first, they lived in round huts made of reeds and covered with mud. Later they lived in houses of mud bricks. They grew rice, raised cattle, and made iron. They traded these goods for gold and copper.

4. What is Djenné-Djeno?

   _____

   _____

As you read about Africa's diverse societies, fill out the chart.

How did each environmental feature affect the peoples of ancient Africa?

Environmental feature	Effect on Africans
1. Waterfalls and rapids	
2. Sahara and Kalahari deserts	
3. Mediterranean coastal areas	
4. Tsetse fly	
5. Fertile land of savannas	

Take notes to explain how the people in each group adapted to their environment.

Group	Methods of Adaptation
6. San of the Kalahari Desert	
7. Nok people	
8. People of Djenné-Djeno	

African Civilizations

Section 2

Migration Case Study: Bantu-Speaking Peoples

Terms and Names

migration A permanent move from one area to another

push-pull factors Reasons attracting or driving people to move

Bantu-speaking peoples People who speak one of a group of languages related to Bantu

Before You Read

In the last section, you read about African societies populating the continent. In this section, you will read about the causes and effects of migration in Africa among Bantu-speaking peoples.

As You Read

Use a chart to identify causes and effects of specific events related to Bantu migration.

PEOPLE ON THE MOVE
(Pages 220–221)
***What* are the main reasons for migrations?**

Throughout human history, many peoples have felt the urge to move from their homes to a new land. This movement is called **migration.** There are many reasons that people make such a move. But they can be grouped into three main causes. They are environmental change, economic pressure, political and religious persecution.

Reasons people move into or out of an area are called **push-pull factors.** People may be attracted or pulled into an area because they see economic advantages. Or they may move because they want freedom. Sometimes people are pushed out of an area because the environment changes and it is impossible to live there. Other times people may leave to find security or peace that

cannot be found in their area. These are examples of push factors.

In studying times before written history, researchers look for clues to migrations. One clue they use is language. People take their language with them when they move to a new place. When historians find two languages from two distant areas that have words that are somewhat similar, they can conclude that those two languages may have both come from the same language. However, some time later the original speakers of the language moved apart. Then the two languages changed independently. This kind of clue has given historians a way of understanding the early history of Africa.

1. Name three key reasons for migration.

_____

_____

_____

MASSIVE MIGRATIONS
(Pages 220–224)
Who were the Bantu-speaking peoples?

Many languages spoken in Africa today developed from the same parent language called Proto-Bantu. The speakers of all these different languages are called the **Bantu-speaking peoples.** The people who spoke Bantu first lived in a part of modern Nigeria. In the first few centuries A.D., they began to move south and east. Over time, they spread throughout Africa south of the Sahara Desert, reaching the southern tip around 500 years ago. They brought their language and their culture with them.

One of the reasons people moved had to do with their style of farming. They would clear an area and use it until the soil no longer could produce good crops. The people then needed to move to a new area to clear new ground.

Another reason they moved was that their farming was so successful. Farming helped them produce more food than they could by hunting and gathering. With more to eat, groups became larger and the land more crowded. They could not move north, where the Sahara Desert made a barrier. So they had to move farther and farther south.

As they reached new areas, the Bantu peoples met other peoples. Sometimes these meetings were violent. The Bantus, who knew how to make iron, had better weapons than those they met, who only had stone tools. Some of the peoples that they met are still found in Africa. But they live in small areas with very harsh environments. The Bantus took the better land.

2. Why did the Bantu peoples keep moving to new areas?

_____

_____

As you read this case study about the Bantu migrations, take notes to answer the questions below.

Bantu-speaking peoples adapted their skills to new environments they encountered in their migrations southward.	

1. a. How did they change their farming in the rain forests?
 	
   b. Why was the change necessary?
	2. a. How did they change their techniques for herding in the savannas?
	
	   b. Why did they make this change?

3. Some of their adaptations caused them to continue their migrations to new places. Why?	

The migrations of the Bantu-speaking peoples helped to shape the cultures of the African continent.	

4. a. Why did the Bantu-speaking peoples move southward, rather than to the north?
 	
   b. What happened to the non-Bantu-speaking hunter-gatherer societies as the newcomers spread south?
	5. a. How did the Bantu speakers relate to the people they did not drive out?
	
	   b. What were some results of their intermingling?

6. How did the Bantu speakers help unify the various peoples of Africa?	

African Civilizations

Section 3

The Kingdom of Aksum

Terms and Names

Aksum African kingdom that reached the height of its power in the fourth century A.D.

Adulis Chief seaport of Aksum

Ezana King of Aksum who conquered Kush

terraces Step like ridges built on slopes to improve farming

Before You Read

In the last section, you read about the migration of Bantu-speakers across parts of southern Africa. In this section, you will learn about the kingdom of Aksum and its role in trade.

As You Read

Use a web diagram to list the achievements of Aksum.

THE RISE OF THE KINGDOM OF AKSUM (Pages 225–226)
How did Aksum arise?

The peoples in East Africa had a great deal of contact with people from other areas. The Kushite kingdom of Nubia had close relations with Egypt. Its kings even ruled Egypt for a while. That kingdom continued for many centuries as a trading power. It was then replaced by the kingdom of **Aksum** in what is now modern Ethiopia. The dynasty that ruled Aksum and later Ethiopia included the 20th-century ruler Haile Selassie.

Aksum may have begun as early as 1000 B.C. when Arabian traders mixed with the people of Kush. It became an important part of world trade. Salt, emeralds, brass, copper, gold, cloth, olive oil, and wine all moved through Aksum. Its trade routes helped link Rome to India. Traders crowded into its chief seaport, **Adulis.**

In the early A.D. 300s, Aksum had a strong new king named **Ezana.** He

brought the kingdom to its height during his rule. Ezana captured more land on the Arabian peninsula, and then conquered Kush in 350.

1. Why was Aksum an important trading center?

_____

_____

_____

AN INTERNATIONAL CULTURE DEVELOPS (Pages 227–228)
What was unique about Aksum's culture?

Aksum was an international trading center. It was home to peoples from many different cultures. There were people from Aksum's widespread trading partners, including Egypt, Arabia, Greece, Rome, Persia, India, and even Byzantium.

At the time of King Ezana, these different peoples all spoke to one another in Greek.

The Aksumites, like other ancient Africans, traditionally believed in one god. They also worshiped the spirits of nature and honored their dead ancestors. During his rule, King Ezana decided to become a Christian. The religion slowly spread throughout the land.

The people of Aksum also developed a special way of building. They made structures out of stone, not mud baked into bricks by the hot sun. Their kings built tall pillars of stone that reached as high as 60 feet. They were among the tallest structures in the ancient world.

Aksum made other advances as well. Aside from Egypt and the city of Meroë, it was the only culture of ancient Africa to have a written language. The language of Aksum had been brought to the land by Arab traders many hundreds of years before. Aksum was also the first state south of the Sahara to mint its own coins.

The people of Aksum also developed a new way of farming. They cut **terraces,** steplike ridges, into the steep mountainsides in their country. The terraces helped the land hold water instead of letting it run down the mountain in a heavy rain. This was called terrace farming. The people of Aksum also used dams and stone tanks to store water and used ditches to channel it to their fields.

2. What achievements and advances were made in Aksum?

   _____

   _____

   _____

THE FALL OF AKSUM (Page 229)
Why did Aksum fall?

Aksum remained an important power in East Africa for 800 years. It was first challenged in the 600s, after the new religion of Islam came to Arabia. The followers of Islam captured the lands that Aksum held in the Arabian peninsula. Within a few decades, they had taken much of North Africa.

At first, these conquerors left Aksum alone. Aksum remained an island of Christianity in a sea of Islam. In 710, however, the conquerors destroyed Adulis. The Aksum kings moved their capital over the mountains to a hard-to-reach area, in present-day northern Ethiopia. Aksum was now cut off from other Christian lands. It was also isolated from the sea trade. Aksum began to decline as a world power.

3. Why did the rulers of Aksum move their capital?

   _____

   _____

   _____

   _____

   _____

As you read about the Kingdom of Aksum, briefly note the causes or effects (depending on which is missing) of each situation.

Causes	Effects
1. Aksum had access to the Red Sea, Blue Nile, and White Nile.	
2. The port city of Adulis included people from Aksum's trading partners.	
	3. The Aksumites created terrace farming, which retained water and prevented erosion.
4. Islamic invaders seized footholds in Africa, destroyed Adulis, and spread the religion of Islam.	
	5. Aksum's new geographic location led to its decline as a power.

The Earliest Americans

Terms and Names

Beringia Land bridge between Asia and the Americas

Ice Age Time when sheets of ice covered large portions of North America

maize Corn; the most important crop of the Americas

Before You Read

In the last chapter, you read about African civilizations.

In this section, you will read about the Americas' first inhabitants.

As You Read

Use a chart to list causes and effects of the development of the Americas.

A LAND BRIDGE (Pages 235–236)
How did the earliest people come to the Americas?

North and South America form a single stretch of land. It stretches from the Arctic Circle in the north to the waters around Antarctica in the south. The Atlantic and Pacific Oceans separate the Americas from Africa, Asia, and Europe.

But that was not always the case. From around 1.6 million years ago until about 10,000 years ago, the earth went through an **Ice Age.** During this time, huge sheets of ice called glaciers spread south from the Arctic Circle. The level of the world's oceans went down. The lowered oceans exposed land that is today again covered by water.

One strip of land, called **Beringia,** connected Asia and North America. Wild animals crossed this rocky land bridge and entered North America for the first time. Some of the Asian people who hunted these animals followed them. The people became the first Americans.

No one knows for sure when these first people arrived. Some scholars say the people came to the Americas as long ago as 40,000 B.C. Others say as late as 12,000 B.C. A discovery in Chile suggests that people were well-settled in that part of the Americas by 10,500 B.C. Since Chile lies far south of the land bridge, some experts say that people needed many thousands of years to travel that far. For this reason, they think that the first people must have crossed the land bridge in about 20,000 B.C.

1. Where did the first Americans come from?

_____

_____

HUNTERS AND GATHERERS
(Page 236)
How did early Americans live?

These first Americans lived as hunters. One of their favorite hunting targets was the huge mammoth. Over time, however, all the mammoths died. People were forced to look for other food. They began to hunt smaller animals and to fish.

Section 1, *continued*

They also began to gather plants and fruits to eat. They no longer had to roam over large areas to search for the mammoth, so they settled for part of the year in one spot.

Between 12,000 and 10,000 B.C., the climate changed. The Ice Age ended, and the world warmed up again. The huge sheets of ice melted, and the oceans rose again to cover the land bridge that connected Asia to the Americas. By this time, though, people lived from north to south in the Americas. They lived in many different environments and found ways of life suited to the place where they lived.

2. What kinds of prey did the first Americans hunt?

_____

_____

AGRICULTURE CREATES A NEW WAY OF LIFE (Page 238–239)
How did agriculture change ways of life?

About 7000 B.C., the people living in central Mexico started a quiet revolution—farming. It was the same kind of radical change that had happened in several spots in Asia and Africa. By 3400 B.C., they had several foods that they grew, including squashes, beans, chilies,

and the most important one—**maize,** or corn. Corn grew so well that a family of three could, in four months, grow enough corn to feed it for two years.

Over many centuries, farming spread throughout the Americas. In what is now the eastern United States and in the region of the Andes, people may have discovered the idea of farming on their own. In central Mexico, farmers became so skilled at growing corn that they could enjoy three harvests each year.

Farming had the same results in the Americas that it did in Asia and Africa. Growing food gave people a larger and more reliable food supply. As more people could be fed, they were healthier and lived longer. As a result, the population grew.

Because farmers produced so much food, some people could concentrate on other ways of making a living. They began to work in different arts and crafts and learned new skills. Some people became rich. They owned more than others and enjoyed a higher position in society. Some people became rulers. Others became their subjects.

3. Why was maize so important?

_____

_____

As you read about the earliest Americans, take notes to answer questions about their way of life.

The earliest Americans lived as hunters and gatherers.

1. According to most experts, when and how did the first Americans arrive in North America?	2. As large animals became extinct, how did hunters adapt to this change in their environment?

The earliest Americans began to experiment with simple methods of farming.

3. How did farming develop in what is now central Mexico?	4. What crops grew well in the tropical climate of Mexico?

Agriculture dramatically changed peoples' way of life.

5. How did farming affect where people lived?	6. How did farming affect the structure of society?

Section 2

Early Mesoamerican Civilizations

Terms and Names

Mesoamerica Area that stretches south from central Mexico to the northern part of modern-day Honduras

Olmec People who flourished along the Mesoamerican coast of the Gulf of Mexico from 1200 B.C. to 400 B.C.

Zapotec Early Mesoamerican civilization that was centered in the Oaxaca Valley of what is now Mexico

Monte Alban First urban center in the Americas, built by the Zapotec

Before You Read

In the last section, you read about the first inhabitants of the Americas.

In this section, you will read about the first civilizations in America.

As You Read

Use a Venn diagram to compare Olmec and Zapotec cultures.

THE OLMEC (Pages 240–241)
Who were the Olmec?

The story of American civilizations begins in Mesoamerica. This area stretches south from central Mexico to the northern part of present-day Honduras.

The earliest known American civilizations arose in southern Mexico, an area of hot rain forests. The people are called the Olmec. They flourished from about 1200 to 400 B.C. Their culture had a great influence on their neighbors and on peoples who lived long after them.

The Olmec lived along the coast of the Gulf of Mexico in a land of dense forests and heavy rains.

The land gave them many benefits. It had good clay that could be used for pottery. Wood and rubber could be taken from the forest. The mountains to the north had stone for building. The rivers

could be used to move people and goods. The soil was excellent for growing food.

Archaeologists have found earthen mounds, courtyards, and pyramids built of stones. On top of the mounds were many monuments made of stone. Some of these stone structures are very large. They weigh as much as 44 tons.

Researchers are not sure whether the Olmec sites were monuments to rulers or areas important for religious reasons. They do think that the Olmec had many gods who stood for important forces of nature. The most important god, it seems, was the jaguar spirit. Many stone monuments show figures that are half-human and half-jaguar.

The Olmec traded goods and their culture with other people in the region. In return for the products they made, they received iron ore and different kinds of stone.

Guided Reading Workbook

For some reason, the Olmec disappeared around 400 B.C. Historians still do not understand why. But their influence lived on.

1. What evidence of Olmec civilization has been found?

_____

_____

_____

_____

ZAPOTEC CIVILIZATION ARISES (Pages 242–243)
Who were the Zapotec?

Another important early culture of Mexico was that of the **Zapotec** people. Their home was to the southwest of the Olmec in a valley that had excellent soil for farming and plenty of rainfall. By about 1000 B.C. the Zapotec built stone platforms and temples. A few hundred years later, they developed a kind of writing and a calendar.

Around 500 B.C., the Zapotec built the first city in the Americas. The city was called **Monte Alban.** As many as 25,000 people lived there. The city lasted as late as A.D. 700. Monte Alban had tall pyramids, temples, and palaces made out of stone. It had an observatory that could be used to look at the stars. But the Zapotec culture collapsed. As with the Olmec, historians do not know why.

2. What evidence of Zapotec civilization has been found?

_____

_____

_____

_____

THE EARLY MESOAMERICANS' LEGACY (Page 243)
How did the early Mesoamericans influence later peoples?

Both of these cultures left their mark on later cultures. The jaguar figure of the Olmec continued to appear in the sculpture and pottery of people who came later. Also, the look of Olmec towns—with pyramids, open space, and huge stone sculptures was repeated in later times. The ritual ball games of the Olmec continued to be played.

The Zapotec also shaped the lives of later peoples. Their way of writing and their calendar were used by other groups. The city of Monte Alban also influenced later peoples, who built their own cities in similar ways. These cities combined religious purposes with the needs of the common people who lived in them.

3. How did the Zapotec influence later peoples?

_____

_____

_____

_____

_____

As you read about early Mesoamerican civilizations, fill out the charts by writing notes that describe aspects of the Olmec and Zapotec civilizations.

Olmec	
1. Geography/Environment	
2. Urban design	
3. Economy	
4. Achievements/Legacy	

Zapotec	
5. Geography/Environment	
6. Urban design	
7. Language	
8. Achievements/Legacy	

Section 3

Early Civilizations of the Andes

Terms and Names

Chavín First influential culture in South America, which flourished from around 900 B.C. to 200 B.C.

Nazca Culture that flourished along the southern coast of Peru from around 200 B.C. to A.D. 600

Moche Culture that flourished along the northern coast of Peru from around A.D. 100 to A.D. 700

Before You Read

In the last section, you read about the first Mesoamerican civilizations.

In this section, you will read about the civilizations of the Andes.

As You Read

Use a chart to record important information about early Andean civilizations.

SOCIETIES ARISE IN THE ANDES
(Pages 246–249)

What geographic factors made it unlikely for a civilization to arise?

Other interesting civilizations arose in the Americas far to the south of the Olmec and Zapotec peoples. These civilizations grew in a very harsh environment—the Andes in South America. This mountain range has many peaks that are more than 20,000 feet high.

Toward the northern part of South America, along these mountains, lies the modern country of Peru. In this area, the mountains are steep and very rocky. Ice and snow cover the tops of the mountains during the entire year. Travel is hard.

The climate changes quickly from being hot during the day to bitter cold at night. The soil is poor.

It was in the mountains of this difficult land that a new civilization arose. That culture is called Chavín. It takes its name

from a major ruin, Chavín de Huántar in the Andes. At this site, researchers have found pyramids, open spaces, and large mounds made of earth. The Chavín culture was at its height from 900 B.C. to 200 B.C. It is considered the first influential civilization in South America.

Scientists have found objects that suggest that the Chavín culture helped shape other cultures to the north and south of this site. At these other sites are the art styles and symbols of religion found at Chavín. Scientists think that the main site was not the center of a political empire but was the chief site of a spiritual or religious movement. People from other areas may have made trips to the main site to pay their respects. The Chavín culture, like the Olmec in Mexico, may have been a "mother culture," one that gave the first form to the ideas and styles of the area.

1. What theories do scientists have about the Chavín culture?

_____

_____

_____

_____

_____

OTHER ANDEAN CIVILIZATIONS FLOURISH (Pages 247–249)

What other Andean civilizations developed?

Two other important cultures arose in Peru. The **Nazca** culture developed along the coast of the Pacific Ocean in the south of Peru. It lasted from 200 B.C. to A.D. 600. The Nazca people built large and complex systems to bring water to their farmlands. They made beautiful cloth and pottery.

The Nazca are most famous for the Nazca Lines. They are huge pictures scraped on the surface of a rocky plain. The drawings include a monkey, a spider, some birds, and other creatures. The pictures are so large that they can be seen and appreciated only from high in the air. Some experts think that the Nazca drew these pictures for their gods to see.

The other culture of early Peru arose along the Pacific Coast but far to the north. This was the **Moche** culture. It lasted from A.D. 100 to A.D. 700. The Moche tapped into rivers that flowed down from the mountains. They built ditches to bring water to their fields. They raised corn, beans, potatoes, squash, and peanuts. They also fished, caught wild ducks and pigs, and hunted deer.

Archaeologists have found some tombs of the Moche people. They show that the culture had great wealth. They have found objects made of gold, silver, and jewels. The Moche people made beautiful pottery that showed scenes of everyday life. So, even though they never had a written language, it is possible to learn much about how they lived.

Eventually, the Moche culture also fell. As with the other peoples of the Americas, the reason for this fall is not known. For the next hundred years, other cultures would rise and fall in the Americas. But most of them remained separate from one another.

2. Name three characteristics of the Moche people.

_____

_____

_____

_____

_____

As you read this section, fill in the chart to compare three early
civilizations that developed in the Andes.

Civilization	Environment	When Flourished	Aspects of Culture
1. Chavín			
2. Nazca			
3. Moche			

Section 1

The Rise of Islam

Terms and Names

Allah One God of Islam

Muhammad Founder of Islam

Islam Religion based on submission to Allah

Muslim Follower of the religion Islam

Hijrah Muhammad's move from Mecca to Yathrib (Medina) in 622

mosque Islamic house of worship

hajj Pilgrimage to Mecca

Qur'an Holy book of Islam

Sunna Islamic model for living based on the life and teachings of Muhammad

shari'a Body of Islamic law

Before You Read

In the last section, you read about early civilizations in South America.

In this section, you will read about the rise of Islam.

As You Read

Use a diagram to list important aspects of Islam.

DESERTS, TOWNS, AND TRADE ROUTES (Pages 263–264)
How did the desert help shape Arab life?

The harsh environment of the Arabian Peninsula left its mark on the Arab peoples. The land is almost completely covered by desert. The desert people were nomads. They herded animals, leading them from one fertile spot, or oasis, to another. Over time, many of these people, called Bedouins, began to live in towns and cities. They also began to trade goods.

By the early 600s, trade became an important activity in the Arabian Peninsula. Merchants from the north brought goods to Arabia. They traded for spices and other goods. They also brought new ideas.

At this time, some Arabs believed in one God, called Allah in Arabic. Others believed in many gods. Religious pilgrims came to Mecca to worship at an ancient shrine called the Ka'aba.

1. When and how did trade become important?

_____

_____

MUHAMMAD, PROPHET OF ISLAM (Pages 264–265)
Who was Muhammad?

Around the year 570, **Muhammad** was born into this Arab society. At around age 40, he took religion as his life's mission.

According to Muslim belief, the angel Gabriel visited Muhammad and told him to speak the word of God to his people. Muhammad believed that he was the last of the prophets.

Muhammad began to teach that **Allah** was the one and only God. The religion based on his teachings is called **Islam.** Its followers are called **Muslims.**

At first many people in Mecca opposed Muhammad's views. They feared Meccans would neglect traditional Arab gods. Muhammad and his followers were forced to leave Mecca for Yathrib (later called Medina) in 622. This became known as the **Hijrah.** The Hijrah was a turning point for Muhammad.

Gradually, Muhammad and his followers gained power. Finally, in 630, Muhammad went to the Ka'aba in Mecca and destroyed the idols. Many of the people of Mecca adopted Islam. They began to worship Allah as the only God. Muhammad died soon after, in 632. Much of the Arabian Peninsula was already united under Islam.

2. What was the Hijrah?

_____

_____

_____

_____

BELIEFS AND PRACTICES OF ISLAM (Pages 267–268)
What do Muslims believe and practice?

Muslims have five duties to perform. These duties include faith, prayer, alms, fasting, and pilgrimage to Mecca. The duties show a person's acceptance of the will of Allah:

- A Muslim must state the belief that, "There is no God but Allah, and Muhammad is the Messenger of Allah."

- A Muslim must pray to Allah, facing Mecca, five times every day. This may be done at a **mosque,** an Islamic house of worship.

- A Muslim must give alms, or money for the poor, through a tax.

- A Muslim must fast during the holy month of Ramadan. Muslims eat only one meal a day, after sunset, every day during this month.

- A Muslim should perform the **hajj**—a trip to the holy city of Mecca—at least once in his or her life.

The central ideas of Islam are found in the **Qur'an.** Muslims believe this book states the will of Allah as revealed to Muhammad. Muslims are also guided by the example of Muhammad's life, called the **Sunna,** and by a set of laws and rules, the **shari'a.**

Muslims believe that Allah is the same God that Jews and Christians worship. To Muslims, the Qur'an perfects the earlier teachings of God found in the Jewish Torah and the Christian Bible. Because their holy books were related to the Qur'an, Jews and Christians were called "people of the book" in Muslim societies.

3. What are the five duties of Muslims?

_____

_____

_____

_____

_____

_____

Section 1, *continued*

As you read about Muhammad's life and the rise of Islam, fill out the charts below to help you understand causes and effects. There can be one or several answers to each question.

The Prophet Muhammad

CAUSE
1. What were Muhammad's revelations?

EFFECTS
2. Why were Muhammad's ideas unpopular in Mecca?
3. In what way(s) was the Hijrah a turning point?
4. Why was Muhammad's return to Mecca important?

Beliefs and Practices of Islam

CAUSE
5. What does Islam teach its followers?

EFFECTS
6. How does carrying out the Five Pillars and other laws of Islam affect the daily lives of Muslims?
7. How did observing Islamic teachings create unity among Muslims?
8. How did Islamic law affect Muslim attitudes toward Christians and Jews?

Islam Expands

Terms and Names

caliph Highest political and religious leader in a Muslim government

Umayyads Dynasty that ruled the Muslim Empire from A.D. 661 to 750

Shi'a Branch of Islam whose members believe the first four caliphs are the rightful successors of Muhammad

Sunni Branch of Islam whose members believe Ali and his descendants are the rightful successors of Muhammad

Sufi Muslim who tries to achieve direct contact with God

Abbasids Dynasty that ruled much of the Muslim Empire from A.D. 750 to 1258

al-Andalus Muslim-ruled area in what is now Spain

Fatimid Member of a Muslim dynasty that traced its ancestry to Muhammad's daughter Fatima

Before You Read

In the last section, you read about the rise of Islam.

In this section, you will read about the spread of Islam.

As You Read

Use a chart to summarize developments that occurred in Islam during the rule of the rightly guided caliphs, the Umayyads, and the Abbasids.

MUHAMMAD'S SUCCESSORS SPREAD ISLAM (Pages 269–270)
How did other leaders spread Islam?

When Muhammad died, his followers elected a new leader, Abu-Bakr. He had been loyal to Muhammad. He was given the title **caliph.** This means "successor" or "deputy." A successor is a person who comes after and takes the place of someone else. A deputy is an assistant who acts on behalf of a leader who is absent.

Abu-Bakr reacted quickly when a group of Arabs abandoned Islam. He defeated them in battle over a two-year period. Abu-Bakr died soon after. But his army began to conquer new lands. By 750, the Muslim Empire stretched from the Indus River in India west to the Atlantic Ocean.

Many of the people conquered by the Muslims accepted Islam. Some found the message of Islam appealing. Others liked the fact that by becoming Muslims they avoided paying a tax put only on non-Muslims. But the Qur'an prevented Muslims from forcing others to accept the religion. Muslim rulers allowed people to follow whatever beliefs they chose.

1. How did Abu-Bakr spread Islam?

_____

_____

_____

INTERNAL CONFLICT CREATES A CRISIS (Pages 270–271)
What disagreements arose?

After the murder of a ruling caliph in 656, different Muslim groups began to struggle for control of the empire. Ali, a cousin and son-in-law of Muhammad, was chosen caliph. After a few years, he was also killed. The system of electing caliphs died with him.

A family known as the **Umayyads** took control of the empire. They did not follow the simple life of earlier caliphs. Instead, they surrounded themselves with wealth. This created a split in the Muslim community.

Most Muslims accepted Umayyad rule. But a different view of the office of caliph also developed. The **Shi'a** group—the "party" of the deceased Ali—felt that caliphs needed to be relatives of Muhammad. Those who did not openly resist Umayyad rule became known as the **Sunni.** Among them were many Muslims who felt that the Umayyads had lost touch with their religion. Another group, the **Sufi,** reacted to the Umayyads' life of luxury. The Sufis emphasized a more spiritual way of life.

2. How did the Shi'a and Sunni groups arise?

_____

_____

_____

CONTROL EXTENDS OVER THREE CONTINENTS (Pages 271–272)
What Muslim states arose?

After 750, there were Muslim caliphates on three continents. The **Abbasids** (750–1258) took power and murdered members of the Umayyad family.

The Abassids controlled the lands of modern Iraq, Iran, and central Asia. They built the city of Baghdad in southern Iraq as their capital. They used their location to control the rich trade between China and Europe.

One Umayyad prince escaped the murders and went to Spain. Muslims known as Berbers already lived there. The prince set up a Muslim state called **al-Andalus.** The Umayyads of al-Andalus (756–976) controlled parts of Spain and North Africa. Another Muslim state—the **Fatimid** caliphate (909–1171)—sprang up in North Africa, This caliphate spread to western Arabia and Syria. Although the Muslims were divided politically, all of the different communities were linked by religion, language, culture, and trade.

3. Who were the Abbasids?

_____

_____

_____

In the years following the death of Muhammad, the Muslims created a huge empire. Take notes to answer the questions about how Muhammad's successors spread Islam during this period of expansion.

The "Rightly Guided" Caliphs	
1. What did the "Rightly Guided" caliphs use as guides to leadership?	
2. What changes did they make during their rule?	
3. Why were they successful in their quest to expand the empire and spread Islam?	

The Umayyads	
4. What ended the elective system of choosing a caliph?	
5. What changes did the Umayyads make during their rule?	
6. What led to the downfall of the Umayyads?	

The Abbasids	
7. How did the Abbasids come to power?	
8. What changes did they make during their rule?	
9. What major problem did the Abbasids face?	

Section 3

Muslim Culture

Terms and Names

House of Wisdom Center of learning established in Baghdad in the 800s

calligraphy Art of beautiful handwriting

Before You Read

In the last section, you read about the expansion of Islam.

In this section, you will read about the cultural achievements of Muslim society.

As You Read

Use a web diagram to take notes on the key elements of Muslim culture.

MUSLIM SOCIETY (Pages 273–274)
Where and how did Muslims live?

The Muslim Empire included people of many different lands and cultures. Major cities arose in the Muslim world. They included Córdoba and Cairo, centers of Muslim rule in Spain and North Africa, and Baghdad, the Abbasid capital.

Muslim society was divided into four groups, At the top were people who were Muslims from birth. Next came those who converted to Islam. The third group included Jews, Christians, and Zoroastrians—protected because Muslims shared some of their beliefs. The fourth group was slaves, none of whom were Muslims.

According to Muslim law, women should obey men. But Muslim women still enjoyed more rights than did those living in European society at the time. The Qur'an gave Muslim women some economic and property rights. In early Muslim society, women could also have an education and take part in public life. Later they lost those rights.

1. Name the four groups of Muslim society.

_____

_____

MUSLIM SCHOLARSHIP EXTENDS KNOWLEDGE (Pages 274–276)
How did Muslim scholars keep learning alive?

Muslims placed a high value on learning and scholarship. Muslim scholars added much to human knowledge. Europe was in chaos and much of the knowledge of Europeans was in danger of being lost. During this time, Muslim scholars collected ancient Greek, Indian, and Persian works of science and philosophy. The scholars translated these works into Arabic. One center of this study was the **House of Wisdom** in Baghdad. Later, this ancient learning returned to Europe when the works of Muslim scholars were translated.

2. Explain how Muslim scholars helped save the learning of the West.

_____

_____

ARTS AND SCIENCES FLOURISH
(**Pages** 276–278)
What **were some achievements of Muslim society?**

Literature was a strong tradition before Islam. Later, the Qur'an became the standard for all Arabic literature and poetry. The collection *The Thousand and One Nights* included many entertaining stories, fairy tales, and legends.

Muslims had their own special practices in art. For instance, artists could not draw pictures of people. Only Allah, the religion said, could create life. Unable to draw these images, Muslims developed a new art form. They practiced **calligraphy,** or the art of beautiful handwriting.

Muslim scholars made great advances in medicine and mathematics, The physician al-Razi wrote an encyclopedia that collected all that was known about medicine from Greece to India. In science, Muslims studied the work of ancient Greek scientists but used logic rather than experiments to reach conclusions. One Muslim scientist made new discoveries about how people see. His findings helped lead to the invention of the telescope and microscope. A mathematician named al-Khwarizmi wrote a textbook that developed algebra.

3. Name four achievements of Muslim scientists and mathematicians.

_____

_____

PHILOSOPHY AND RELIGION BLEND VIEWS (**Pages** 278–279)
How **did philosophy blend with Islam?**

Philosophers at the House of Wisdom also translated works of the ancient Greek philosophers. Muslim philosopher Ibn Rushd was criticized for trying to join their ideas with Muslim ideas. But he argued that Greek philosophy and Islam both searched for the truth. The Jewish philosopher Maimonides, who lived in the Muslim Empire, was also criticized for his ideas. He wrote a book that blended philosophy, religion, and science. Philosophers reflected the different people who lived in the Muslim Empire. Muslims came to recognize the value of their differences.

4. Why was Ibn Rushd criticized?

_____

_____

As you read about Muslim culture, write notes to help you summarize
Muslim achievements in each area.

1. Muslim society	2. Medicine, math, and science
3. Philosophy	4. Literature and the arts

Byzantines, Russians, and Turks Interact

Section 1

The Byzantine Empire

Terms and Names

Justinian Powerful ruler of Byzantine Empire

Justinian Code Body of Roman law collected and organized by Justinian around A.D. 534

Hagia Sophia Church destroyed by mobs of rioters in 532 and rebuilt by Justinian

patriarch Leader of the Eastern church

icon Religious image used in practices by eastern Christians

excommunication Formal declaration that someone is no longer a member of the Church

Cyrillic alphabet Alphabet invented by Saints Cyril and Methodius, in which most Slavic languages, including Russian, are written

Before You Read

In the last chapter, you read about the Muslim world.

In this section, you will learn about the Byzantine Empire.

As You Read

Use a diagram to show Justinian's accomplishments as emperor of the New Rome.

A NEW ROME IN A NEW SETTING
(Page 301)
How did the Roman Empire change?

In the A.D. 300s, the emperor Constantine moved the capital of the Roman Empire to the east. He built a great new capital city, Constantinople. It was on the site of the old port city of Byzantium. Constantinople became the center of the empire. Power moved eastward.

The Roman Empire was officially divided in 395. The western area was overrun by German tribes. It did not exist after 476. However, the Byzantine, or eastern, part remained strong. It lasted for hundreds of years.

In 527, **Justinian** became the Byzantine emperor. He sent an army to try to regain control of Italy. He hoped to restore the

Roman Empire once again. By about 550, Justinian ruled over almost all of the territory of the old Roman Empire.

1. Who was Justinian?

_____

_____

LIFE IN THE NEW ROME
(Pages 302–303)
What changes did Justinian bring?

Justinian directed legal experts to create a complete code of laws based on the laws of ancient Rome. This body of civil law—**the Justinian Code**—served the empire for 900 years.

Justinian also worked at making Constantinople a strong but also a beautiful capital. He built high, sturdy walls to protect the city from attack. The main street of the city was lined with shops and open-air markets. People bought and sold goods from Asia, Africa, and Europe there.

In 532, riots broke out against the emperor. Justinian's troops maintained control of the city, killing thousands of rioters. A church called **Hagia Sophia** ("Holy Wisdom," in Greek) had been destroyed by the mobs. Justinian rebuilt it to become the most beautiful church in the Christian world.

2. How did Justinian make Constantinople a strong and beautiful capital?

_____

_____

THE EMPIRE FALLS (Page 304)
What weakened the empire?

The Byzantine Empire faced many dangers. A terrible disease broke out in 542. The illness killed thousands of people and returned every 8 to 12 years until about 700. This weakened the empire.

Also, the empire was forced to confront many enemies over the centuries. Constantinople remained safe during this time despite many attacks. Eventually, though, the empire shrank. By 1350, the empire included only the capital city and lands in the Balkans—part of southeastern Europe.

3. What were the two biggest problems the empire faced?

_____

_____

THE CHURCH DIVIDES
(Pages 304–306)
Why did the church divide?

Although it was based on the Roman Empire, the Byzantine Empire had developed a culture of its own. People in the Byzantine Empire spoke Greek, not Latin. They belonged to the Eastern Orthodox Church, not the Catholic Church. The Eastern Church was led by the **patriarch,** the leading bishop. However, even the patriarch had to obey the emperor.

The feeling of separateness from Rome grew worse when one emperor banned the use of **icons.** Icons are religious images used by eastern Christians to aid their devotions. The emperor thought this was like idol worship. Iconoclasts, or "icon breakers" went into churches destroying images. The pope supported the use of icons. One pope even ordered the **excommunication** of a Byzantine emperor. That means that the pope said the emperor could no longer be a member of the Church.

Slowly the Eastern and Roman churches grew further apart. In 1054, the schism, or split, became permanent.

Some missionaries traveled from the Byzantine Empire to the north. Two missionaries, Saint Methodius and Saint Cyril developed an alphabet for the Slavic languages. Many Slavic languages, including Russian, are now written in what is called the **Cyrillic alphabet.**

4. What are two differences between the Eastern and Roman churches?

_____

_____

Guided Reading Workbook

As you read about the history of Constantinople, the leading city of the
Byzantine Empire, take notes to answer questions about the time line.

527	Justinian becomes ruler of the eastern empire.	1. What did Justinian accomplish during his reign?
537	Justinian completes building the Hagia Sophia.	
542	Deadly plague sweeps through Constantinople.	2. How did the plague affect Constantinople?
674	Arab armies attack Constantinople.	
		3. How did the Byzantines first try to prop up their shaky empire?
860	Russians invade Constantinople for the first of three times.	
		4. What factors led to the schism?
1054	Christianity splits into the Roman Catholic Church in the west and the Orthodox Church in the east.	
		5. What was the effect of the split?
1204	Crusading knights from Europe pillage Constantinople.	
		6. What factors enabled the city to survive foreign attacks for hundreds of years before finally falling?
1453	Constantinople falls to Ottoman Turks.	

Byzantines, Russians, and Turks Interact

The Russian Empire

Terms and Names

Slavs People from the forests north of the Black Sea

Vladimir Grandson of Olga who ordered all his subjects to adopt Christianity

Yaroslav the Wise Russian ruler who helped Kiev gain power and wealth

Alexander Nevsky Russian noble who gained power in Moscow

Ivan III Moscow prince who led rebellion against Mongol rule

czar Russian emperor

Before You Read

In the last section, you read about the establishment and decline of the Byzantine Empire.

In this section, you will learn about the emergence of Russia.

As You Read

Use a chart to show how Mongol rule affected different parts of Russian society.

RUSSIA'S BIRTH (Pages 307–308)
Who were the Slavs?

The **Slavs** lived in what is today eastern Russia. The area was bounded by the Ural Mountains and the Black Sea on the south and the Baltic Sea on the north.

The Slavs lived in the forest areas. They worked as farmers and traders. In the 800s, some Vikings called the Rus came from the north. They built forts along the rivers and blended with the Slavic people. They founded the cities of Novgorod and Kiev and became the rulers of the land. They began to trade in Constantinople. With them, they brought furs, timber, and the Slavs who were their subjects. They sold these people as slaves. In fact, the word *slave* comes from *Slav*.

Over time, the Vikings adopted the culture of the Slavs. Divisions between Vikings and Slavs disappeared. In 957

Princess Olga of Kiev converted to Christianity. Her grandson, **Vladimir,** also converted to Byzantine Christianity. He was the ruler of Russia. He ordered all of his subjects to adopt this religion. Now more than trade linked Russia to the Byzantine Empire.

Russia also looked to Constantinople for religious leadership. Teachers from the empire gave the Russian people instructions in the new religion. The king liked the idea that the ruler of the empire was also the head of the church.

1. How did Olga and Vladimir influence the Slavic people?

_____

_____

Guided Reading Workbook

KIEV'S POWER AND DECLINE
(Pages 308–309)
What caused Kiev's rise?

Under the influence of Byzantine culture, Kiev grew to be a large, wealthy, and cultured city. It continued to grow as Vladimir took land to the west and to the north. His son, **Yaroslav the Wise,** came to power in 1019. He proved to be an able ruler as well. Under him, Kiev grew even more wealthy through trade and alliances made with western nations.

Then the state centered in Kiev began to have problems. After Yaroslav's death in 1054, his sons fought one another for control of the land. Trade declined, cutting the wealth of Kiev.

2. What caused Kiev's decline?

_____

_____

THE MONGOL INVASIONS; RUSSIA BREAKS FREE (Pages 309–311)
How did the Mongol invasions change Russia?

In the middle 1200s, the Mongols reached Kiev. They quickly overran the Russian state, killing many people. The Mongols held control of the area for more than 200 years.

The Mongols had been fierce conquerors, but they were not harsh rulers. As long as the Russian people did not rebel, the Mongols let them keep their customs, including their Eastern Christian religion.

The Mongols made the Russians pay tribute, a sum of money that was owed every year. They used Russian nobles to collect the tribute. One of those nobles, **Alexander Nevsky,** gained power. His heirs became princes of Moscow. They later used this city as their base of power.

Control by the Mongols had important effects on Russia. It isolated the Russians from western Europe. Russian society developed in its own way. Rule by the Mongols united many different areas of Russia under one central authority. Before then, what is now Russia had been ruled by a number of princes. Mongol rule also led to the rise of Moscow, which had a good location near three major rivers—the Dnieper, the Don, and the Volga.

Ivan I increased the influence of Moscow. Overtime, Ivan and his successors added to the land that Moscow controlled. In the late 1400s, under **Ivan III,** Russia grew to be a mighty empire. In 1453, the Byzantine Empire had fallen, defeated by the Turks. In 1472, Ivan married the niece of the last Byzantine emperor. From that time, he called himself **czar**—the Russian version of Caesar. In 1480, Ivan finally broke with the Mongols.

3. Name three effects of Mongol rule on Russia.

_____

_____

Section 2, continued

As you read about the Byzantine culture that developed in Russia, take notes to answer the questions in the box.

1. What ties linked Kiev to Byzantium?	2. How did Vladimir and his son Yaroslav contribute to the power of Kiev?
3. What factors brought about Kiev's decline?	4. How did the Mongols treat the Russian people?
5. What were some effects of Mongol rule on Russia?	6. What events marked the beginning of an independent Russian Empire?

Byzantines, Russians, and Turks Interact

Turkish Empires Rise in Anatolia

Terms and Names

Seljuks Turkish group that migrated into the Abbasid Empire in the 10th century and later established their own empire

vizier Prime minister in a Muslim kingdom or empire

Malik Shah Famous Seljuk sultan

Before You Read

In the last section, you read about the growth of Russia.

In this section, you will learn about the Turks in Anatolia.

As You Read

Use a chart to show important events and features of the various occupations of Baghdad.

THE RISE OF THE TURKS
(Pages 314–315)
Who were the Seljuk Turks?

The Turks were nomads from central Asia. They lived by herding sheep and goats. They traded with the settled peoples of the Abbasid Empire.

Beginning in the 900s, they moved into the lands of that empire and began converting to Islam.

The Turks were fierce and highly skilled fighters. The rulers of the empire began to buy them as children to train them for their armies. These Turkish military slaves were known as mamelukes. The Turks became an important political factor in the empire. Turkish soldiers many times removed caliphs from the throne in Baghdad and put new rulers in their place.

While the Turkish influence was growing, the empire itself was shrinking. Local leaders in several areas split off to

establish their own states. In 945, a Persian army seized control of the empire. Members of the Abbasid family continued to hold the position of caliph and act as religious leaders. The new rulers of the government were from outside the dynasty. They were called sultans.

Large numbers of Turks settled in the empire as these changes took place. They were called **Seljuks** after the name of the family that led them. In 1055, the Seljuks captured Baghdad and took control of the government. The Seljuks used their force to take land from another empire—the Byzantine Empire. They won almost all of Anatolia. Anatolia was the name for the peninsula where modern Turkey is located. In this position, the Seljuks stood almost at the gates of Constantinople.

The Seljuks relied on the government experience of Persians in ruling their empire. They chose the Persian city of Isfahan as the capital of their kingdom.

They gave Persians important positions in the government. For example, Nizam al-Mulk was a Persian who served as **vizier,** or prime minister. In return, Persians became loyal supporters of Turkish rule.

The Turks also adopted Persian culture. The nomadic Seljuk Turks had arrived in Southwest Asia as basically illiterate. They were not familiar with the traditions of Islam, which they had just adopted. They looked to Persian scholars to teach them the proper way to follow Islam. They began to use the Persian language for art and education. Turkish rulers even took the Persian word for "king"—shah—as their title.

One of the greatest Seljuk rulers, **Malik Shah,** became a patron of the arts. He made the capital city more beautiful by building many mosques, or Muslim houses of worship. Persian became so important that Arabic—the language of the Qur'an—almost died out in Seljuk lands.

1. What influence did Persians and Persian culture have on the Seljuks?

   _____

   _____

   _____

   _____

SELJUKS CONFRONT CRUSADERS AND MONGOLS (Pages 316–317)
Why did the Seljuk Empire collapse?

After Malik Shah died unexpectedly in 1092, the Seljuk Empire collapsed quickly. Weak rulers could not maintain it. Collapse was also due to the Crusades. Rulers in western Europe sent armies to capture the holy lands of the Middle East. These were places sacred to Christians.

The First Crusade began in 1095, and the Christian armies captured Jerusalem. They established a Latin Kingdom that lasted about a century. Eventually, the Turks gathered enough strength to fight back. They retook the city in 1187.

Just when the Crusades became less of a threat to the Muslim world, the Mongols moved in from the east. They were led by a brutal leader, Genghis Khan. They killed tens of thousands of people and overran huge stretches of territory. Baghdad was captured in 1258. The Mongols killed the last caliph and took control of the government from the Seljuk Turks.

2. What brought the Seljuk Empire to an end?

   _____

   _____

   _____

   _____

As you read about the rise and decline of the Turkish Empire in Anatolia, make notes in the chart to describe the outcome of each action or situation.

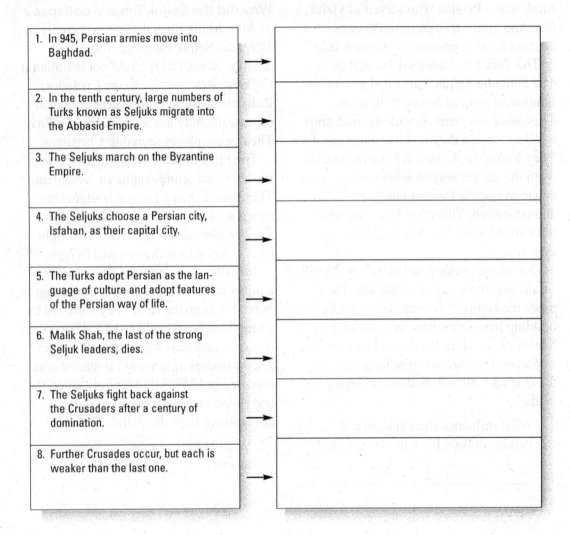

1. In 945, Persian armies move into Baghdad.	
2. In the tenth century, large numbers of Turks known as Seljuks migrate into the Abbasid Empire.	
3. The Seljuks march on the Byzantine Empire.	
4. The Seljuks choose a Persian city, Isfahan, as their capital city.	
5. The Turks adopt Persian as the language of culture and adopt features of the Persian way of life.	
6. Malik Shah, the last of the strong Seljuk leaders, dies.	
7. The Seljuks fight back against the Crusaders after a century of domination.	
8. Further Crusades occur, but each is weaker than the last one.	

Empires in East Asia

Section 1

Tang and Song China

Terms and Names

Tang Taizong Great emperor of the Tang Dynasty

Wu Zhao Tang ruler and only woman in China ever to assume the title of emperor

movable type Wood or metal blocks, each with a single character, that can be arranged to make up a page for printing

gentry Powerful upper class

Before You Read

In the last section, you read about the Turkish empires. In this section, you will read about changes in China during the Tang and Song dynasties.

As You Read

Use a Venn diagram to note the similarities and differences between the Tang and Song dynasties.

THE TANG DYNASTY EXPANDS CHINA (Pages 323–324)
***What* changes occurred during the Tang Dynasty?**

Starting in A.D. 220, China went through a long period of troubles. There were no strong rulers. China was not united. Then in 589, Wendi brought order. He united the northern and southern regions. He also named himself the first emperor of the Sui Dynasty.

This dynasty lasted only about 30 years. Just two rulers reigned. Both were important. They built the Grand Canal. This waterway connected China's two major rivers. The canal was a trade route between northern and southern China. Cities were in the north. Areas that grew rice were in the south.

The Tang Dynasty followed. It lasted for 300 years. **Tang Taizong** was a mighty emperor. He and other Tang rulers made the empire larger. They gained back lands lost since the fall of the Han Dynasty. **Wu**

Zhao was another great Tang leader. She was the only woman ever to rule China as emperor. During her reign, parts of Korea were added to the dynasty.

Early Tang rulers made the government stronger. They extended the network of roads and canals, helping to tie the empire together.

Schools were set up to train people for political jobs. They had to pass tough tests. Only then could people work for the government.

By the mid-700s, the Tang Dynasty had begun to weaken. Rulers charged heavy taxes. The Chinese people faced more hardship. Invaders attacked the empire's lands. Chinese rebels became violent. In 907, they killed the last Tang ruler.

1. How did Tang rulers change China?

_____

_____

_____

THE SONG DYNASTY RESTORES CHINA (Pages 324–325)
What happened during the Song Dynasty?

The Song Dynasty replaced the Tang Dynasty. The Song Dynasty also lasted about 300 years. Its empire was smaller than the Tang. But China was still strong under Song rule.

This dynasty did have military troubles, though. Invaders forced the Song to move south. The dynasty of the Southern Song arose in 1127.

2. How was the Song Dynasty related to the Tang Dynasty?

_____

_____

_____

AN ERA OF PROSPERITY AND INNOVATION (Pages 325–326)
What advances occurred during the Tang and Song periods?

During the Tang and Song rule, the Chinese made many advances. They invented useful things. **Movable type** made printing faster. Gunpowder was another important invention. It led to the design of exploding weapons. The Chinese made progress in farming, too. They improved ways of growing rice.

Trade increased under the Tang and Song emperors. Goods were carried over land routes. Later, ocean trade became important. Ideas were also exchanged.

Buddhism spread. This religion traveled from China to Japan, Korea, and Vietnam.

The Tang and Song dynasties were creative periods. Great poets wrote about life. Artists made beautiful paintings.

3. Name three advances in technology.

_____

_____

_____

CHANGES IN CHINESE SOCIETY (Page 327)
How did China change under the Tang and Song?

Chinese society changed during the Tang and Song periods. The old noble families lost power. Key officials in government gained power. They formed a new upper class. This wealthy group is called the **gentry.**

Next came the middle class. They lived in the cities. People such as store owners and traders belonged to this group. Below them were workers, soldiers, and servants. In country areas, peasants made up the largest class. The position of women became worse.

4. What social changes occurred in China during the Tang and Song periods?

_____

_____

_____

As you read this section, take notes to answer the questions about how the Tang and Song dynasties transformed China.

What impact did the Tang and Song dynasties have on the following areas of Chinese society?		
1. Transportation	2. Government	3. Foreign trade
4. Agriculture	5. Science/Technology	6. Art

What changes did the two dynasties bring about for the following groups?		
7. Old Aristocratic Families	8. Gentry	9. Women

The Mongol Conquests

Terms and Names

pastoralist Person who herds tamed animals

clan Large group of people related to a common ancestor

Genghis Khan Leader who brought together the Mongol clans

Pax Mongolica "Mongol Peace," a period from mid-1200s to mid-1300s when Mongols imposed order across much of Eurasia

Before You Read

In the last section, you read about the Tang and Song dynasties.

In this section, you will read about the rise and conquests of the Mongols.

As You Read

Use a chart to list the series of events leading to the creation of the Mongol Empire.

NOMADS OF THE ASIAN STEPPE
(Pages 330–331)
How did the nomads of the Asian steppe live?

Much of Central Asia is covered by dry grassland. Such a region is called the steppe. Very little rain falls on the steppe. Only short hardy grasses grow in this dry region. It gets very cold in winter and very hot in the summer.

Herders lived in this area. They were **pastoralists.** They herded domesticated animals. The herders were nomads. They moved from place to place. They searched for grass to feed the sheep and goats.

Herders often rode on horseback. They traveled together in large groups. These groups formed **clans.** The clans were made up of people related to a common ancestor.

The nomads often rode out from the steppes and made contact with the settled peoples who lived in towns and villages.

Often they traded peacefully with one another. But sometimes the nomads attacked the villages and took what they wanted by force. A nomadic group, called the Mongols, became very powerful.

1. Name three characteristics of the nomads of the steppes.

_____

_____

_____

THE RISE OF THE MONGOLS
(Pages 331–332)
Who united the Mongols?

Around 1200, a leader tried to bring the Mongol clans together. His name was Temujin. In 1206, he took the title **Genghis Khan.** This means "universal ruler." Over the next 21 years, he ruled the Mongols. They conquered much of Central Asia, including parts of China.

Section 2, *continued*

Genghis Khan enjoyed military success for several reasons. First, he organized his soldiers well. He followed the Chinese model of creating armies of 10,000 men. The armies were broken into brigades of 1,000 men, companies of 100 men, and platoons of 10 men.

Second, Genghis Khan was able to trick his enemies. He set traps for his opponents. He sometimes had his cavalry retreat. Then, when the enemy gave chase, the rest of the Mongol army would appear and charge the enemy.

Third, he used cruelty. His terror made many of his enemies surrender.

2. Name three reasons for the success of the Mongols as conquerors.

_____

_____

_____

THE MONGOL EMPIRE
(Pages 332–334)
How **did the Mongol Empire spread and divide?**

Genghis Khan died in 1227. In less than 50 years, his successors conquered territory from China to Poland. In doing so, they created the largest unified land empire in history.

By 1260, the Mongol Empire was divided into four areas. These were called khanates. Each was ruled by a descendant of Genghis Khan.

The Mongols destroyed many things in their invasions. Some towns were completely wiped out. They destroyed irrigation systems in the Tigris and Euphrates valleys. People could no longer live in some of those areas.

Over time, Mongol rulers borrowed from the cultures in the areas they ruled. Rulers in the west became Muslims. Those in China used Chinese inventions. Differences in culture split up the Empire.

The Mongols were able rulers. They brought about a long period of peace, called the **Pax Mongolica,** in Central Asia. Trade thrived. The exchange of ideas between Asia and Europe increased. However, the Mongols may have also brought the bubonic plague to Europe. In the 1300s, this deadly disease killed many people in Europe.

3. What were two effects of the Mongol empire on Central Asia?

_____

_____

_____

As you read about the Mongols, take notes to answer the questions.

The Rise of the Mongols
1. What was the primary cause of conflict between steppe nomads and settled communities?
2. How was Genghis Khan able to unite the nomadic Mongols?
3. What traits enabled Genghis Khan to conquer most of Asia?

The Khanates
4. Into what four khanates did the successors of Genghis Khan divide the Mongol Empire?
5. How did the Mongols rule?
6. How did the cultural differences among the khanates eventually affect the empire?

The Pax Mongolica
7. What was the Mongol peace?
8. How did this peace affect trade and cultural interaction?

Guided Reading Workbook

Section 3

The Mongol Empire

Terms and Names

Kublai Khan Mongol leader and Chinese emperor

Marco Polo Traveler from Venice who served Kublai Khan for 17 years

Before You Read

In the last section, you read about the rise of the Mongols and their conquests.

In this section, you will read about the Mongol leader who became emperor of China.

As You Read

Use a diagram to show the impact of Kublai Khan on East Asia.

KUBLAI KHAN BECOMES EMPEROR (Pages 335–336)
How did Kublai Khan rule China?

Genghis Khan began the conquest of China in 1215. His grandson, **Kublai Khan,** conquered all of China in 1279. He was the first foreigner to rule the whole country.

Kublai Khan became China's new emperor. He began the Yuan Dynasty. It ruled China for less than 100 years. This era was important. Kublai Khan united China for the first time in 300 years. He opened China to more foreign trade. The Mongols did not disrupt Chinese government or culture. Kublai Khan built a new capital. It was located in the modern city of Beijing.

The Mongols tried to conquer other lands. Kublai Khan attacked Japan in 1274 and 1281. The Mongols forced the Koreans to build and supply ships for the planned invasions. It was very expensive and almost ruined Korea. Both attacks failed. The second failed because a typhoon destroyed the Mongol fleet.

1. Why was the Yuan Dynasty important in Chinese history?

_____

_____

_____

MONGOL RULE IN CHINA
(Pages 336–337)
What changes occurred under Mongol rule?

Mongol rulers were very different from the Chinese. The Mongols kept the top government jobs for themselves. They also hired many people from other lands for these posts. Mongol rulers did not trust the Chinese.

Kublai Khan was a great leader. He restored the Grand Canal. He helped foreign trade increase. Chinese goods such as silk and porcelain were in demand. Western Asia and Europe wanted Chinese inventions. These included gunpowder and paper money.

Kublai Khan welcomed merchants from other countries to China. **Marco Polo** was a trader from Venice, Italy. He came to Kublai Khan's court around 1275. Polo learned several Asian languages and served under Kublai Khan for 17 years. Polo traveled to different Chinese cities in his work for Kublai Khan.

Polo returned to Italy in 1292. He told amazing stories about his journeys. He described China's cities, riches, and customs. He also recorded the way the Khan's government worked. Later, Polo's tales were collected in a book. The book was popular in Europe.

2. How did Kublai Khan help China?

_____

_____

_____

_____

_____

THE END OF MONGOL RULE
(Pages 337–338)
How did Mongol rule end?

In the last years of his rule, Kublai Khan ran into trouble. Attacks on Southeast Asia failed. Many lives and much equipment were lost.

To pay for these wars, as well as public works and the luxuries enjoyed by the Yuan court, the Khan raised taxes. The Chinese resented the heavy burden these taxes placed on them.

Kublai Khan died in 1294. Afterward, Mongol leaders struggled for power. They fought over control of the empire. These fights weakened Mongol rule.

Rebellions broke out in many parts of China in the 1300s. In 1368, Chinese rebels took over the government. Mongol rule ended. The rebels set up a new dynasty. It was called the Ming.

By this time, the whole Mongol Empire was falling apart. Mongols lost control of Persia and Central Asia. The Mongols held on to Russia, though, until 1480.

3. Name two reasons why Mongol rule came to an end.

_____

_____

_____

_____

_____

_____

As you read this section, use the questions to help you summarize information about Mongol rule in China.

1. **Who?** Who was Kublai Khan? Who was Marco Polo?	
2. **When?** When did the Mongols gain control of all of China? When did Kublai Khan rule?	
3. **Where?** Where did Kublai Khan build palaces? Where did Kublai Khan move the capital of his empire?	
4. **How?** How did the Mongol rulers treat their Chinese subjects? How did Kublai Khan expand foreign trade?	
5. **Why?** Why did the Mongols give most high government posts to foreigners? Why were the Mongols unable to conquer Japan? Why is the Yuan Dynasty important in Chinese history?	
6. **What?** What brought about the fall of the Yuan Dynasty?	

Section 4

Feudal Powers in Japan

Terms and Names

Shinto Japan's earliest religion, based on respect for nature and worship of ancestors

samurai Japanese warrior who served a lord

Bushido Code that samurai lived by—"the way of the warrior"

shogun Highest military commander in feudal Japan, ruling in the name of the emperor

Before You Read

In the last section, you read about Mongol rule in China.

In this section, you will learn about the early Japanese and their system of government.

As You Read

Use a time line to record the main periods and events in Japanese history from 300 to 1300.

THE GROWTH OF JAPANESE CIVILIZATION (Pages 339–340)
How did geography help shape Japan?

Japan benefited from its location. It was near China. Thus Chinese culture influenced Japan. However, there was enough distance between these two countries to make Chinese attacks difficult.

Japan is made up of about 4,000 islands. They vary in size. Most people live on the four largest islands. The country has many mountains. There is not much good farmland. The islands have few natural resources, such as coal and oil.

Early Japan was broken up into many small areas. Each was controlled by a clan. These clans believed in their own gods. Later, all these beliefs became combined. They formed Japan's earliest religion, called **Shinto.** The main ideas of Shinto are respect for nature and the worship of ancestors.

In the 400s, the Yamato clan became the most powerful clan. The Yamato claimed that they were related to a sun goddess. By the 600s, Yamato leaders began to call themselves emperors. The emperor remained an important figure in Japan.

1. Who were the Yamato?

_____

_____

JAPANESE CULTURE; LIFE IN THE HEIAN PERIOD (Pages 340–341)
How did Chinese culture influence Japanese culture?

By the 400s, contact between China and Japan grew. Japan became more aware of Chinese ways. Buddhism from China reached Japan. It became an important religion in Japan.

Japan's emperor sent people to China to learn about its culture. The Japanese adopted the Chinese system of writing.

Japanese artists imitated Chinese paintings. For a while, Japan even used China's government as a model. Yet Japan still held on to its own traditions.

The years from 794 to 1185 are called the Heian Period. Heian was the new capital of the royal court. Japanese culture thrived there.

The gentleman and ladies of the court lived in splendor. Art and good manners formed the center of their lives. The best accounts of Heian society come from the writings of women of the court.

2. Name two parts of Chinese culture that Japan adopted.

_____

_____

FEUDALISM ERODES IMPERIAL AUTHORITY (Pages 341–343)
How did feudalism arise in Japan?

Over time, the power of Japan's central government decreased. Wealthy landowners lived away from the capital.

They set up their own armies. These soldiers began to terrorize farmers.

In exchange for protection, farmers gave up some of their land to the lords. This is how the feudal system began in Japan. It was similar to the feudal system in Europe during the Middle Ages.

Each lord used a group of trained soldiers. They were called **samurai.** They protected their lord from attacks by other lords. Samurai followed a strict code of behavior. It was called **Bushido.** This word means "way of the warrior."

After a period of war, one of these lords arose as the most powerful. The emperor named him the **shogun.** This means "supreme general of the emperor's army." The emperor remained in power in name. But the new shogun ran the country. This pattern continued in Japan from 1192 to 1868.

3. Who were the samurai?

_____

_____

As you read about the development of Japanese civilization, take notes to answer the questions and fill out the charts.

How did these factors help shape Japanese civilization?
1. Geography
2. Yamato clan
3. Korean travelers
4. Chinese culture
5. Heian period

How did these groups weaken Japan's imperial government?
6. Samurai warriors
7. Shoguns

Empires in East Asia

Section 5

Kingdoms of Southeast Asia and Korea

Terms and Names

Khmer Empire Empire that ruled what is now Cambodia

Angkor Wat Temple complex of the Khmer Empire

Koryu Dynasty Dynasty that ruled Korea from 935 to 1392

Before You Read

In the last section, you read about early Japan and the rise of feudalism.

In this section, you will learn about smaller kingdoms in East and Southeast Asia.

As You Read

Use a chart to note important information on the kingdoms discussed in this section.

KINGDOMS OF SOUTHEAST ASIA
(Pages 344–347)

What was the Khmer Empire?

The region of Southeast Asia lies to the south of China. It includes mainland areas and many islands.

The region has never been united culturally or politically. Rivers and valleys cut through the mainland from north to south. Between the valleys are hills and mountains that make travel difficult in the region.

Political power in the area has often come from control of trade routes. This is because Southeast Asia lies on the most direct sea route between the Indian Ocean and the South China Sea.

India had a great influence on Southeast Asia. Hindu and Buddhist missionaries spread their faiths. Kingdoms in the area followed these religions as well as Indian political ideas. This early Indian influence on Southeast Asia is seen today in the region's religions, languages, and art forms.

Chinese ideas spread to the area through trade and migration. Sometimes the Chinese exerted political influence over the region.

From about 800 to 1200, the **Khmer Empire** was the main power. It was located on the mainland of Southeast Asia in what is now Cambodia. Growing rice was its chief source of wealth. The Khmer used large irrigation works to bring water to their fields. Rulers built huge temples and palaces. One of these is called **Angkor Wat.** It is among the world's greatest achievements in architecture.

At the same time, a dynasty called Srivijaya arose on Java. Java is an island. This dynasty reached its height from the 600s to the 1200s. Nearby islands fell under its rule. The capital, Palembang, was located on Sumatra. Palembang was a center for the study of Buddhism.

Vietnam fell under the influence of China. China controlled the area from about 100 B.C. to A.D. 900. Vietnam became an independent kingdom, known as Dai Viet, in 939.

The Vietnamese borrowed from Chinese culture. For example, Buddhism became important. The Vietnamese, though, kept their own culture. Women in Vietnam, for instance, had more rights than women in China.

1. What kingdoms arose in Southeast Asia?

_____

_____

_____

_____

KOREAN DYNASTIES (Pages 346–347)
How did China influence Korea?

Korea, like Japan and Vietnam, was influenced by China. Korea also preserved its own traditions. In 108 B.C., the Han Dynasty of China conquered Korea. Leaders set up a military government. From China, the Koreans learned about two religions—Buddhism and Confucianism. Koreans also learned about China's central government and system of writing.

Korean tribes began to gather into groups. One group, the Silla, chased out the Chinese in the 600s and took control of the Korean peninsula.

By the 900s, Silla rule had weakened. A rebel leader named Wang Kon took power and set up the **Koryu Dynasty.** It ruled Korea from 935 to 1392. It had a government similar to China's. Korea used examinations to fill government jobs. But this did not keep wealthy landowners from controlling society. The dynasty, though, produced great works of art—including celadon pottery, fine poetry, and wood blocks to print the entire Buddhist canon.

Korea fell to the Mongols. They were under the Mongols until the 1350s. The Mongols demanded heavy taxes. The Koreans rebelled. The Mongols lost power. Then a new dynasty, the Choson, took over Korea. It ruled for 518 years.

2. What was the Koryu Dynasty?

_____

_____

_____

As you read about the kingdoms that prospered in Southeast Asia and Korea, write notes to fill in the chart.

Dynasty/Kingdom	Location	Achievements
1. Khmer Empire		
2. Sailendra Dynasty		
3. Srivijaya Empire		
4. Ly Dynasty		
5. Koryu Dynasty		

In each box, cite examples that illustrate the influence of India and China on the kingdoms of Southeast Asia and Korea.

Indian Influence	Chinese Influence

Charlemagne Unites Germanic Kingdoms

Terms and Names

Middle Ages Period of European history from 500 to 1500

Franks Germanic people who held power in the Roman province called Gaul

monastery Religious community of people devoting their lives to worship and prayer

secular Concerned with worldly things

Carolingian Dynasty Dynasty of Frankish rulers, lasting from 751 to 987

Charlemagne Powerful Frankish ruler who built a huge empire

Before You Read

In the last section, you read about Southeast Asian kingdoms and Korean dynasties.

In this section, you will read about the rise and fall of Charlemagne's empire.

As You Read

Use a time line to note important events in the unification of the Germanic kingdoms.

INVASIONS OF WESTERN EUROPE
(**Page** 353)
How did invasions by Germanic groups change Europe?

The slow decline of the Roman Empire marked the beginning of a new era in European history called the **Middle Ages.** It lasted from around 500 to 1500.

By the end of the fifth century, various Germanic groups invaded the Roman Empire in the west. These invasions led to a series of changes. Trade was halted. Moving goods from place to place became unsafe. Cities were no longer centers of trade and government. Many people fled to the countryside and returned to rural ways of life. People also became less educated.

As Germanic groups settled in different areas, they began to blend Latin with phrases of their own language. Many kinds of dialects developed. Europe no longer had a single language understood by all.

1. Name three effects of the Germanic invasions.

_____

_____

GERMANIC KINGDOMS EMERGE
(**Page** 354)
Who were these Germanic peoples?

As Rome's power faded, a new kind of government appeared. Warring Germanic groups carved out kingdoms. The borders of these kingdoms changed often because of warfare. There was no central rule.

Family ties and loyalty to a local leader bound Germanic peoples together. Europe was in chaos. The Church provided a sense of order, though.

The **Franks,** a Germanic people, established a large kingdom. It was located in the Roman province of Gaul. In 496, Clovis, the king of the Franks, and his warriors became Christian. From then on, the pope in Rome supported Clovis.

2. What new kind of government arose during Rome's decline?

_____

_____

GERMANS ADOPT CHRISTIANITY
(Pages 354–355)
How did Christianity spread?

Other Frankish rulers helped spread Christianity. The Church also tried to convert people. It set up religious communities called **monasteries.** There Christian men called monks devoted their lives to God. Nuns were women who led this religious way of life. Monasteries became centers of learning. Their libraries preserved some writings of ancient Rome.

The Church grew in importance when Gregory I became pope in 590. He made the pope the guardian of the spiritual lives of all Christians. He also made the pope a worldly, or **secular,** power in governing part of Italy. His influence in politics grew.

3. What role did monasteries play during this period?

_____

_____

AN EMPIRE EVOLVES (Pages 355–356)
How did the Carolingian Dynasty arise?

The kingdom of the Franks covered much of modern France. By the 700s, the most powerful official was the mayor of the palace. He made laws and controlled the army.

In 719, Charles Martel became mayor of the palace. He expanded the lands controlled by the Franks. He also won a battle in 732. He defeated a Muslim force moving north from Spain. This victory ended the Muslim threat to Europe.

His son, Pepin, was crowned king. Pepin began the reign of the Frankish rulers called the **Carolingian Dynasty.** One of Pepin's sons, **Charlemagne,** became king of the whole Frankish kingdom in 771.

4. Who were Charles Martel and Pepin?

_____

_____

CHARLEMAGNE BECOMES EMPEROR (Pages 356–357)
What did Charlemagne achieve?

Charlemagne had great military skill. He made his kingdom larger than any other known since ancient Rome. By 800, he held most of modern Italy, all of modern France, and parts of modern Spain and Germany. Pope Leo III crowned him emperor. This event marked the joining of Germanic power, the Church, and the heritage of the Roman Empire.

Charlemagne cut the power of the nobles in his empire and increased his own. He traveled throughout his lands, visiting the people and judging cases. He revived learning. However, Charlemagne's empire fell apart soon after his death.

5. What was important about Charlemagne's being crowned as emperor?

_____

_____

As you read this section, take notes to answer questions about the
unification of western Europe after the fall of the Roman Empire.

Between 400 and 600, small Germanic kingdoms replaced Roman provinces.

1. What role did the Church play in helping Clovis conquer other Germanic peoples?	2. What role did Pope Gregory the Great play in spreading the idea of a vast unified kingdom?

Clovis's successors extended Frankish rule.

3. What was important about Charles Martel's victory at the Battle of Tours?	4. How did Pepin the Short strengthen the Frankish kingdom?

Charlemagne reunited western Europe and spread Christianity throughout his lands.

5. What was the importance of Charlemagne's coronation as emperor?	6. How did Charlemagne govern his unified kingdom?

Section 2

Feudalism in Europe

Terms and Names

lord Landowner

fief Land granted by a lord to a vassal

vassal Person receiving a fief from a lord

knight Warrior on horseback who promised to defend his lord's land in exchange for a fief

serf Peasant who could not lawfully leave the place where he or she was born

manor Lord's estate

tithe Church tax; usually one-tenth of a peasant family's income

Before You Read

In the last section, you read about Charlemagne and his empire.

In this section, you will read about feudalism.

As You Read

Use a diagram to show the causes and effects of feudalism.

INVADERS ATTACK WESTERN EUROPE (Pages 358–360)
Who invaded Western Europe?

Between 800 and 1000, new invasions threatened Europe. From the north came the most feared fighters of all. They were the Vikings, or Norsemen.

The Vikings raided villages and monasteries. By around the year 1000, though, the Vikings had settled down in many parts of Europe. They adopted Christianity and stopped raiding to become traders and farmers.

The Magyars were Turkish nomads. They attacked from the east and reached as far as Italy and western France. They sold local people as slaves. The Muslims struck from the south. They attacked areas along the Atlantic and Mediterranean coast.

The attacks by Vikings, Muslims, and Magyars made life in western Europe difficult. People suffered and feared for their futures. With no strong central government, they went to local leaders for protection.

1. Why did the people need to turn to local leaders for help?

_____

_____

A NEW SOCIAL ORDER: FEUDALISM (Page 360)
How did feudalism affect society?

Europe's feudal system arose around the ninth and tenth centuries. Feudalism was based on an agreement between a **lord,** or landowner, and a **vassal,** a person who received land from a lord. In exchange for land, or a fief, a vassal promised to help his lord in battle.

Under feudalism, society in western Europe was divided into three groups. Those who fought were the nobles and **knights.** Those who prayed were the officials of the Church. Those who worked were the peasants. Peasants were by far the largest group. Most peasants were **serfs,** who were not free to move about as they wished. They were tied to the land of their lord.

2. What were the three main groups of feudal society?

_____

_____

MANORS: THE ECONOMIC SIDE OF FEUDALISM (Pages 360–363)
What was life like on a manor?

The lord's land was called the **manor.** Manors became the centers of economic life. The lord gave peasants some land, a home, and protection from raiders. The lord controlled much of their lives. The peasants worked the land to grow food, giving part of each year's crop to the lord. They paid taxes on their grain. Peasants also paid a tax, called a **tithe,** to the Church.

Peasants lived in small villages of 15 to 30 families. They produced almost everything they needed. Peasants rarely traveled far from their homes.

Life on the manor was often harsh. Peasants' cottages had just one or two rooms with only straw mats for sleeping. They had poor diets. Peasants endured these conditions. They believed that God had set their place in society.

3. What was the job of peasants on the manor?

_____

_____

As you read about the development of feudalism in Europe, fill out the
charts by writing notes in the appropriate spaces.

Social Structure of Feudalism	
1. Explain the mutual obligations of the feudal system.	
2. Explain why the feudal system often resulted in complicated alliances.	
3. Describe feudal social classes.	

Economic Structure of Feudalism	
4. Explain the mutual obligations between lord and serfs under the manor system.	
5. Explain why the serfs rarely had to leave their manor.	
6. Explain why the serfs accepted their economic hardships.	

The Age of Chivalry

Terms and Names

chivalry Code of behavior for knights, stressing ideals such as courage, loyalty, and devotion

tournaments Staged battles for entertaining audiences and training knights

troubadours Poet-musicians at the castles and courts of Europe

Before You Read

In the last section, you read how feudalism shaped society.

In this section, you will read about the code of chivalry for knights and its influence.

As You Read

Use a web diagram to identify the ideas associated with chivalry.

KNIGHTS: WARRIORS ON HORSEBACK (Pages 364–365)
What was the role of knights?

Nobles were constantly at war with one another. They raised private armies. The armies included knights, soldiers who fought on horseback. These knights became the most important warriors during the Middle Ages.

By the 11th century, nobles used their armies of mounted knights to fight for control of land. When nobles won battles, they gave some of the new land to their knights. The knights could use the wealth from this land to pay for weapons, armor, and horses. Knights devoted much of their time to improving their skill at fighting.

1. What was the main duty of knights?

_____

_____

KNIGHTHOOD AND THE CODE OF CHIVALRY (Pages 365–367)
What was required of a knight?

By the 1100s, a new code of conduct for knights arose. This code of **chivalry** required that knights fight bravely for three masters: their lord, God, and their chosen lady. Knights were also required to protect the weak and poor. While the code set high standards, most knights failed to meet all of the standards.

The son of a noble began training to become a knight at an early age. At around age 7, his parents sent him off to the castle of another lord. There he would learn good manners. The boy would also practice fighting skills. At around age 14, he would become the servant of a knight. Then at age 21, he would finally become a knight himself.

Knights gained experience by fighting in combats called **tournaments.** These were fierce, but real battles, especially those fought at castles, were far more violent.

Guided Reading Workbook

To protect their lands and homes, nobles built stone castles.

2. Give two examples of training for knighthood.

_____

_____

THE LITERATURE OF CHIVALRY
(**Pages** 367–368)
What was the literature of chivalry about?

The literature about knights did not reflect real life. Many stories glorified castle life. Others centered on the code of chivalry. Songs and poems were often about a knight's loyalty to the woman he loved. Some long poems, called epics, told the story of legendary kings, such as King Arthur and Charlemagne.

Troubadours were poet-musicians at the castles and courts of Europe. They wrote and sang about the joys and sorrows of romantic love. Many troubadours traveled to the court of Eleanor of Aquitaine. She was the rich, powerful ruler of a land in southern France.

3. Who were the troubadour's songs about?

_____

_____

WOMEN'S ROLE IN FEUDAL SOCIETY (**Pages** 368–369)
What were the roles of women?

Most women in feudal society had little power. The Church taught that they were inferior. But they played important roles in the lives of both noble and peasant families.

Noblewomen could sometimes rule the land when their husbands were away from home. But they could not inherit land. It usually passed from father to son. In reality, most noblewomen, young and old, were limited to activities in the home or in convents.

The vast majority of women during the Middle Ages were poor peasants. They held no power. They worked in the fields and took care of their families. Poor women struggled to survive—just as they had for centuries.

4. How were noble and poor women alike?

_____

_____

As you read about knighthood and chivalry, take notes to fill in the web diagram below.

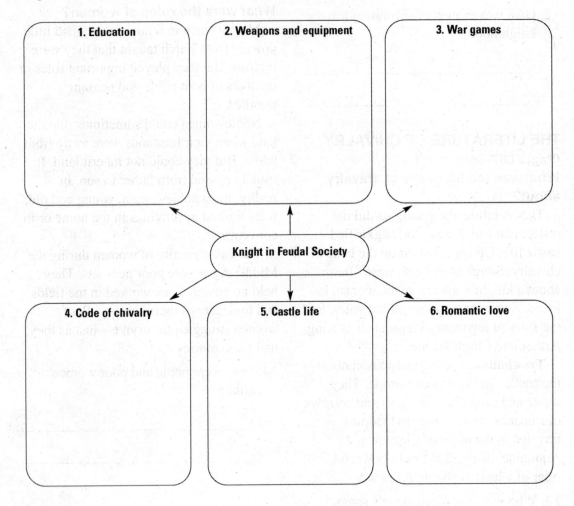

1. Education

2. Weapons and equipment

3. War games

Knight in Feudal Society

4. Code of chivalry

5. Castle life

6. Romantic love

Section 4

The Power of the Church

Terms and Names

clergy Religious officials

sacrament Important religious ceremony

canon law Law of the church

Holy Roman Empire Kingdom originally made up of what is now Germany and Italy

lay investiture Appointment of religious officials by kings or nobles

Before You Read

In the last section, you read about knighthood and the literature of chivalry.

In this section, you will learn about power struggles between church leaders and political leaders.

As You Read

Use a chart to list the significant dates and events for the Holy Roman Empire.

THE FAR-REACHING AUTHORITY OF THE CHURCH (Pages 370–371)
***How* did the Church control most aspects of life?**

With the central governments of Europe weak, the Church became the most important force in unifying European society. An early pope believed that God had made two areas of influence in the world—religious and political. The pope was in charge of spiritual matters. The emperor and other rulers were in charge of political affairs. Over the years, though, the difference was not so clear. Popes often tried to influence the actions of rulers, who clashed with them in struggles for power.

The Church established its own organization. It consisted of different ranks of **clergy,** or church officials. At the bottom were the priests who led services at local churches. Above them were

bishops, who oversaw all the priests in a large area. At the top was the pope. He was the head of the Church.

The Middle Ages was an Age of Faith. People were bound together by their belief in God and the teachings of the Church. Though their lives were hard, Christians during this time hoped for salvation— eternal life in heaven. One path for achieving this goal was through the **sacraments.** These were important religious ceremonies.

The law of the Church, called **canon law,** was a set of standards that applied to all Christians during the Middle Ages. These standards guided such matters as marriage and religious practices. The Church also set up courts. People who broke canon law were put on trial.

Two punishments were especially harsh. If the Church excommunicated a person, he or she was out of the Church.

The person was denied the chance for eternal life in heaven. Popes often used this power to threaten rulers. The other punishment was interdiction. When a ruler disobeyed the pope, the Church leader could place the land under interdiction. That meant that no sacred actions of the Church could officially take place there. The people of the area deeply feared this. They might then be doomed to eternal suffering in hell.

1. What powerful punishments could the Church hand down?

_____

_____

THE CHURCH AND THE HOLY ROMAN EMPIRE; THE EMPEROR CLASHES WITH THE POPE
(Pages 371–372)
How did conflict develop between the pope and the Holy Roman emperor?

Otto I was the strongest ruler of medieval Germany. He set up an alliance with the Church. In 962, the pope crowned him emperor of what became the Holy Roman Empire.

The **Holy Roman Empire** was the strongest kingdom that arose from Charlemagne's fallen empire. It was mainly made up of what is now Germany and Italy. One of Otto's successors was Henry IV. He and Pope Gregory VII became caught in a conflict.

For a long time, rulers had the power to name the bishops who led the Church in their lands. This power was known as **lay**

investiture. In 1075, Pope Gregory VII banned this practice. Henry IV was angry. He persuaded his bishops to say that this pope had no real authority. Gregory then excommunicated Henry. Henry's nobles supported Gregory. So Henry begged the pope for forgiveness. The pope forgave him.

The larger issue of lay investiture was left open until 1122. Then an agreement stated that only the pope could name bishops. However, the emperor had the right to turn down any appointment he did not like.

2. Why did Henry IV beg Pope Gregory VII for forgiveness?

_____

_____

DISORDER IN THE EMPIRE
(Page 373)
Who was Frederick I?

In the late 1100s, a strong German king came to power. His name was Frederick I. He repeatedly invaded the cities of Italy but lost an important battle in 1176. He then made peace with the pope.

When Frederick died in 1190, his empire fell apart. It was broken up into feudal states. These German states did not unify during the Middle Ages.

3. What happened to the Holy Roman Empire after Frederick I's death?

_____

_____

As you read about the clashes between the Church and European rulers, note the causes and outcomes of each action listed in the chart.

Causes	Actions	Outcomes
	1. Otto invades Italy on pope's behalf.	
	2. Pope Gregory bans lay investiture.	
	3. Henry IV travels to Canossa.	
	4. Representatives of Church and emperor meet in Worms.	
	5. Lombard League fights Battle of Legnano.	

Church Reform and the Crusades

Terms and Names

simony Practice of selling positions in the church

Gothic Style of architecture of the cathedrals during the Middle Ages

Urban II Pope who called for the first Crusade

Crusade A holy war

Saladin Famous Muslim leader of the1100s

Richard the Lion-Hearted English king who fought Saladin in the Third Crusade

Reconquista Effort by Christian leaders to drive the Muslims out of Spain

Inquisition Church court that tried people suspected of having opposing religious beliefs

Before You Read

In the last section you read about the authority and role of the Church during the Middle Ages.

In this section you will read about changes in the Church and the launching of the Crusades.

As You Read

Use a time line to note important events in the Age of Faith.

THE AGE OF FAITH (Pages 379–380)
What **changes did the Church undergo?**

Starting in the 1000s, a new Age of Faith arose in Europe. It led to many changes.

Popes tried to end certain practices. One was the marriage of priests. Another was **simony,** or the selling of positions in the Church. A third problem was the appointment of bishops by kings. The Church felt it alone could appoint bishops.

In the early 1200s, a new Church group arose. They were called friars. They moved from place to place spreading the ideas of the Church. Women also played a role

during the Age of Faith. Many entered convents to devote themselves to God.

1. What three practices showed the Church needed reforming?

_____

_____

CATHEDRALS—CITIES OF GOD
(Pages 380–381)
How **did the new cathedrals reflect the new Age of Faith?**

The Age of Faith was shown in the building of great cathedrals. In the early 1100s, these huge churches were built in a style of architecture called **Gothic.**

The cathedrals were towering. Light streamed in through colorful stained-glass windows.

2. What was the new style of church architecture?

_____

_____

THE CRUSADES (Pages 382–383)
Why were the Crusades fought?

In 1093, the Byzantine emperor asked for help against Muslim Turks. They were threatening to conquer Constantinople. Pope **Urban II** urged the leaders of Western Europe to begin a holy war—a **Crusade.** He wanted Christians to gain control of Jerusalem and the entire Holy Land. Both knights and common people joined the Crusades. Their motive was deep religious feeling.

The First Crusade began in 1095. The Crusaders captured some of the Holy Land, including Jerusalem. Muslims won back some of this land. Then other Crusades followed. During the Second Crusade, the Muslim leader **Saladin** recaptured Jerusalem.

Three powerful European rulers led the Third Crusade. One was the English king **Richard the Lion-Hearted.** He fought Saladin. The two reached a truce. But the Crusades were not over.

The Fourth Crusade ended in disaster. In 1204, knights looted Constantinople. This helped make a lasting split between western and eastern Christian churches.

3. Why did people support the Crusades?

_____

_____

THE CRUSADING SPIRIT DWINDLES (Pages 383–384)
What happened to Muslims and Jews in Spain?

Christian rulers tried to drive the Muslims out of Spain. This long fight was called the **Reconquista.** It lasted from the 1100s until 1492.

Thousands of Jews lived in Spain. During the late 1400s, many Spanish Jews and Muslims became Christians. Jewish and Muslim converts were suspected of holding beliefs that differed from the teachings of the Church. Queen Isabella and King Ferdinand of Spain conducted the **Inquisition.** Suspects might be questioned for weeks and even tortured. Those who confessed were often burned at the stake.

4. What was the Reconquista?

_____

_____

THE EFFECTS OF THE CRUSADES (Pages 383–384)
What changes did the Crusades bring?

The Crusades had many effects on Europe. At first the Crusades showed the power of the Church in the lives of the believers. The failure of later Crusades cut the pope's power. The deaths of many knights reduced the nobles' power. Contact with the East revived trade. The Christians' harsh treatment of Muslims in the Holy Land led to bitterness that has lasted to the present.

5. What are four effects of the Crusades?

_____

_____

Guided Reading Workbook

As you read about reforms in the Catholic Church and the Crusades, note one or more reasons for each of the following developments.

1. The Benedictine monastery was founded at Cluny.	2. The power of the pope was extended.
3. Nearly 500 Gothic cathedrals were built and decorated between 1170 and 1270.	4. The Byzantine emperor appealed to the Count of Flanders for help.
5. Pope Urban II issued a call for a Crusade.	6. There was an outpouring of support for the First Crusade.
7. Four feudal Crusader states were formed, each ruled by a European noble.	8. Jerusalem remained under Muslim control, though unarmed Christian pilgrims could visit the city's holy places.
9. In Spain, Isabella and Ferdinand used the Inquisition to suppress heretics.	10. European kings strengthened their own power as a result of the Crusades.

Section 2

Changes in Medieval Society

Terms and Names

three-field system Farmland divided into three equal-sized fields, in which crops were rotated

guild An organization working to get the best prices or working conditions

Commercial Revolution The expansion of trade and changes in business practices

burgher Merchant class person who lived in a town

vernacular Everyday language.

Thomas Aquinas Scholar who argued that the most basic religious truths could be proved by sound reasoning

scholastics Scholars who gathered and taught at universities

Before You Read

In the last section, you read about the Crusades.

In this section, you will read about the rise of towns and trade.

As You Read

Use a diagram to identify changes in medieval society.

A GROWING FOOD SUPPLY
(Page 387)
Why did the food supply increase?

The climate in Europe became warmer between 800 and 1200. This helped farming. Farmers also developed better ways to produce crops. Horses pulled plows and did twice the work of oxen.

Farmers also used a new method of rotating the crops planted in an area. They planted two-thirds of their fields, leaving one-third unplanted. This **three-field system** help farmers grow more food.

1. Give three reasons why the food supply increased.

_____

_____

THE GUILDS **(Page 388)**
What were the guilds?

Changes in the way goods were produced and sold happened in the medieval period. Merchants banded together in an organization called a **guild.** A merchant guild worked to get the best prices for their goods.

Craft guilds were made up of groups of workers who did the same job. These included bakers, tailors, and glassmakers. Members set standards and prices for their products. They also made rules for young people learning the craft.

2. What were the two kinds of guilds?

_____

_____

THE COMMERCIAL REVOLUTION
(Pages 389–390)
Why did trade and finance increase?

Along with the growth in the food supply, trade and finance increased. Craft workers began to make more goods. These goods were traded all over Europe. Towns held fairs each year. There merchants sold cloth, food, leather, and other wares.

With more trade, merchants needed more cash. They needed new ways to get cash and loans and to exchange different types of money. The Church had rules against charging a fee for loaning money. Jews, who were outside the Church, became the chief sources of loans. Later, the Church relaxed its rules. Then Christians began to form banks. The expansion of trade and changes in banking practices was called the **Commercial Revolution.**

3. How did ways of doing business change?

_____

_____

URBAN LIFE FLOURISHES
(Pages 390–391)
Why did towns grow larger?

In the early 1100s, the population of western Europe grew quickly. Trade was booming. Towns grew larger and more important. Towns were dirty places, with narrow streets. Wooden houses in the towns were fire hazards.

Many peasants fled to the towns. After living there a year and a day, they became free. Other town dwellers, known as **burghers,** organized themselves. The burghers were of the merchant class. They demanded more rights for town dwellers.

4. Why did peasants move to the towns?

_____

_____

THE REVIVAL OF LEARNING
(Pages 391–392)
Why did learning spread?

Growing trade and wealth helped lead to a growing interest in education. New centers of learning arose in Europe. They were called universities.

At this time, most writers were still using Latin. However, some began to use the **vernacular.** This was their native, everyday language. Dante Alighieri wrote *The Divine Comedy* in Italian. Geoffrey Chaucer wrote *The Canterbury Tales* in English. These writers brought literature to many people.

During the Crusades, contact with Muslims helped increase learning. Muslim scholars had preserved books from ancient Rome and Greece. These works then became available in Europe.

Ancient writings influenced Christian thinkers, such as **Thomas Aquinas.** He reasoned that the most basic religious truths could be proved by logic. Aquinas and his fellow scholars met at the great universities. They were known as schoolmen, or **scholastics.**

5. How did the use of the vernacular help spread learning?

_____

_____

As you read this section, make notes in the chart to explain the results of
each change or trend in medieval society.

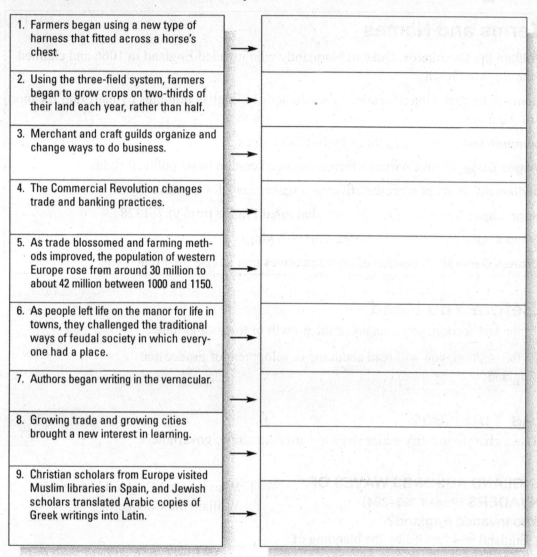

1. Farmers began using a new type of harness that fitted across a horse's chest.	
2. Using the three-field system, farmers began to grow crops on two-thirds of their land each year, rather than half.	
3. Merchant and craft guilds organize and change ways to do business.	
4. The Commercial Revolution changes trade and banking practices.	
5. As trade blossomed and farming methods improved, the population of western Europe rose from around 30 million to about 42 million between 1000 and 1150.	
6. As people left life on the manor for life in towns, they challenged the traditional ways of feudal society in which everyone had a place.	
7. Authors began writing in the vernacular.	
8. Growing trade and growing cities brought a new interest in learning.	
9. Christian scholars from Europe visited Muslim libraries in Spain, and Jewish scholars translated Arabic copies of Greek writings into Latin.	

England and France Develop

Terms and Names

William the Conqueror Duke of Normandy who invaded England in 1066 and claimed the English crown

Henry II English king who added French lands to English holdings by marrying Eleanor of Aquitaine

common law A body of rulings by English judges

Magna Carta Great Charter, which guaranteed certain basic political rights

parliament Body of representatives that makes laws for a nation

Hugh Capet Founder of the dynasty that ruled France from 987–1328

Philip II One of the most powerful Capetian kings

Estates General A council of representatives that advise the French king

Before You Read

In the last section, you read about the growth of towns and trade.

In this section, you will read about the development of France and England.

As You Read

Use a chart to identify major steps toward democratic government.

ENGLAND ABSORBS WAVES OF INVADERS (Pages 393–394)
Who **invaded England?**

England was formed by the blending of cultures. Danish Vikings invaded the island in the 800s. Some Germanic groups arrived there much earlier. Over time, the Vikings and Anglo-Saxons were united under one rule and kingdom.

In 1066, King Edward died. A power struggle followed. This led to one last invasion. The invader was **William the Conqueror.** He was the duke of Normandy, a land in northern France. He won control of England and declared it his personal realm.

1. Who invaded England before the William the Conqueror?

_____

_____

ENGLAND'S EVOLVING GOVERNMENT (Pages 394–395)
What **were some of England's earliest steps toward democracy?**

Later English kings, descendants of William, tried to hold and add to the land they still had in France.

They also wanted to increase their control over the government and the Church in England.

Henry II ruled from 1154 to 1189. He was one of the strongest of William's descendants. He married Eleanor of Aquitaine, who had been married to King Louis VII of France. From this marriage, Henry gained more territory in France. In England, he began the practice of trial by jury. Over the years, the ruling of the English judges formed a body of law called **common law.** These laws form the basis of law in many English-speaking countries.

One of Henry's sons, King John, had serious problems. He was a poor military leader. His harsh rule caused nobles to rebel against him. In 1215, they forced John to sign an important paper called the **Magna Carta.** It put limits on the power of the king. The document protected the power of nobles only. Common people, though, said that parts of the Magna Carta also applied to them.

Another step toward limiting the king came in the 1200s. Edward I needed to raise taxes for a war against the French. He called a meeting of representatives from all parts of England. It was called a **parliament.** The purpose of this meeting was to approve his tax plan. His Model Parliament met in 1295. This was the first time bishops, nobles, and common people attended together.

2. Why was the Magna Carta important?

_____

_____

CAPETIAN DYNASTY RULES FRANCE (Pages 396–397)
What was the Capetian Dynasty?

In France, a new dynasty of kings came to power. They were called the Capetians. They were named for the first of these rulers, **Hugh Capet**, who had been a duke from the middle of France. This dynasty ruled from 987 to 1328.

France was split into 30 separate small territories. Each was ruled by a different lord. The kings held only a small area centered in Paris. They tried to gain control of all the land. Gradually, the growth of royal power would unite France.

One of the most successful kings was **Philip II.** He ruled from 1180 to 1223. He tripled the land sunder his control. He also made a stronger central government. This gave the king more control over his lands and the people who lived there.

His grandson, Louis IX, ruled from 1226 to 1270. He carried on Philip's work. Louis set up royal courts. There, people could appeal their lords' decisions. These courts increased the king's power. In 1302, Philip IV called for a meeting of representatives. Like Edward I in England, Philip invited common people. This meeting and the council of representatives was called the **Estates General.**

3. How did the kings of France gain more control over their subjects?

_____

_____

Guided Reading Workbook

As you read about the democratic traditions that evolved as England and
France developed into nations, answer questions about the time line below.

1066	The Battle of Hastings is fought.	→	1. How did this event affect the course of English history?
1154	Henry II becomes ruler of England.		2. How did Henry II strengthen England's legal system?
1204	Philip II of France regains Normandy from the English.		3. How did Philip strengthen the central government in France?
1215	The Magna Carta is signed by King John of England.		4. Why is this document so important?
1226	Louis IX becomes king of France.		5. How did Louis strengthen the monarchy while weakening feudal ties?
1295	Model Parliament meets during reign of Edward I of England.	→	6. How was this meeting a major step toward democratic government?

The Formation of Western Europe

The Hundred Years' War and the Plague

Terms and Names

Avignon City in France where the pope moved temporarily

Great Schism Division in the Church created by having popes in both Avignon and Rome

John Wycliffe English scholar who argued that the Bible was the final authority for Christian life

John Huss Bohemian scholar who taught that the Bible was the final authority for Christian life

bubonic plague Deadly disease that spread across Asia and Europe in the mid-14th century

Hundred Years' War War between England and France waged from 1337 to 1453

Joan of Arc English peasant who led the French army to victory at Orleans

---

Before You Read

In the last section, you read about developments in the governments of France and England.

In this section, you will learn about the plague, religious conflict, and war between England and France.

As You Read

Use a chart to identify causes and effects of major events at the end of the Middle Ages.

A CHURCH DIVIDED (Pages 398–399)
How was the Church divided?

In 1300, the pope said he had supreme authority over King Philip IV of France. Philip would not obey him. He held the pope prisoner. Philip planned to put him on trial. The pope was rescued but died soon after. The king then forced the election of a French cardinal as pope. In 1305, the new pope moved to **Avignon,** a city in France. There, the new pope was to lead the Church. This action weakened the Church.

In 1378, the French pope at that time died. An Italian was elected the next pope. But the French elected their own pope. Confusion resulted. Church officials had two popes, one in France and the other in Rome. This situation, called the **Great Schism,** lasted 39 years.

At the same time, the pope's authority was challenged. The English scholar **John Wycliffe** and the Bohemian **John Huss** argued that the Bible, not the pope, was the final authority for Christian teaching.

Guided Reading Workbook

1. What created the Great Schism?

_____

_____

THE BUBONIC PLAGUE STRIKES
(Pages 399–401)
What happened when the plague struck?

People of the late 1300s experienced an even greater shock than the schism in the Church. A deadly disease—the **bubonic plague**—struck. It swept across Europe. The plague started in 1347. It lasted for decades. Millions of people died. The disease wiped out about one-third of Europe's population.

The plague affected Europe's economy. Trade declined, and prices rose. Towns became smaller. Fewer people meant fewer workers. Peasants demanded wages or their freedom. When nobles resisted these demands, peasants often revolted.

The Church lost prestige because it could not stop the plague. Jews were persecuted all over Europe. The plague helped bring an end to the Middle Ages.

2. Name three effects of the plague.

_____

_____

_____

THE HUNDRED YEARS' WAR
(Pages 401–403)
Why was the Hundred Years' War fought?

A century-long war also helped bring the Middle Ages to an end. The last Capetian king of France died in 1328. He left no heirs. Edward III of England claimed the throne. In 1337, he began a war to win control of France. This conflict is known as the **Hundred Years' War.**

English forces won three important battles. At one, their archers used longbows. These weapons launched arrows that killed one-third of the French troops—even armored knights.

By 1429, France was desperate. The French army held the town of Orleans. But England was about to capture it. A teenage peasant girl named **Joan of Arc** arrived on the scene. She led the army of France to victory. Then the French crowned a new king, Charles VII. Later, Joan was captured in battle by allies of the English. She was turned over to Church authorities. She was tried as a witch and burned at the stake.

The Hundred Years' War finally ended in 1453. Most of the fighting took place in France. The war brought France much suffering. However, the war produced a strong national feeling in both England and France. It provided the sense that the king was not just a feudal lord. He was also the leader of a nation.

3. What role did Joan of Arc play in the Hundred Years' War?

_____

_____

_____

As you read this section, take notes to answer the questions about three events that led to the end of medieval society.

➤ **Factor 1: The Great Schism**

1. When and how did the Great Schism begin?	2. When and how was the Great Schism resolved?	3. How did the Great Schism affect medieval life?

➤ **Factor 2: The Bubonic Plague**

4. Where did the plague begin and how did it spread?	5. What were some economic effects of the plague?	6. How did the plague affect the Church?

➤ **Factor 3: The Hundred Years' War**

7. What was the primary reason for the war?	8. What was the outcome of the war?	9. How did the war affect medieval society?

Guided Reading Workbook

Section 1

North and Central African Societies

Terms and Names

lineage Group of people descended from a common ancestor

stateless societies Societies without central governments

patrilineal Tracing ancestry though the father

matrilineal Tracing ancestry though the mother

Maghrib Part of North Africa that is today the Mediterranean coast of Morocco

Almoravids Islamic group that established an empire in North Africa and southern Spain during the 11th century

Almohads Islamic group that overthrew the Almoravids in the 12th century

Before You Read

In the last section, you read about disasters in Europe during the 1300s.

In this section, you will read about various societies that arose in North and Central Africa.

As You Read

Use a web diagram to list characteristics of stateless societies.

HUNTING-GATHERING SOCIETIES
(**Page** 409)
What is life like for hunter-gatherers?

People in early African societies depended on hunting and gathering for their food supply. Some societies, such as the Efe, still use these methods today. The Efe live in central Africa. They live in groups of around 50 people. All members of the groups are related to one another. Each family has its own shelter. It is made of grass and brush. The Efe move often in search for food. That is why they keep few belongings.

Women gather plant foods. They look for roots, yams, mushrooms, and wild seeds. These are found in the forest. Men and older boys hunt animals. Sometimes they form groups to hunt. At other times, a hunter goes alone. He uses a poison-tipped arrow as a weapon. The Efe also collect honey.

An older male leads the group. But he does not give orders or act like a chief. Each family makes its own decisions. Families, though, do ask the leader for his advice.

1. How do the Efe get food?

_____

_____

_____

STATELESS SOCIETIES (Page 410)
What are stateless societies?

Family organization is important in African society. In many African societies, families form groups called **lineages.** Members of a lineage believe that they are all descended from a common ancestor. Lineage also includes relatives of the future. These are the children who are not yet born.

Lineage groups sometimes take the place of rulers. They do not have central governments. Such societies are called **stateless societies.** Power in these societies is spread among more than one lineage. This prevents any one family from having too much control and power.

The Igbo people are from southern Nigeria. They first began living in a stateless society in the 800s. Sometimes there were disagreements within an Igbo village. Then the older members from different villages would meet. Together they would solve the problem.

In **patrilineal** societies, lineages are traced through fathers. In **matrilineal** societies, lineages are traced through mothers.

In some societies, children of similar ages belong to groups called age sets. All members of the age set take part in ceremonies. These rites mark the movement from one stage of life to the next. Men and women have different life stages.

2. How does lineage help balance the power in some stateless societies?

_____

_____

_____

_____

MUSLIM STATES (Pages 410–412)
How did Islam spread in North Africa?

Islam was an important influence on African history. Muslims came to northwest Africa in the 600s. By 670, Muslims ruled Egypt. They entered the **Maghrib,** a part of North Africa. This area today is the Mediterranean coast of Libya, Morocco, Tunisia, and Algeria.

In their new states, the Muslims set up theocracies. In them, the ruler served as both political and religious leader. The Islamic tradition of obeying the law was important. It helped promote order in the government. The common influence of Islamic law also set up ties between the different North African states.

The Berbers were a group of North Africans. They converted to Islam. In the 11th century, a group of Berbers devoted themselves to spreading Islam. They were called the **Almoravids.** They had many conquests. They conquered modern Morocco, the empire of Ghana, and parts of Spain.

The **Almohads** were another group of Berbers. They overthrew the Almoravids in the 1100s. The Almohads also captured Morocco and then Spain. Their empire reached east to the cities of Tripoli and Tunis. This empire lasted about 100 years. Then it broke up into smaller states.

3. Who were the Berbers?

_____

_____

_____

_____

As you read this section, take notes to answer questions about three types of societies that developed in the various topographical regions of Africa.

Hunting-gathering societies formed close-knit family groups.

1. What are some characteristics of a hunting-gathering society?	2. Why are written laws not necessary in these societies?

Stateless societies, which existed near the coast, were based on extended family ties.

3. What are some characteristics of a stateless society?	4. What are some advantages of an age-set system?

Muslim societies developed in North Africa.

5. What are some characteristics of a Muslim theocracy?	6. How did Muslim law affect individual Islamic states?

Section 2

West African Civilizations

Terms and Names

Ghana West African empire that grew rich from trade

Mali West African empire that grew rich from trade

Sundiata Founder and first emperor of the kingdom of Mali

Mansa Musa Mali ruler who created a large kingdom and adopted Islam

Ibn Battuta 14th century traveler who visited most of the Islamic world

Songhai West African empire that conquered Mali

Hausa West African people who lived in several city-states of what is now northern Nigeria

Yoruba West African people who formed several kingdoms in what is now Benin

Benin Kingdom that arose near the Niger River delta and became a major West African state

Before You Read

In the last section, you read about societies in North and Central Africa.

In this section, you will read about kingdoms in West Africa.

As You Read

Use a Venn diagram to compare and contrast information about the Mali and Songhai empires.

EMPIRE OF GHANA (Pages 413–415)
How did the kingdom of Ghana arise?

Traders crossed the Sahara Desert of North Africa as early as A.D. 200. The desert was harsh. This limited trade. Then the Berbers began using camels. Trade increased.

By the 700s, the rulers of the kingdom of **Ghana** were growing rich. They taxed the goods that traders carried through their land. The two most important trade goods were gold and salt. Gold was taken from mines and streams in the western and southern parts of West Africa. It was traded for salt from the Sahara region. Arab traders also brought cloth and manufactured goods. These came from cities on the Mediterranean Sea.

The king of Ghana was powerful. Only the king could own gold nuggets. He was the religious, military, and political leader. By the year 800, Ghana had become an empire. It controlled the people of nearby lands.

Over time, Muslim merchants and traders brought their religion to Ghana. By the 1000s, the kings converted to Islam. Many common people in the empire, though, kept their traditional beliefs. Later, Ghana fell to the Almoravids of North Africa. Ghana never regained its former power.

1. What goods were traded in Ghana?

_____

_____

EMPIRE OF MALI (Pages 415–417)
How did Mali rise to power?

By 1235, a new kingdom began—**Mali**. It arose south of Ghana. Mali's wealth and power were also based on the gold trade. **Sundiata** became Mali's first emperor. He was a great military and political leader.

Later Mali rulers adopted Islam. One of them was **Mansa Musa**. He made Mali twice the size of the old empire of Ghana. To rule this large empire, he named governors to head several provinces. Mansa Musa was a devoted Muslim. He built mosques in two cities. One was Timbuktu. It became a leading center of Muslim learning.

Ibn Battuta was a later traveler to the area. He described how peaceful Mali was. Mali, though, declined in the 1400s. Mali was replaced by another empire that grew wealthy from gold.

2. What did Mansa Musa achieve?

_____

_____

EMPIRE OF SONGHAI (Page 417)
How did Songhai arise?

The next trading empire was **Songhai**. It was farther to the east than Mali. Songhai arose in the 1400s. It had two great rulers. One was Sunni Ali. He gained control of new areas. His conquests included the city of Timbuktu.

Songhai's other great ruler was Askia Muhammad. He was a devoted Muslim. He ran the government well.

The Songhai Empire fell, however. Its army lacked modern weapons. In 1591, Moroccan troops used gunpowder and cannons to beat Songhai soldiers. They had only swords and spears. This defeat ended the period when empires ruled West Africa.

3. Why did Songhai fall?

_____

_____

OTHER PEOPLES OF WEST AFRICA (Pages 417–419)
What other states and kingdoms arose?

In other parts of West Africa, city-states developed. The **Hausa** people lived in the region that is now northern Nigeria. Their city-states first arose between the years 1000 and 1200. The Hausa rulers depended on farmers' crops. They also relied on trade goods. These included salt, grain, and cotton cloth.

The **Yoruba** people also first lived in city-states. These were located in what is now Benin and southwestern Nigeria. Over time, some of the small Yoruba communities joined together. Many Yoruba kingdoms were formed. Yoruba people believed their kings were gods.

The kingdom of **Benin** arose in the 1200s. It was located near the delta of the Niger River. In the 1400s, a ruler named Ewuare led Benin. He made the kingdom more powerful. During his reign, Benin became a major West African state. He strengthened Benin City, his capital. High walls surrounded the city. The huge palace contained many works of art.

In the 1480s, trading ships from Portugal came. They sailed into a major port of Benin. Their arrival was historic. It marked the start of a long period of European involvement in Africa.

4. What was important about Benin?

_____

_____

Name _____ Class _____ Date _____

Section 2, *continued*

As you read about the empires and states that arose in West Africa, briefly note the causes or effects (depending on which is missing) of each situation.

Causes	Effects
1. Berbers discovered that camels could cover greater distances than other pack animals and could travel up to ten days without water.	
2. The Muslim Almoravids disrupted the gold-salt trade that Ghana had controlled.	
3.	The people of Mali, who lived in the region of the new trade routes, were able to seize power.
4.	The empire of Mali weakened.
5.	Moroccan troops quickly defeated the Songhai warriors.
6. The city-states of Kano and Katsina were located along the route that linked other West African states with the Mediterranean.	
7. The largest Yoruba kingdoms produced surplus food, which was sent to cities.	

Section 3

Eastern City-States and Southern Empires

Terms and Names
Swahili Language that is a blend of Arabic and Bantu
Great Zimbabwe City that grew into an empire built on the gold trade
Mutapa Southern African empire established by the leader Mutota

Before You Read

In the last section, you read about West African kingdoms and states.

In this section, you will read about East African city-states and southern African empires.

As You Read

Use a chart to explain one example of cultural interaction resulting from trade.

EAST COAST TRADE CITIES
(**Pages** 422–424)
What cultures blended in East Africa?

The east coast of Africa became a region where cultures blended. Africans speaking Bantu languages moved to this area from central Africa. Muslim Arab and Persian traders settled in port cities along the coast. A new blended language formed. It was called **Swahili.**

Arab traders sold porcelain bowls from China. They sold jewels and cotton cloth from India. They bought ivory, gold, and other African goods. The traders took these goods back to Asia. By 1300, trade was thriving in over 35 cities on the coast. Some cities also manufactured products for trade. These goods included woven cloth and iron tools.

Kilwa was one of the richest trading ports. It was located far to the south. Trade goods from southern lands passed through Kilwa.

In 1497, though, the situation changed. Ships arrived on the east coast of Africa from Portugal. Portuguese sailors were looking for a route to India. They wanted to join in the trade for spices and other goods desired in Europe. Soon the Portuguese attacked Kilwa. They also attacked other trading centers along the East African coast.

For the next two centuries, the Portuguese remained a powerful force in the region.

1. Why did Kilwa become an important center of trade?

_____

_____

ISLAMIC INFLUENCES
(Pages 424–425)
How **did Muslim traders influence East Africa?**

On the east coast of Africa, contact with Muslim traders grew. This resulted in the spread of Islam. A sultan, or governor, ruled each city. Most government officials and wealthy merchants were Muslims. As in West Africa, though, most common people kept their traditional beliefs.

Muslim traders also sold slaves from the East African coast. These slaves were brought to markets in areas such as Arabia and Persia. Some slaves did household tasks. Other were sent to India to be soldiers. This slave trade was still small. Only about 1,000 slaves a year were traded. The later European-run slave trade was much larger.

2. Describe the Muslim slave trade.

_____

_____

SOUTHERN AFRICA AND GREAT ZIMBABWE **(Pages** 425–426)
What **empires arose in southern Africa?**

In southern Africa, a great city-state arose in the1000s. The Shona people grew crops in their rich land. They also raised cattle. Their city, **Great Zimbabwe,** linked the gold fields inland with the trading cities on the coast. From the 1200s through the 1400s, the city controlled this trade. The city grew wealthy.

Around 1450, though, the people left the city. No one knows why. One explanation is that overuse had destroyed the grasslands, soil, and timber. About 60 acres of ruins remain. The ruins include stone buildings. A high wall carved with figures of birds also still stands.

3. What happened to Great Zimbabwe around 1450?

_____

_____

THE MUTAPA EMPIRE **(Page** 427)
Who **founded the Mutapa empire?**

The **Mutapa** Empire followed. It began around 1420. A man named Mutota left the area. He moved farther north looking for salt. Mutota and his successors took control of a large area. It was almost all of the land of the modern Zimbabwe. This empire gained wealth from its gold. The rulers forced the conquered to mine the gold. The southern region of the empire formed its own kingdom.

In the 1500s, the Portuguese moved in. They failed to conquer the empire. Later, through political schemes, they took over the government.

4. How did Mutapa rulers obtain luxury goods from coastal city-states?

_____

_____

As you read this section, make notes to answer the questions.

1. How did the monsoons help change the existing villages of East Coast Africa into bustling seaports?

2. How did Kilwa's location contribute to its wealth and power?

3. What was the importance of the Portuguese conquest of Sofala, Kilwa, and Mombasa?

4. What were the geographical advantages of Great Zimbabwe?

5. How did the Muslims influence the development of East African cities?

6. How did the Mutapa Empire become great? List four reasons.			
a.	b.	c.	d.

Section 1

North American Societies

Terms and Names

potlatch Ceremonial giving practiced by some Native American societies in the Pacific Northwest

Anasazi Early Native American people who lived in the Southwest

pueblos Villages of large apartment-like buildings made of clay and stone by peoples of the American Southwest

Mississippian Related to the Mound Builder culture that flourished in North America between A.D. 800 and 1500

Iroquois Native American peoples from the eastern Great Lakes region of North America who formed an alliance in the late 1500s

totems Animals or other natural objects that serve as symbols of clans or other groups

---

Before You Read

In the last section, you read about diverse societies in Africa.

In this section, you will read about diverse societies in North America.

As You Read

Use a Venn diagram to compare and contrast the Native Americans of the Northwest and the Southwest.

COMPLEX SOCIETIES IN THE WEST; MOUND BUILDERS AND OTHER WOODLAND CULTURES
(Pages 441–444)
Where did different Native American societies arise?

Between about 40,000 and 12,000 years ago, hunter-gatherers moved from Asia to North America. (At that time the two continents had a land connection.) These were the first Americans. They spread throughout North and South America. They had many different ways of life, each suited to the place where they lived.

The Pacific Northwest stretches from modern Oregon to Alaska. The peoples who lived there used the rich resources of the region. The sea was the most

important of these resources. The people there hunted whales. They also gathered food from the forests on the coast. The people of the Pacific Northwest developed societies in which differences in wealth led to the creation of social classes. From time to time, they performed a ceremony called the **potlatch.** In this ceremony, wealthy families could show their rank and prosperity by giving food, drink, and gifts to the community.

The peoples of the Southwest faced a harsh environment. The Hohokam people irrigated, or watered, their crops. Their use of pottery and baskets showed that they had contact with the Mesoamerican people to the south.

The **Anasazi** lived where the present-day states of Utah, Arizona, Colorado, and New Mexico meet. They built groups of houses in the shallow caves that broke up the rocky walls of deep canyons. By the 900s, the Anasazi were living in **pueblos.** Pueblos were villages with large, apartment-style groupings. They were made of stone and clay baked in the sun. The Anasazi did not have horses, mules, or the wheel. They relied on human power to make their pueblos. They had small windows to keep out the hot sun. One of the largest pueblos had more than 600 rooms and probably housed about 1,000 people.

Many Anasazi pueblos were abandoned around 1200. Later peoples—including the Hopi and Zuni—living in this area continued the traditions of the Anasazi.

In the woods east of the Mississippi River, another culture arose. These people are called the Mound Builders. They built large mounds of earth that were filled with copper and stone art work. When seen from above, some mounds revealed the shapes of animals. The **Mississippians** were a people who lived later in this area. They built thriving villages, such as Cahokia. In the center of Cahokia was a flat-topped pyramid with a temple on top.

The peoples of the northeastern woodlands had many different cultures. They often fought for control of land. Some groups formed alliances to put an end to this fighting. The most successful of these alliances was set up in the late 1500s by the Iroquois and was called the **Iroquois** League. The league linked five tribes in upper New York.

1. Explain the cultural differences between the Anasazi and the Mississippians.

_____

_____

CULTURAL CONNECTIONS
(Pages 444–445)
How were Native American groups similar culturally?

These North American groups had some common features. Trade linked people of all regions of North America. Religious ideas were similar across the continent as well. Nearly all native North Americans thought that the world was full of spirits and that people had to follow certain rituals and customs to live in peace. Native Americans also shared great respect for the land, which they did not believe that people could own.

They also shared an emphasis on the family as the most important social unit. Family included parents, children, grandparents, and other relatives. In some tribes, families were linked together with others who shared a common ancestor. These larger groups are called clans. Clans were often identified with a **totem.** A totem is a natural object or animal that a person, clan, or family uses to show its identity.

2. Name three features shared by Native American groups.

_____

_____

_____

Name _____ Class _____ Date _____

As you read this section, fill out the chart below to describe early North American societies.

People	Environment	Achievements
1. Pacific Northwest peoples		
2. Pueblo builders		
3. Mound Builders		
4. Northeastern tribes		

Give examples to show how North American societies were linked to each other.

Political Links	Economic Links	Cultural Links

Section 2

Maya Kings and Cities

Terms and Names

Tikal Maya city in present-day Guatemala

glyph Picture symbol used as part of a writing system

codex Book with bark-paper pages; only three of these ancient Maya books have survived

Popul Vuh Book containing a Maya story of creation

Before You Read

In the last section, you read about societies in North America.

In this section, you will read about the Maya civilization in Mexico and Central America.

As You Read

Use a chart to take notes on the major features of the Maya civilization.

MAYA CREATE CITY-STATES
(Pages 446–447)
Who were the Maya?

A great civilization arose in what is today southern Mexico and northern Central America. This was the Maya civilization. It appeared around A.D. 250. Between then and 900, the Maya built large cities such as **Tikal** and Copán. Each city was independent and ruled by a god-king. Each city was a religious center as well as a trade center for the area around it. These cities were large. Tens of thousands of people lived in these cities. The cities were full of palaces, temples, and pyramids. Archaeologists have found at least 50 Maya cities.

Trade linked these cities. Among the trade goods were salt, flint, feathers, shells, cotton cloth, and ornaments made of jade. Cacao beans, which are used to make chocolate, were sometimes used as money. Maize, beans, and squash were the main foods.

Maya society was divided into social classes. The best warriors and priests were at the top. The merchants and craft workers were at the next level. Peasant farmers—the majority of the people—were at the bottom.

1. What is known about Maya cities?

_____

_____

RELIGION SHAPES MAYA LIFE
(Pages 447–448)
How did religion shape Maya life?

The Maya religion was at the center of their society. There were many gods, including one for each day. The actions of the day's god could be predicted, they thought, by following a calendar. The Maya sometimes cut themselves to offer their blood to the gods in sacrifice. Sometimes they killed enemies and sacrificed them.

The Maya religion led to the development of mathematics, calendars, and astronomy. Maya math included the idea of zero. They had two calendars. One calendar was religious, and it had thirteen 20-day months. The other calendar was based on the sun. It had 18 months consisting of 20 days each. The Maya linked the two together to identify days that would bring good fortune.

Maya astronomy was very accurate. They observed the sun, moon, and stars to make their calendars as accurate as possible. They calculated the time it takes the earth to revolve around the sun almost perfectly.

The Maya also developed the most advanced writing system in the ancient Americas. Maya writing was made up of about 800 symbols, or **glyphs.** They used their writing system to record important historical events. They carved in stone or recorded events in a bark-paper book known as a **codex.** Three of these ancient books still survive. A famous Maya book called the *Popul Vuh* records a Maya story of the creation of the world.

2. How does Maya writing reflect Maya culture?

_____

_____

_____

_____

_____

MYSTERIOUS MAYA DECLINE
(**Page** 449)
Why did the civilization decline?

In the late 800s, the Maya civilization began to decline. Historians do not know why. One explanation may be that warfare between the different city-states disrupted Maya society. The wars interrupted trade and drove many people out of the cities into the jungle. Another may be that the soil became less productive due to intensive farming over a long time. Whatever the cause, the Maya became a less powerful people. They continued to live in the area, but their cities were no longer the busy trade and religious centers they had been.

3. Name two reasons that may explain the Maya civilization's decline.

_____

_____

_____

_____

As you read about the rise and fall of Maya civilization, fill out the web diagram below.

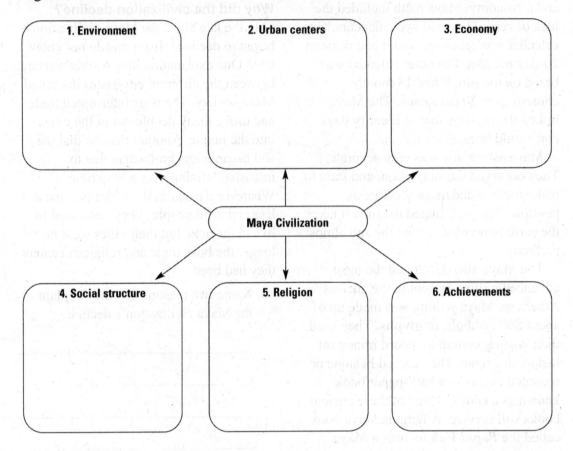

1. Environment

2. Urban centers

3. Economy

Maya Civilization

4. Social structure

5. Religion

6. Achievements

Section 3

The Aztecs Control Central Mexico

Terms and Names

obsidian Hard, volcanic glass used by early peoples to make sharp weapons

Quetzalcoatl Toltec god

Triple Alliance Association of city-states that led to the formation of the Aztec Empire

Montezuma II Ruler under whom the Aztec Empire weakened

Before You Read

In the last section, you read about Maya civilization. In this section, you will read about societies that arose in central Mexico, including the Aztecs.

As You Read

Use a diagram to list events in the establishment and growth of the Aztec Empire.

THE VALLEY OF MEXICO
(Pages 452–453)
What **civilizations arose in the Valley of Mexico?**

The Valley of Mexico is more than a mile above sea level. It is a good place for people to settle because it has lakes and fertile soil. An early city-state called Teotihuacán ("City of the Gods") arose in this area in the first century A.D. The city had between 150,000 and 200,000 people at its peak in the sixth century.

The city was the center of a major trade network. The most important trade item was **obsidian.** This green or black volcanic glass was used to make sharp weapons. The huge Pyramid of the Sun, which measured some 200 feet high and 3,000 feet around its base, dominated the city. By 750, Teotihuacán was abandoned. The reasons why are not clear.

The next people to dominate the area were the Toltecs. They rose to power around 900 and ruled over central Mexico for about 300 years. The Toltecs were warlike and worshiped a warlike god.

One Toltec king, Topiltzin, tried to replace the warlike god with a peaceful one. The peaceful god was called **Quetzalcoatl,** the Feathered Serpent. Followers of the warlike god rebelled and chased Topiltzin away. The Toltecs became warlike again. Over time, Topiltzin and Quetzalcoatl became one in Toltec legends. In these legends, someday Quetzalcoatl would return and bring a new reign of peace. This legend lived on in central Mexico for centuries.

1. What was Teotihuacán?

_____

_____

THE AZTEC EMPIRE; TENOCHTITLÁN: A PLANNED CITY
(Pages 453–455)
How did the Aztecs build an empire?

Around 1200, the Toltecs were losing control of the region. But another people—the Aztecs—began to gain power. The Aztecs founded a city and, in 1428, they joined with two other city-states to form the **Triple Alliance.** The Triple Alliance became the leading power of the Valley of Mexico. It soon gained control over neighboring regions.

By the early 1500s, the Aztecs controlled a large empire that included somewhere between 5 and 15 million people. This empire was based on military conquest and collecting tribute from conquered peoples.

Military leaders held great power in Aztec society. Along with government officials and priests, they made up a noble class. Below them were commoners—merchants, craft workers, soldiers, and farmers who owned their land. At the bottom of society were the slaves taken as captives in battle. At the top was the emperor. He was treated as a god as well as a ruler.

The capital city—Tenochtitlán—was built on an island in a lake. The Aztecs made long causeways to connect the city to the mainland. The city contained between 200,000 and 400,000 people. It was well-planned and had a huge religious complex at its center.

2. How was Aztec society organized?

_____

_____

RELIGION RULES AZTEC LIFE
(Page 456)
What was the role of religion in Aztec life?

Religion played a major role in Aztec society. Temples were built in cities for the many different gods. Priests led religious rituals. The most important rituals were for the sun god. Priests made the sacrifice of human blood to make sure that the sun god was happy, and the sun would rise every day. People taken captive in war were sacrificed. The need for a steady supply of victims pushed the Aztecs to fight their neighbors.

3. Why and how did the Aztecs sacrifice to the sun god?

_____

_____

PROBLEMS IN THE AZTEC EMPIRE
(Pages 456, 458)
What weakened the Aztec Empire?

Montezuma II became emperor in 1502. The Aztec Empire began to have problems during his reign. The Aztecs ordered the other peoples they had conquered to hand over even more people to sacrifice. These other peoples finally rebelled against the Aztecs. In the midst of this conflict, the Spanish arrived and made contact with the Aztecs for the first time. Some saw their arrival as the legendary return of Quetzalcoatl.

4. Why did conquered peoples rebel against the Aztecs?

_____

_____

As you read this section, note one or more reasons why the Aztecs took each of the following actions.

1. The Aztecs first worked for local rulers as soldiers-for-hire.	2. The Aztecs joined two other city-states to form a Triple Alliance.
3. In Tenochtitlán, the Aztec capital, the Aztecs built hundreds of temples and religious structures dedicated to the gods.	4. Aztec engineers built three causeways over water and marshland.
5. Aztec priests sacrificed humans atop the Great Temple.	6. The Aztecs built a calendar in the main ceremonial plaza of Tenochtitlán.
7. Some of the conquered provinces rebelled against Aztec rule.	8. Montezuma II reduced the number of public officials.

People and Empires in the Americas

The Inca Create a Mountain Empire

Terms and Names

Pachacuti Ruler under whom the Incan Empire grew quickly

ayllu Small community or clan whose members worked together for the common good

mita Requirement for all Incan subjects to work for the state a certain number of days each year

quipu Arrangement of knotted strings on a cord used by the Inca to record numerical information

Before You Read

In the last section, you read about the Aztec Empire.

In this section, you will learn about the empire of the Inca.

As You Read

Use a web diagram to identify the methods the Inca used to build their vast, unified empire.

THE INCA BUILD AN EMPIRE
(**Pages** 459–460)
Who **were the Inca?**

The Inca civilization arose in the Andes of South America. It was built on the foundations made by several earlier cultures.

The Inca united much of the Andes under their rule. They first settled in the Valley of Cuzco, in modern Peru. They built a kingdom there by the 1200s. The Inca believed that their ruler was related to the sun god, who would bring wealth and power to them. Only men from one of 11 noble families believed to be descendants of the sun god could serve as king.

In 1438, **Pachacuti** became the ruler of the Inca. He made conquest after conquest. By 1500, the Inca ruled an empire that stretched along the Andes from modern Ecuador all the way south to Chile and

Argentina. It held about 16 million people. The empire did not grow only through military conquest. Often the Inca offered new peoples the chance to join the empire peacefully as long as they swore loyalty to the emperor. Many peoples became part of the empire in this way. Even when force was needed, afterward the Inca tried to win the loyalty of the conquered peoples through friendship rather than fear.

1. What beliefs and practices related to Inca rulers?

_____

_____

INCAN GOVERNMENT CREATES UNITY (Pages 460–461)
How did the government unite the empire?

The Inca had a highly organized system to govern their empire. Small groups of people known as **ayllu** worked together for the common good. For example, they built irrigation ditches together. The Inca applied this idea to their empire. Families were placed in groups of 10, 100, 1,000, and so on. A chief led each group.

The Inca usually let local rulers stay in place when they conquered a people—as long as the conquered people met any Incan demands. The most important demand was for all adult workers to spend some days each year working for the state. They might work on state farms or build state roads or buildings. This payment of labor was known as **mita.**

The Inca built a complex network of roads. The roads linked all parts of the empire. The Inca also built all government buildings in the same style. This created a common identity for the government throughout the empire. They made all people speak a common language—the Incan tongue, called Quechua.

The Inca controlled the economy. They told people what to grow or make and how it would be distributed. The government also took care of people who needed help, such as the very old or ill.

In spite of all these advances, the Inca never developed a system of writing. All records were kept in peoples' memories. They did have a device for counting. It was a set of knotted strings called a **quipu.** The Inca also had day and night calendars for information about their gods.

2. What was mita, and what forms did it take?

_____

_____

_____

RELIGION SUPPORTS THE STATE; DISCORD IN THE EMPIRE
(Pages 462–463)
How were religion and government connected?

The Incan religion played a central role in Inca life. The Inca believed in fewer gods than the peoples of Mexico. The most important of the Incan gods were the creator god and the sun god. Cuzco, the capital, was the most important religious center. It was decorated with gold and other precious objects.

In the early 1500s, the Incan Empire reached the height of its power under the rule of Huayna Capac. However, he died while traveling through the empire. After Huayna Capac's death, civil war broke out between his two sons, Atahualpa and Huascar. Atahualpa eventually won, but the war tore the empire apart. When the Spanish arrived, they took advantage of Incan weakness to divide and conquer the empire.

3. Why did the Incan Empire fall?

_____

_____

_____

Original content © Houghton Mifflin Harcourt Publishing Company. Additions and changes to the original content are the responsibility of the instructor.

As you read this section, take notes to answer questions about the Incan Empire.

What role did each of the following play in the building of the Incan Empire?		
1. Ancient cultures	2. Incan traditions and beliefs	3. Pachacuti

How did each of the following help to unify or support the Incan Empire?		
4. System of government	5. Language	6. Cities
7. Road system	8. Economy	9. Religion

European Renaissance and Reformation

Italy: Birthplace of the Renaissance

Terms and Names

Renaissance Period of rebirth of art and learning in Europe lasting from about 1300 to 1600

humanism Focus on human potential and achievements

secular Concerned with worldly rather than spiritual matters

patrons People who financially supported artists

perspective Art technique that re-creates three dimensions

vernacular Use of native language instead of classical Latin

Before You Read

In the last section, you read about the development of the Incan Empire.

In this section, you will learn about the beginning of the Renaissance.

As You Read

Use an outline to organize each summary's main ideas and details.

ITALY'S ADVANTAGES
(Pages 471–472)
Why did the Renaissance begin in Italy?

The years 1300 to 1600 saw a rebirth of learning and culture in Europe called the **Renaissance.** This rebirth spread north from Italy. It began there for three reasons. First, Italy had several important cities. Cities were places where people exchanged ideas. Second, these cities included a class of merchants and bankers who were becoming wealthy and powerful. This class strongly believed in the idea of individual achievement. Third, Italian artists and scholars were inspired by the ruined buildings and other reminders of classical Rome.

1. What are three reasons why the Renaissance began in Italy?

_____

_____

CLASSICAL AND WORLDLY
VALUES (Pages 472–473)
What new values did people hold?

Interest in the classical past led to an important value in Renaissance culture—**humanism.** This was a deep interest in what people have already achieved as well as what they could achieve in the future. Scholars did not try to connect classical writings to Christian teaching. Instead, they tried to understand them on their own terms.

In the Middle Ages, the emphasis had been mostly on spiritual values. Renaissance thinkers stressed **secular** ideas. These ideas centered on the things of the world. One way that powerful or wealthy people showed this interest in worldly things was by paying artists, writers, and musicians to create beautiful works of art. Wealthy people who supported artists were known as **patrons.**

People tried to show that they could master many fields of study or work. Someone who succeeded in many fields was admired greatly. The artist Leonardo da Vinci was an example of this ideal. He was a painter, a scientist, and an inventor. Men were expected to be charming, witty, well educated, well mannered, athletic, and self-controlled. Women were expected to have many accomplishments, too. But women were not to show them in public.

2. What are secular ideas?

_____

_____

_____

THE RENAISSANCE REVOLUTIONIZES ART
(Pages 474–475)
How did art change during the Renaissance?

Renaissance artists sometimes used new methods. Sculptors made figures more realistic than those from the Middle Ages. Painters used **perspective** to create the illusion that their paintings were three-dimensional. The subject of artwork changed also. Art in the Middle Ages was mostly religious. Renaissance artists

reproduced other views of life. Michelangelo showed great skill as an architect, a sculptor, and a painter.

3. How did the methods and subjects in art change?

_____

_____

_____

RENAISSANCE WRITERS CHANGE LITERATURE (Pages 475–477)
How did literature change during the Renaissance?

Renaissance writers also achieved greatness. Several wrote in the **vernacular.** This means they wrote in their native languages. It was a change from the Middle Ages, when most writing was done in Latin. Writers also changed their subject matter. They began to express their own thoughts and feelings. Sometimes they gave a detailed look at an individual. Dante and others wrote poetry, letters, and stories that were more realistic. Niccoló Machiavelli took a new approach to understanding government. He focused on telling rulers how to expand their power. He believed rulers should do what was politically effective, even if it was not morally right.

4. What did Renaissance writers write about?

_____

_____

_____

As you read about the rebirth of learning and the arts in Italy, write notes to answer the questions.

In Italy, thriving urban centers, a wealthy merchant class, and the classical heritage of Greece and Rome encouraged the development of new ideas and values.

1. How did humanism influence the growth of learning?	
2. How did ideas about piety and a simple life change?	
3. What role did patrons of the arts play in the development of Renaissance ideas?	

Styles in art and literature changed as artists and writers emphasized the individual.

4. What effects did the emphasis on individuals have on painters and sculptors?	
5. How did writers reflect Renaissance values in their work?	
6. How did the writing of Petrarch, Boccaccio, and Machiavelli demonstrate the values of humanism?	

European Renaissance and Reformation

Section 2

The Northern Renaissance

Terms and Names

Utopia An ideal place

William Shakespeare Famous Renaissance writer

Johann Gutenberg German craftsman who developed the printing press

Before You Read

In the last section, you read how the Renaissance began in Italy.

In this section, you will learn how Renaissance ideas spread in northern Europe.

As You Read

Use a time line to note important events of the northern Renaissance.

THE NORTHERN RENAISSANCE BEGINS (Page 480)
Why was the time right for the northern Renaissance to begin?

By 1450, the bubonic plague had ended in northern Europe. Also, the Hundred Years' War between France and England was ending. This allowed new ideas from Italy to spread to northern Europe. They were quickly adopted. Here, too, rulers and merchants used their money to sponsor artists. But the northern Renaissance had a difference. Educated people combined classical learning with interest in religious ideas.

1. How was the northern Renaissance different from the Renaissance in Italy?

_____

_____

ARTISTIC IDEAS SPREAD
(Pages 480–481)
What ideas about art developed in northern Europe?

The new ideas of Italian art moved to the north, where artists began to use them. Major artists appeared in parts of Germany, France, Belgium, and the Netherlands. Dürer painted religious subjects and realistic landscapes. Holbein, Van Eyck, and Bruegel painted lifelike portraits and scenes of peasant life. They revealed much about the times. They began to use oil-based paints. Oils became very popular, and their use spread to Italy.

2. What did northern European artists paint?

_____

_____

_____

NORTHERN WRITERS TRY TO REFORM SOCIETY; THE ELIZABETHAN AGE (Pages 482–483)
What did northern writers write?

Writers of the northern Renaissance combined humanism with a deep Christian faith. They urged reforms in the Church. They tried to make people more devoted to God. They also wanted society to be more fair. In England, Thomas More wrote a book about **Utopia,** an imaginary ideal society where greed, war, and conflict do not exist.

William Shakespeare is often called the greatest playwright of all time. His plays showed a brilliant command of the English language. They also show a deep understanding of people and how they interact with one another.

3. Who were two of the most famous writers of the northern Renaissance?

_____

_____

_____

PRINTING SPREADS RENAISSANCE IDEAS; THE LEGACY OF THE RENAISSANCE (Pages 484–485)
Why was the printing press such an important development?

One reason that learning spread so rapidly during the Renaissance was the invention of movable type. The Chinese had invented the process of carving characters onto wooden blocks. They then arranged them in words, inked the blocks, and pressed them against paper to print pages.

In 1440, a German, **Johann Gutenberg,** used this same practice to invent his printing press. He produced his first book—the Gutenberg Bible—in 1455 on this press. The technology then spread rapidly. By 1500, presses in Europe had printed nearly 10 million books.

Printing made it easier to make many copies of a book. As a result, written works became available far and wide. Books were printed in English, French, Spanish, Italian, or German. More people began to read. The Bible was a popular book. After reading the Bible, some people formed new ideas about Christianity. These ideas were different from the official teachings of the Church.

The Renaissance prompted changes in both art and society. Artists and writers portrayed people in more realistic ways and celebrated individual achievement. In a larger sense, the Renaissance opened up a world of new ideas to people and led them to examine and question things more closely.

4. What effects did the printing press have on northern European life?

_____

_____

_____

As you read about the ways that northern Europeans adapted the ideas of the Renaissance, take notes to answer each question.

1. What factors led to the beginning of the Renaissance in northern Europe?
2. How did the invention of the printing press help spread learning and Renaissance ideas?

Describe briefly how each of the following showed Renaissance influences in his work.

3. Albrecht Dürer
4. Jan van Eyck
5. Pieter Bruegel the Elder
6. Desiderius Erasmus
7. Thomas More
8. William Shakespeare

Section 3

Luther Leads the Reformation

Terms and Names

indulgence Release from punishments due for a sin

Reformation 16th-century movement for religious reform, leading to the founding of new Christian churches

Lutheran Member of a Protestant church founded on the teachings of Martin Luther

Protestant Member of a Christian church founded on the principles of the Reformation

Peace of Augsburg Agreement in 1555 declaring that the religion of each German state would be decided by its ruler

annul Cancel or put an end to

Anglican Relating to the Church of England

Before You Read

In the last section, you saw how the Renaissance spread to northern Europe.

In this section, you will see how Renaissance ideas helped bring about the Reformation.

As You Read

Use a chart to identify the effects of Martin Luther's protests.

CAUSES OF THE REFORMATION
(Pages 488–489)
Why was the Church criticized?

By 1500, the influence of the Church on the lives of people had weakened. Some people resented paying taxes to support the Church in Rome. Others sharply criticized the Church for some of its practices. Popes seemed more concerned with luxury and political power than with spiritual matters. Many local priests lacked education and were not able to teach people. Some lived immoral lives.

Reformers urged the Church to change its ways to become more spiritual and humble. Christian humanists such as Erasmus and Thomas More added their

voices to calls for change. In the early 1500s, the calls grew louder.

1. What kinds of changes did Church critics want to make?

_____

_____

LUTHER CHALLENGES THE CHURCH (Page 489)
How did the Reformation begin?

In 1517, a German monk named Martin Luther protested against a Church official who was selling **indulgences.** An indulgence was a kind of forgiveness. By paying money to the Church, people thought they could win salvation.

Luther challenged this practice and others. He posted a protest on the door of a castle church. His words were printed and spread throughout Germany. This was the beginning of the **Reformation**, a movement for reform that led to the founding of new Christian churches.

2. What role did Martin Luther play in the Reformation?

_____

_____

THE RESPONSE TO LUTHER
(Pages 490–492)
What effects did Luther's protest have?

Pope Leo X punished Luther for his views, but he refused to change them. Holy Roman Emperor Charles V, a strong Catholic, called Luther an outlaw. Luther's books were burned. But it was too late. Many of his ideas were already being practiced. The **Lutheran** Church started around 1522.

In 1524, peasants in Germany hoped to use Luther's ideas about Christian freedom to change society. They demanded an end to serfdom—a condition like slavery. When it was not granted, they revolted. Luther disagreed with this revolt. German princes killed thousands in putting the revolt down.

Some nobles supported Luther's ideas. They saw a chance to weaken the emperor's power over them. Other German princes joined forces against Luther's supporters. They signed an agreement to remain loyal to the pope and the emperor. Supporters of Luther's ideas protested this agreement. They were called the Protestants. Eventually, the term **Protestant** meant Christians who belonged to non-Catholic churches.

War broke out between Catholic and Protestant forces in Germany. It finally ended in 1555 with the **Peace of Augsburg.** This treaty granted each prince the right to decide whether his subjects would be Catholic or Protestant.

3. Why did Luther's ideas lead to war?

_____

_____

ENGLAND BECOMES PROTESTANT (Page 492–494)
How did England become Protestant?

The Catholic Church faced another challenge in England. Henry VIII, the king, was married to a Spanish princess. She gave birth to a daughter. England had never had a female ruler. Henry feared a civil war would start if he had no son. He believed his wife was too old to have another child. He tried to get the pope to **annul**, or put an end to, the marriage so he could remarry. The pope refused.

To remarry, Henry had to get out of the Catholic church. In 1534, Henry had Parliament pass laws that created the Church of England. These laws made the king or queen, not the pope, head of the Church. Henry no longer had to obey the pope. Henry remarried five times. His only son was from his third wife.

One of Henry's daughters, Elizabeth, became queen in 1558. She finished creating a separate English church. The new church was called **Anglican.** It had some practices that would appeal to both Protestants and Catholics. In this way, Elizabeth hoped to end religious conflict.

4. What role did Henry VIII play in creating the Church of England?

_____

_____

As you read this section, note some of the causes and effects of the events identified.

Causes	Event or Situation	Effects
	1. In 1517, Luther posts his 95 theses on the church door at Wittenberg.	
	2. In 1520, Luther is excommunicated. In 1521, he is declared an outlaw and a heretic.	
	3. The German peasants revolt in 1524.	
	4. The Peace of Augsburg is signed in 1555.	
	5. The English Parliament approves the Act of Supremacy in 1534.	
	6. Parliament establishes the Anglican Church in 1559.	

European Renaissance and Reformation

The Reformation Continues

Terms and Names

predestination Doctrine that God has decided all things beforehand, including which people will be saved

Calvinism Religious teachings based on the ideas of the reformer John Calvin

theocracy Government controlled by religious leaders

Presbyterian Member of a Protestant church governed by elders and founded by John Knox

Anabaptist Member of a Protestant group during the Reformation who believed only adults should be baptized. Also believed that church and state should be separate

Catholic Reformation 16th-century Catholic reform movement in response to Protestant Reformation

Jesuits Members of the Society of Jesus, a Roman Catholic religious order founded by Ignatius of Loyola

Council of Trent Meeting of Roman Catholic leaders to rule on doctrines criticized by the Protestant reformers

---

Before You Read

In the last section, you read how the Reformation began.

In this section, you will learn how it developed and spread.

As You Read

Use a chart to compare the ideas of the reformers who came after Luther.

CALVIN CONTINUES THE REFORMATION (Pages 495–496)
***What* did Calvin teach?**

Protestantism arose elsewhere in the 1530s under the leadership of John Calvin. Calvin taught that people are sinful by nature. He also taught **predestination,** the idea that God determines beforehand who will be saved. The religion based on Calvin's teachings is called **Calvinism.**

Calvin created a **theocracy** in Geneva, Switzerland. It was government run by religious leaders. It had strict rules of behavior.

A preacher named John Knox put these ideas into practice in Scotland. This was beginning of the **Presbyterian** Church. Others in Holland, France, and Switzerland adopted Calvin's ideas as well. In France, his followers were called Huguenots. Conflict between them and Catholics often turned into violence. In 1572, mobs killed about 12,000 Huguenots.

1. What is Calvinism?

_____

OTHER PROTESTANT REFORMERS (Pages 496–498)
What other reformers were important during the Reformation?

Another new Protestant group was the **Anabaptists.** They preached that people should be baptized into the faith as adults. Anabaptists also taught that the church and state should be separate. In addition, they refused to fight in wars.

Many women played key roles in the Reformation. Marguerite of Navarre protected John Calvin from being killed for his beliefs. Katherina von Bora was the wife of Martin Luther. She supported an equal role for women in marriage.

2. Who were two women who played important roles in the Reformation?

_____

_____

THE CATHOLIC REFORMATION (Pages 498–499)
What was the Catholic Reformation?

Protestant churches grew all over Europe. To keep Catholic believers loyal, the Catholic Church took steps to change itself. This was called the **Catholic Reformation.**

One Catholic reformer was a Spanish noble named Ignatius. He founded a new group in the Church based on deep devotion to Jesus. Members of this group, called the **Jesuits,** started schools across Europe. They sent missionaries to convert people to Catholicism. In addition, they tried to stop the spread of Protestant faiths.

Two popes of the 1500s helped bring about changes in the Church. Pope Paul III set up a kind of court called the Inquisition. It was charged with finding, trying, and punishing people who broke the rules of the Church. He also called a

meeting of church leaders, the **Council of Trent.** The council, which met in 1545, passed doctrines. These doctrines stated that the Church's interpretation of the Bible was final and that Christians needed to perform good works to win salvation. They also gave the Bible and the Church equal authority in setting out Christian beliefs and supported indulgences.

The next pope, Paul IV, put these doctrines into practice. They helped revive the Church and allowed it to survive the challenge of the Protestants.

3. What happened at the Council of Trent?

_____

_____

THE LEGACY OF THE REFORMATION (Page 500)
What was the legacy of the Reformation?

The Reformation had an enduring impact on society. In the wake of the movement, Protestant churches flourished. Meanwhile, the Catholic Church became more unified as a result of the reforms started at the Council of Trent.

The Reformation caused an overall decline in the authority of the church. As a result, individual monarchs and states gained greater power. This in turn led to the development of modern nation-states.

Women thought that their status in society might improve as a result of the Reformation. However, this did not happen. Women were still mainly limited to the concerns of home and family.

4. What was the result of the declining authority of the church?

_____

_____

As you read about new Protestant churches and reforms within the Catholic Church, take notes to answer the questions.

What were some religious or social beliefs of each new Protestant religion?
1. Calvinism
2. Presbyterianism
3. Anabaptism

4. What were the three major activities of the Jesuits?
5. Why were the effects of the work of Jesuit missionaries so long lasting?
6. What role did Popes Paul III and Paul IV play in reforming the Catholic Church?
7. What were some important effects of the Reformation?

The Ottomans Build a Vast Empire

Terms and Names

ghazis Warriors for Islam

Osman Successful ghazi who built a small state in Anatolia

sultans Rulers of Muslim states

Timur the Lame Conqueror of Persia and Russia

Mehmed II Conqueror who made Istanbul his capital

Suleyman the Lawgiver Ruler who brought Ottoman Empire to its height

devshirme Policy for creating the sultan's army

janissary Soldier slave drawn from conquered Christian territories

Before You Read

In the last chapter, you read about changes in Europe during 1300-1600.

In this section, you will read about the rise of the Ottoman Empire during the same period.

As You Read

Use a chart to list the main rulers of the Ottoman Empire and their successes.

TURKS MOVE INTO BYZANTIUM
(Pages 507–508)
How did the Ottoman Empire begin?

In 1300, the world of the eastern Mediterranean was also changing. The Byzantine Empire was fading. The Seljuk Turk state had been destroyed. Anatolia, the area of modern Turkey, was now inhabited by groups of nomadic Turks. They saw themselves as **ghazis,** or Muslim warriors for Islam. They raided the lands where non-Muslims lived.

The most successful ghazi was **Osman.** Western Europeans thought his name was Othman. They called his followers Ottomans. Between 1300 and 1326,

Osman built a strong but small kingdom in Anatolia. Leaders who came after Osman called themselves **sultans,** or "ones with power." They extended the kingdom by buying land. They also formed alliances with other chieftains and conquered everyone they could.

The Ottomans ruled in a kindly way. Muslims had to serve in the army but paid no taxes. Non-Muslims paid tax but did not serve in the army. Many joined Islam just to avoid the tax. Most people adjusted easily to their new rule.

One warrior did not. He was **Timur the Lame.** He conquered Russia and Persia. In 1402, he defeated the Ottoman forces.

Timur captured the sultan and took him to Samarkand in a cage.

1. Who were the Ottomans?

_____

_____

_____

_____

POWERFUL SULTANS SPUR DRAMATIC EXPANSION
(Pages 508–509)
How did the empire grow?

In Anatolia, the four sons of the last sultan fought for control of the empire. Mehmed I won control. His son and the four sultans who came after him brought the Ottoman Empire to its greatest power. One of them—**Mehmed II**—took power in 1451. He built a force of 100,000 foot soldiers and 125 ships to gain control of Constantinople. In 1453, he took the city and the waterway it controlled. Mehmed made the city his capital. He renamed it Istanbul. The rebuilt city became home to people from all over the Ottoman Empire.

Other emperors used conquest to make the empire grow. After 1514, Selim the Grim took Persia, Syria, and Palestine. He then captured Arabia, took the Muslim holy cities of Medina and Mecca, and gained control of Egypt.

2. Who was Mehmed II?

_____

_____

SULEYMAN THE LAWGIVER; THE EMPIRE DECLINES SLOWLY
(Pages 510–511)
Why was Suleyman the Lawgiver a great leader?

Suleyman I took power in 1520 and ruled for 46 years. He brought the Ottoman Empire to its greatest size and most impressive achievements. He conquered parts of southeastern Europe. He won control of the entire eastern Mediterranean Sea and took North Africa as far west as Tripoli.

Suleyman revised the laws of the empire. His people called him **Suleyman the Lawgiver.** Suleyman ruled his empire with a highly structured government. Thousands of slaves served the royal family. The policy of making people slaves was called *devshirme.* The **janissaries** were an enslaved group of soldiers. They were Christians taken as children and made slaves. They were trained as soldiers and fought fiercely for the sultan. Other slaves held important government jobs.

The empire allowed people to follow their own religion. Jews and Christians were not mistreated. His empire was also known for great works of art and many fine buildings.

Although the empire lasted long after Suleyman, it spent the next few hundred years in decline. That means its power slipped. None of the sultans were as accomplished as Suleyman had been.

3. What were two of Suleyman's accomplishments?

_____

_____

_____

Section 1, *continued*

As you read this section, fill out the chart below by writing answers in the appropriate boxes.

What role did each ruler play in the building and expansion of the Ottoman Empire?
1. Osman
2. Murad II
3. Mehmed II
4. Selim the Grim
5. Suleyman

List the achievements of Suleyman in the boxes below.

Social Achievements	Cultural Achievements

The Muslim World Expands

Cultural Blending
Case Study: The Safavid Empire

Terms and Names

Safavid Member of a Shi'a Muslim group that built an empire in Persia

Isma'il Safavid warrior who seized most of what is now Iran

shah Persian title meaning king

Shah Abbas Leader during the Safavid golden age

Esfahan Capital city of the Safavid Empire

Before You Read

In the last section, you read about the Ottomans.

In this section, you will learn about the development of another empire, the Safavid.

As You Read

Use a diagram to identify examples of cultural blending in the Safavid Empire.

PATTERNS OF CULTURAL BLENDING (Pages 512–513)
What is cultural blending?

Throughout history, different peoples have lived together. Their cultures have influenced one another. Often these people have blended one culture with another. This can happen because of migration, trade, conquest, or pursuit of religious freedom or conversion.

Cultural blending results in changes in society. Some results of cultural blending are changes in language, religion, styles of government, or arts and architecture.

Societies that are able to benefit from cultural blending are open to new ways. They are willing to adapt and change.

1. What are the four causes of cultural blending?

_____

_____

THE SAFAVIDS BUILD A SHI'A EMPIRE (Pages 513–514)
How did the Safavids rise to power?

Cultural blending took place in the Safavid Empire of Persia. The **Safavids** were members of the Shi'a, a branch of Islam. The major group of Muslims, the Sunnis, persecuted the Shi'a for their views. The Safavids feared the Sunni Muslims. They decided to build a strong army to protect themselves.

In 1499, a 14-year-old leader named **Isma'il** led this army to conquer Iran. He took the traditional Persian title of **shah,** or king, and made Shi'a the religion of the new empire. He destroyed Baghdad's Sunni population. Ottoman Turk rulers—who were Sunni Muslims—in turn killed all the Shi'a that they met. This conflict between the two groups of Muslims continues today.

Guided Reading Workbook

2. Why are the Shi'a and Sunni Muslims enemies?

_____

A SAFAVID GOLDEN AGE
Who was Shah Abbas?

The Safavids reached their height in the late 1500s under **Shah Abbas.** He created two armies that were loyal to him and him alone. He also gave new weapons to the army to make them better fighters. He got rid of corrupt officials in the government. He also brought gifted artists to his empire.

Shah Abbas drew on good ideas from other cultures. The main elements of that culture were the joining together of the Persian tradition of learning and sophistication with the strong faith of the Shi'a. He used Chinese artists. They helped create gorgeous artwork that decorated the rebuilt capital of **Esfahan.**

Under Shah Abbas, the Safavids enjoyed good relations with nations of Europe. The demand for Persian rugs increased greatly in Europe. In this period, rug-making, which had been a local craft in Persia, became a major industry for the country.

3. What were four reforms made by Shah Abbas?

_____

THE DYNASTY DECLINES QUICKLY
(Pages 515)
Why did the Safavids lose power?

Like the Ottoman Empire, the Safavid Empire began to decline soon after it had reached its greatest height. Shah Abbas had killed or injured his most talented sons—just as Suleyman had done. Shah Abbas feared that his sons would seize power from him. As a result, a weak and ineffective grandson became shah after him.

4. Why weren't there strong leaders after Shah Abbas?

_____

_____

As you read this case study, take notes to answer the questions about patterns of cultural blending.

Interaction among peoples can create a blending of cultures.

1. What activities cause cultural blending to occur?	2. Which of those activities contributed to the culture of the Ottomans?

The Safavids built a Shi'a Empire.

3. How did Isma'il help the Safavids rise to power?	4. How did Isma'il's rule affect the Islam religion?

Shah Abbas helped create a Safavid culture.

5. How did Shah Abbas promote cultural blending in his empire?	6. What was probably the most important result of Western influence on the Safavid Empire?

Guided Reading Workbook

Section 3

The Mughal Empire in India

Terms and Names

Babur Founder of the Mughal Empire

Mughal One of the nomads who invaded the Indian subcontinent and established a powerful empire there

Akbar Mughal ruler with a genius for cultural blending, military conquest, and art

Sikh Nonviolent religious group that became the enemy of the Mughals

Shah Jahan Mughal ruler who built Taj Mahal

Taj Mahal Tomb built by Shah Jahan for his wife

Aurangzeb Last important Mughal ruler

Before You Read

In the last section, you learn about how the Safavids established an empire in what is present-day Iran.

In this section, you will learn about the establishment of the Mughal Empire in what is now India.

As You Read

Use a time line to identify the Mughal emperors and their successes.

EARLY HISTORY OF THE MUGHAL EMPIRE (Page 516)
How did the Mughal Empire begin?

Starting in the 600s, India went through a long, unsettled period. Nomads from central Asia invaded the area and created many small kingdoms. In the 700s, Muslims arrived on the scene. This began a long history of fighting with the Hindus who had lived in India for centuries.

After about 300 years, a group of Muslim Turks conquered a region around the city of Delhi. They set up a new empire there. They treated the Hindus in their area as conquered peoples. Their rule was brought to an end in 1398.

A little over a hundred years later, a new leader named **Babur** raised an army and began to win large parts of India. He had many talents. He was a lover of poetry

and gardens. He was also an excellent general. His empire was called the **Mughal** Empire because he and his families were related to the Mongols.

1. Who was Babur?

_____

_____

THE GOLDEN AGE OF AKBAR (Pages 517–518)
Who was Akbar?

Babur's grandson was **Akbar**. His name means "Greatest One." He ruled with great wisdom and fairness for almost 40 years.

Akbar was a Muslim. However, he believed strongly that people should be allowed to follow the religion they choose.

Both Hindus and Muslims worked in the government. He hired people in his government based on their ability.

Akbar ruled fairly. He ended the tax that Hindu pilgrims and all non-Muslims had to pay. To raise money, he taxed people on a percentage of the food they grew. This made it easier for peasants to pay the tax. His land policy was less wise. He gave much land to government officials. However, when they died he took it back. As a result, workers did not see any point in caring for the land.

He had a strong, well-equipped army that helped him win and keep control of more lands. His empire held about 100 million people—more than lived in all of Europe at the time.

During Akbar's reign, his policy of blending different cultures produced two new languages. One was Hindi, which is widely spoken in India today. The other was Urdu. It is now the official language of Pakistan. The empire became famous for its art, literature, and architecture. He also sponsored the building of a new capital city.

2. What are some examples of Akbar's policy of fair rule?

_____

_____

AKBAR'S SUCCESSORS

(Pages 518–521)

Who ruled after Akbar?

After Akbar's death in 1605, his son Jahangir took control of the empire. During his reign, the real power was his wife, Nur Jahan. She plotted with one son to overthrow another son. She had a bitter political battle with the **Sikhs,** members of a separate, nonviolent religion, who became the target of attacks.

The next ruler was **Shah Jahan.** He too chose not to follow Akbar's policy of

religious toleration. Shah Jahan was a great patron of the arts and built many beautiful buildings. One was the famous **Taj Mahal,** a tomb for his wife. His ambitious building plans required high taxes, though. People suffered under his rule.

His son **Aurangzeb** ruled for almost 50 years. He made the empire grow once again with new conquests. His rule also brought new problems. He was a devout Muslim, and he punished Hindus and destroyed their temples. This led to a rebellion that took part of his empire. At the same time, the Sikhs won control of another part of the empire.

3. How did Aurangzeb deal with Hindus?

_____

_____

THE EMPIRE'S DECLINE AND DECAY **(Page** 521)

How did the Mughal Empire lose its power?

Aurangzeb used up the empire's resources. People did not feel loyalty to him. As the power of the state weakened, the power of local lords grew. Soon there was only a patchwork of independent states. There continued to be a Mughal emperor, but he was only a figurehead, not a ruler with any real power. As the Mughal empire was rising and falling, Western traders were building power. They arrived in India just before Babur did. Shah Jahan let the English build a trading fort in Madras. Aurangzeb handed them the port of Bombay. This gave India's next conquerors a foothold in India.

4. How did the Mughal Empire change after Akbar?

_____

_____

As you read about the Mughal Empire, make notes in the chart to describe
the outcome of each action listed.

Action	Outcome
1. Babur leads troops to victories over an army led by the sultan of Delhi and the rajput army.	
2. Akbar governs through a bureaucracy of officials in which natives and foreigners, both Hindus and Muslims, can rise to high office.	
3. Akbar prohibits inheritance of land granted to bureaucrats.	
4. Akbar appoints rajputs as officers in Mughal army.	
5. Akbar practices cultural blending.	
6. The Sikhs defend Khusrau in his rebellion against his father, Jahangir.	
7. Shah Jahan orders the building of the Taj Mahal.	
8. Aurangzeb strictly enforces Islamic laws and reinstates tax on non-Muslims.	
9. Aurangzeb dies.	

Section 1

Europeans Explore the East

Terms and Names

Bartolomeu Dias Portuguese explorer who rounded the tip of Africa

Prince Henry Portuguese supporter of exploration

Vasco da Gama Explorer who gave Portugal a direct sea route to India

Treaty of Tordesillas Treaty between Spain and Portugal dividing newly discovered lands between them

Dutch East India Company Dutch company that established and directed trade throughout Asia

Before You Read

In the last chapter, you read about empire building in Asia.

In this section, you will learn why and how Europeans began an age of exploration.

As You Read

Use a time line to take notes on important events in the European exploration of the East.

FOR "GOD, GLORY, AND GOLD"
(Pages 529–530)
Why did Europeans begin to explore new lands?

For many centuries, Europeans did not have much contact with people from other lands. That changed in the 1400s. Europeans hoped to gain new sources of wealth. By exploring the seas, traders hoped to find new, faster routes to Asia— the source of spices and luxury goods. Another reason for exploration was spreading Christianity to new lands.

Bartolomeu Dias, an early Portuguese explorer, explained his motives: "to serve God and His Majesty, to give light to those who were in darkness and to grow rich as all men desire to do."

Advances in technology made these voyages possible. A new kind of ship, the caravel, was stronger than earlier ships. It had triangle-shaped sails that allowed it to sail against the wind. Ships could now travel far out into the ocean. The magnetic compass allowed sea captains to stay on course better.

1. What were the two main reasons for European exploration?

_____

_____

_____

PORTUGAL LEADS THE WAY; SPAIN ALSO MAKES CLAIMS
(Pages 530–533)
How did Portugal lead the way in exploration?

Portugal was the first nation to develop the caravel and magnetic compass.

Prince Henry was committed to the idea of exploring. In 1419, he started a school of navigation. Sea captains, mapmakers, and navigators met and exchanged ideas there.

Over the next few decades, Portuguese captains sailed farther and farther down the west coast of Africa. In 1488, Bartolomeu Dias reached the southern tip of Africa. Ten years later, **Vasco da Gama** led a ship around Africa, to India and back. The Portuguese had found a sea route to Asia.

The Spanish, meanwhile, had plans of their own. Christopher Columbus convinced the king and queen that he could reach Asia by sailing west. In 1492, instead of landing in Asia, Columbus touched land in the islands of the Americas. Spain and Portugal argued over which nation had the rights to the land that Columbus had claimed. In 1494, they signed the **Treaty of Tordesillas.** It divided the world into two areas. Portugal won the right to control the eastern parts—including Africa, India, and other parts of Asia. Spain got the western parts—including most of the Americas.

2. How did Spain and Portugal solve their differences over claims to new lands?

_____

_____

TRADING EMPIRES IN THE INDIAN OCEAN (Pages 533–535)
Who established trading empires in the Indian Ocean?

Portugal moved quickly to make the new Indian Ocean route pay off. Through military might, Portugal gained power over islands that were rich in desirable spices. They were called the Spice Islands. Spices now cost Europeans one-fifth of what they had cost before, while still making Portugal very wealthy.

Other European nations joined in this trade. In the 1600s, the English and Dutch entered the East Indies. They quickly broke Portuguese power in the area. Then both nations set up an East India Company to control Asian trade. These companies were more than businesses. They were like governments. They had the power to make money, sign treaties, and raise their own armies. The **Dutch East India Company** was richer and more powerful than England's company.

By 1700, the Dutch ruled much of Indonesia. They had trading posts in many other Asian countries and commanded the southern tip of Africa. At the same time, both England and France finally gained footholds in India.

Nevertheless, even though Europeans controlled the trade between Asia and Europe, they had little impact on most people living in these areas.

3. How did the Dutch and English become Indian Ocean trading powers?

_____

_____

_____

Guided Reading Workbook

As you read about the age of exploration, take notes to answer questions about events listed in the time line.

Time Line	Questions
1400	1. What technological advances made possible the age of exploration?
1419 Prince Henry starts a navigation school.	
	2. What were some immediate and some long-term outcomes of Columbus' voyage?
1487 Bartolomeu Dias rounds the southern tip of Africa.	
1492 Christopher Columbus reaches the Caribbean.	3. What was the most important result of this agreement?
1494 Spain and Portugal sign the Treaty of Tordesillas.	
1498 Vasco da Gama reaches the port of Calicut on the Indian Ocean.	4. How did Portugal benefit from his voyage?
1500	
1521 Ferdinand Magellan leads a Spanish expedition to the Philippines.	5. Why did Spain set up trading posts in Asia?
1565 Spain begins settlements in the Philippines.	
	6. How did the Dutch gain control of much of the Indian Ocean trade?
1600	
1619 The Dutch establish a trading center on Java.	7. How did the European battles for Indian Ocean trade affect the peoples of Asia before the nineteenth century?
1664 France sets up its own East India Company.	

An Age of Explorations and Isolation

China Limits European Contacts

Terms and Names

Hongwu Commander of the rebel army that drove the Mongols out of China in 1368

Ming Dynasty Chinese dynasty that ruled from 1368 to 1644

Yonglo Ming ruler; son of Hongwu

Zheng He Muslim admiral who led seven voyages of exploration during the Ming Dynasty

Manchus People from Manchuria

Qing Dynasty Chinese dynasty that followed the Ming Dynasty and was begun by the Manchus

Kangxi Powerful Manchu emperor of the Qing Dynasty

Before You Read

In the last section, you read about European exploration in the East.

In this section, you will read about China's reactions to the world around it.

As You Read

Use a chart to summarize relevant facts about each emperor discussed in this section.

CHINA UNDER THE POWERFUL MING DYNASTY (Pages 536–539)
What occurred during the Ming Dynasty?

Mongol rule in China ended in 1368 when **Hongwu** led a rebel army that took control of the country. He declared himself the first emperor of the **Ming Dynasty,** which was to last for almost 300 years. Hongwu began his rule by increasing the amount of food produced and improving the government. Later he grew suspicious and untrusting. He caused the deaths of many people whom he suspected of plotting against him.

His son **Yonglo** continued his better policies. He also launched a major effort at making contact with other Asian peoples. Beginning in 1405, an admiral named **Zheng He** led several voyages to Southeast Asia, India, Arabia, and Africa. Wherever he went, he gave away gifts to show Chinese superiority.

Eventually the Chinese began to isolate themselves. China allowed Europeans to trade at only three ports, but illegal trade took place all along the coast. Europeans wanted Chinese silk and ceramics, and they paid silver for them. Manufacturing never grew very large in China, however.

The Confucian ideas that shaped Chinese thinking said that farming was a better way of life, so manufacturing was heavily taxed. Missionaries entered China at this time, bringing both Christianity and technology.

1. How was China influenced by foreigners during the Ming Dynasty?

_____

_____

MANCHUS FOUND THE QING DYNASTY (Pages 539–540)
How did China change during the Qing Dynasty?

The Ming Dynasty lost power because the government could not solve several problems. Manchus, people who came from a land north of China called Manchuria, took control of the country in 1644. They started the **Qing Dynasty.** Two important emperors were **Kangxi** and his grandson Qian-long. They brought China to its largest size, increased its wealth, and sponsored an increase in artistic production.

The Chinese insisted that Europeans had to follow certain rules in order to continue trading with them. These rules included trading only at special ports and paying fees. The Dutch were willing to do so, and they carried on the largest share of trade with China. The British, though, did not agree to following these rules.

At the same time, a feeling of national pride was rising in Korea, which had long been dominated by China.

2. Why was trade a problem during the Qing Dynasty?

_____

_____

LIFE IN MING AND QING CHINA
(Page 541)
What was life like in China under the Ming and Qing?

In China, the production of rice and the long period of peace gave the people better lives. In the1600s and 1700s, the number of people in China almost doubled. The majority of these people were farmers. Because of the use of fertilizer and better irrigation, they could grow more food. The level of nutrition improved. This caused the population to grow.

In Chinese families, sons were valued over daughters. It was believed that only sons could carry out family religious duties and tend to the family farm. For that reason, many infant girls were killed, and adult women had few rights.

The invasions by the foreigners from Manchuria and the pressure from European traders bothered the Chinese. They tried to preserve their traditions and their isolation. Artists created books and paintings that showed traditional Chinese values and ideas. Plays about Chinese history and heroes were popular. They helped to unify the Chinese people.

3. Which parts of society improved during this time, and which continued to be the same?

_____

_____

As you read this section, take notes to answer questions about the Ming
and Qing dynasties.

The rulers of the Ming Dynasty drive out the Mongols and bring peace and prosperity to China.

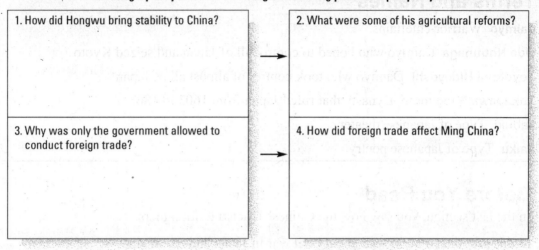

1. How did Hongwu bring stability to China?

2. What were some of his agricultural reforms?

3. Why was only the government allowed to conduct foreign trade?

4. How did foreign trade affect Ming China?

The Manchus invade China and begin the Qing Dynasty.

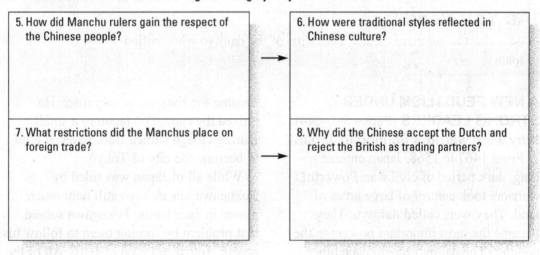

5. How did Manchu rulers gain the respect of the Chinese people?

6. How were traditional styles reflected in Chinese culture?

7. What restrictions did the Manchus place on foreign trade?

8. Why did the Chinese accept the Dutch and reject the British as trading partners?

Section 3

Japan Returns to Isolation

Terms and Names

daimyo Warrior-chieftains

Oda Nobunaga Daimyo who hoped to control all of Japan and seized Kyoto

Toyotomi Hideyoshi Daimyo who took control of almost all of Japan

Tokugawa Shogunate Dynasty that ruled Japan from 1603 to 1868

kabuki Type of Japanese theater

haiku Type of Japanese poetry

Before You Read

In the last section, you saw how the Chinese reacted to foreigners.

In this section, you will read about civil war in Japan and its effects.

As You Read

Use a chart to compare the achievements of the daimyo who unified Japan.

A NEW FEUDALISM UNDER STRONG LEADERS (Pages 542–544)
Why were warriors fighting in Japan?

From 1467 to 1568, Japan entered a long, dark period of civil war. Powerful warriors took control of large areas of land. They were called **daimyo.** They became the most important powers in the country. The daimyo fought each other constantly to gain more land for themselves.

In 1568, one of the daimyo, **Oda Nobunaga,** took control of Kyoto. It was the site of the emperor's capital. Another general, **Toyotomi Hideyoshi,** continued the work of bringing all of Japan under one rule. Using military conquest and clever diplomacy, he won that goal in 1590. He failed in his effort to capture Korea, however.

The work of unifying Japan was completed by Tokugawa Ieyasu. He became the shogun, or sole ruler. He moved the capital of Japan to a small fishing village named Edo. Later, it grew to become the city of Tokyo.

While all of Japan was ruled by Tokugawa, the daimyo still held much power in their lands. Tokugawa solved that problem by forcing them to follow his orders. Tokugawa died in 1616. All of the shoguns to follow him were from his family. They maintained a strong central government in Japan. This system of rule, called the **Tokugawa Shogunate,** lasted until 1867.

1. Which three leaders helped bring Japan under one rule?

_____

_____

LIFE IN TOKUGAWA JAPAN
(**Page** 544)
How **was Tokugawa society organized?**

The new government brought about a long period of peace and prosperity for most people. Peasant farmers suffered greatly during this time, however. They worked long and hard on the farms and paid heavy taxes. Many left the countryside to move to the cities. By the mid-1700s, Edo had more than a million people. It was perhaps the largest city in the world. Women found more opportunities for work in this and other cities than they had in the country.

A traditional culture thrived, characterized by ceremonial dramas, stories of ancient warriors, and paintings of classical scenes. However, in cities, new styles emerged. Townspeople attended **kabuki,** dramas of urban life. They hung woodblock prints of city scenes in their homes. They also read **haiku,** poetry that presents images instead of expressing ideas.

2. What kinds of old and new culture were found in the cities?

_____

_____

CONTACT BETWEEN EUROPE AND JAPAN; THE CLOSED COUNTRY POLICY (Pages 545–547)
Who **came to Japan?**

In 1543, Europeans began to arrive in Japan. The Portuguese were first. In the beginning, Japanese merchants and the daimyo welcomed them. They even welcomed the Christian missionaries who came after 1549. Some missionaries scorned traditional Japanese beliefs. They also got involved in local politics. Tokugawa became worried. In 1612, he banned Christianity from the country. Christians were persecuted. Over the next 20 years or so, Japan managed to rid the country of all Christians. This was part of a larger plan to protect the country from European influence.

In 1639, leaders sealed Japan's borders except for one port city. It was open to only the Chinese and the Dutch. The Tokugawa shoguns controlled that port city, so they had tight control over all foreign contact. For the next 200 years, Japan remained closed to just about all European contact.

3. Why did the Japanese seal almost all of their borders?

_____

_____

Name _____ Class _____ Date _____

As you read this section, take notes to answer the questions.

How did each of the following help to unify Japan?	
1. daimyo	2. Oda Nobunaga
3. Toyotomi Hideyoshi	4. Tokugawa Ieyasu

How did each of the following influence Japanese society and culture?	
5. Tokugawa Shogunate	6. Portuguese
7. Christian missionaries	8. "Closed country" policy

Guided Reading Workbook

The Atlantic World

Spain Builds an American Empire

Terms and Names

Christopher Columbus Italian explorer who landed in the Americas

colony Land controlled by another nation

Hernando Cortés Conquistador who defeated the Aztec

conquistadors Spanish explorers in the Americas

Francisco Pizarro Conquistador who defeated the Inca

Atahualpa Last Incan emperor

mestizo Person with mixed Spanish and Native American blood

encomienda System of mining and farming using natives as slave labor

Before You Read

In the last chapter, you read about European exploration in the East.

In this section, you will study the Spanish and Portuguese exploration of the Americas.

As You Read

Use a diagram to trace the major events in the establishment of Spain's empire in the Americas.

THE VOYAGE OF COLUMBUS
(**Pages** 553–554)
How did the voyage of Columbus change the Americas?

In 1492, **Christopher Columbus,** an Italian sailor, led a voyage for Spain. He sailed west hoping to reach Asia. Instead, he landed in the Americas. Columbus thought that he had reached the East Indies in Asia. He misnamed the natives he met there, calling them Indians. He claimed the land for Spain. From then on, Spain began to create **colonies.** Colonies are lands controlled by another nation.

In 1500, a Portuguese explorer claimed Brazil. In 1501, Amerigo Vespucci

explored the eastern coast of South America. He said that these lands were a new world. Soon after, a mapmaker showed the lands as a separate continent. He named them America after Vespucci.

Other voyages gave Europeans more knowledge about the world. Balboa reached the Pacific Ocean. Ferdinand Magellan sailed completely around the world.

1. Which voyages gave Europeans new knowledge of the world?

_____

_____

SPANISH CONQUESTS IN MEXICO
(Pages 554–556)
Why did Spain conquer the Aztecs?

Hernando Cortés was one of the Spanish **conquistadors,** or conquerors. In the 16th century, they began to explore the lands of the Americas. They were seeking great riches. In 1519, Cortés came to Mexico and defeated the powerful Aztec Empire led by Montezuma II.

2. What was the main goal of Cortéz in his conquests?

_____

_____

SPANISH CONQUESTS IN PERU
(Pages 556–557)
How did Spain build an empire?

About 15 years later, **Francisco Pizarro** led another Spanish force. It conquered the mighty Inca Empire of South America, led by **Atahualpa,** the last of the Incan emperors. Once again, the Spanish found gold and silver. By the mid-1500s, Spain had formed an American empire that stretched from modern-day Mexico to Peru. After 1540, the Spanish looked north of Mexico and explored the future United States.

The Spanish lived among the people they conquered. Spanish men married native women. Their children and descendants were called **mestizo**—people with mixed Spanish and Native American blood. The Spanish also formed large farms and mines that used natives as slave labor. This system was known as *encomienda.*

One large area of the Americas— Brazil—was the possession of Portugal. In the 1830s, colonists began to settle there. Colonists built huge farms called

plantations to grow sugar, which was in demand in Europe.

3. Give two examples of conquistadors and explain what they did.

_____

_____

SPAIN'S INFLUENCE EXPANDS
(Page 558)
Where did Spain hope to gain more power?

Soon Spain began to want even more power in the Americas. It started to look at land that is now part of the United States. Explorers like Coronado led expeditions to the area. Catholic priests went along.

4. What area did Coronado explore?

_____

_____

OPPOSITION TO SPANISH RULE
(Page 559)
Who opposed Spanish rule?

Spanish priests began to make some protests, however. One thing they criticized was the *encomienda* system. A monk named Bartolomé de Las Casas and others successfully called for the end of the system.

Native Americans also resisted new or continued Spanish rule. One of the most serious rebellions occurred in New Mexico. A Pueblo leader named Popé led a well-organized effort. It involved about 17,000 warriors and drove the Spanish back into New Spain for 12 years.

5. What challenges to their power did the Spanish face?

_____

Section 1, *continued*

As you read about the empire Spain built in the Americas, take notes to answer questions about the time line below.

1492	Christopher Columbus sails westward from Spain, hoping to reach Asia.	1. What was the significance of Columbus's voyages?
		2. Magellan himself died in the Philippines. What was the importance of the voyage his crew completed?
1519	Ferdinand Magellan sets sail on a voyage that rounds the southern tip of South America.	3. What factors helped the Spanish defeat the Aztec?
1521	Hernando Cortés conquers the Aztec.	
		4. How did the Spanish treat the peoples they conquered?
1533	Francisco Pizarro conquers the Inca Empire.	5. What was unique about the Spanish colonization of the lands of New Mexico?
1540	Francisco Vásquez de Coronado explores the Southwest.	6. What was the long-term consequence of this action?
1542	Spain abolishes the *encomienda* system.	

Guided Reading Workbook

Section 2

European Nations Settle North America

Terms and Names

New France Area of the Americas explored and claimed by France

Jamestown First permanent settlement in America

Pilgrims Group of English people who founded a colony in Plymouth

Puritans People who did not agree with the practices of the Church of England

New Netherland Dutch colony begun in modern New York City

French and Indian War War between Britain and France over land in North America

Metacom Native American leader who led an attack on the villages of Massachusetts; also called King Philip

Before You Read

In the last chapter, you read about Spanish conquests.

In this section, you will see how other nations competed for power in North America.

As You Read

Use a chart to record information about early settlements.

COMPETING CLAIMS IN NORTH AMERICA (Pages 561–562)
What new colonies were formed in North America?

In the early 1500s, the French began to explore North America. Jacques Cartier discovered and named the St. Lawrence River. He then followed it to the site of what is now Montreal. In 1608, Samuel de Champlain sailed as far as modern-day Quebec. In the next 100 years, the French explored and claimed the area around the Great Lakes and the Mississippi River all the way to its mouth at the Gulf of Mexico. The area became known as **New France**. The main activity in this colony was trade in beaver fur.

1. What was the main economic activity in New France?

_____

_____

THE ENGLISH ARRIVE IN NORTH AMERICA (Pages 562–563)
Why did the English settle in Massachusetts?

The English also began to colonize North America. The first permanent settlement was at **Jamestown,** in modern Virginia, in 1607. The colony struggled at first. Many settlers died from disease, hunger, or war with the native peoples.

Soon, farmers began to grow tobacco to meet the high demand for it in Europe.

In 1620, a group known as **Pilgrims** founded a second English colony in Plymouth, in Massachusetts. These settlers and others who followed were deeply religious people who did not agree with the practices of the Church of England. They were called **Puritans.**

Meanwhile, the Dutch also started a new colony. They settled in the location of modern New York City and called it **New Netherland.** Like the French, they traded fur. The colony became known as a home to people of many different cultures. Europeans also took possession of many islands of the Caribbean. There they built tobacco and sugar plantations that used enslaved Africans as workers.

2. In which two places did English colonists first settle?

_____

_____

THE STRUGGLE FOR NORTH AMERICA (Pages 563–564)
Who fought for control of North America?

The European powers began to fight for control of North America. First, the English forced the Dutch to give up their colony. New Netherland was renamed New York. The English also started other colonies along the Atlantic coast, from New Hampshire to Georgia. These English colonists interfered with the French settlers in Canada.

The British and the French clashed over the Ohio Valley in 1754. The fight was called the **French and Indian War.** When it ended in 1763, France was forced to give up all its land in North America to England.

3. How did England gain land from the French?

_____

_____

_____

NATIVE AMERICANS RESPOND
(**Pages** 564–565)
How did native peoples respond to the colonists?

The native peoples responded to the colonists in many different ways. Many worked closely with the French and Dutch, joining in the fur trade and benefiting from it. Those who lived near the English, though, had stormier relations with colonists. More than just trade, the English were interested in settling the land and farming it. This was land that Native Americans would not be able to use for hunting or growing their own food.

Conflicts over land erupted into war several times. One of the bloodiest times was known as King Philip's War. The Native American ruler **Metacom** (also known as King Philip) led an attack on 52 colonial villages throughout Massachusetts. However, Metacom's forces were no match for the settlers' guns and cannons.

As in Spanish lands, the native peoples suffered even more from disease than from warfare. Thousands upon thousands of Native Americans died from European illnesses. This made it impossible for them to resist the growth of the colonies.

4. Why did Native Americans lose their way of life?

_____

_____

As you read this section, fill out the chart below by writing notes that describe aspects of each European settlement.

1. New France	
Explorers	Reasons for exploration

2. Jamestown	
Founders	Significance of colony

3. Plymouth and Massachusetts Bay colonies	
Settlers	Reasons for colonization

4. New Netherland	
Land claims	Reasons for colonization

The Atlantic Slave Trade

Terms and Names

Atlantic slave trade Buying and selling of Africans for work in the Americas

triangular trade European trade between the Americas, Africa, and Europe involving slaves and other goods

middle passage Voyage that brought captured Africans to the West Indies and the Americas

Before You Read

In the last section, you saw how different European nations settled in North America.

In this section, you will read about the slave trade that brought Africans to the Americas.

As You Read

Use an outline to list effects of the Atlantic slave trade.

THE CAUSES OF AFRICAN SLAVERY (Pages 566–567)
What was the Atlantic slave trade?

Slavery has had a long history in Africa and in the world. For most of that history in Africa, though, large numbers of people had not been enslaved. That changed in the 600s, when Muslim traders started to take many slaves to Southwest Asia.

Most worked as servants, and they did have certain rights. Also, the sons and daughters of slaves were considered to be free. The European slave trade that began in the 1500s was larger. The enslaved Africans also were treated far more harshly.

In the Americas, Europeans first used Native Americans to work farms and mines. When the native peoples began dying from disease, the Europeans brought in Africans. The buying and selling of Africans for work in the Americas became known as the **Atlantic slave trade.** From

1500 to 1870, when the slave trade in the Americas finally ended, about 9.5 million Africans had been imported as slaves.

The Spanish first began the practice of bringing Africans to the Americas. However, the Portuguese increased the demand for slaves. They were looking for workers for their sugar plantations in Brazil.

1. Why were slaves brought to the Americas?

_____

_____

SLAVERY SPREADS THROUGHOUT THE AMERICAS (Pages 567–568)
What sorts of plantations existed in the Americas?

Other European colonies also brought slaves to work on tobacco, sugar, and coffee plantations. About 400,000 slaves were brought to the English colonies in North America. Their population had increased to about 2 million in 1830.

Many African rulers joined in the slave trade. They captured people inland and brought them to the coast to sell to European traders.

2. How did some African rulers participate in the slave trade?

_____

_____

A FORCED JOURNEY (Pages 568–569)
What kinds of trade included human beings?

Africans taken to the Americas were part of a **triangular trade** between Europe, Africa, and the Americas. European ships brought manufactured goods to Africa, trading them for people. They carried Africans across the Atlantic to the Americas, where they were sold into slavery. The traders then bought sugar, coffee, and tobacco to bring back to Europe.

Another triangle involved ships sailing from the northern English colonies in North America. They carried rum to Africa, people to the West Indies, and sugar and molasses back to the colonies to make more rum.

The part of the voyage that brought people to the Americas was called the **middle passage.** It was harsh and cruel.

People were crammed into ships, beaten, and given little food. About 20 percent of the people on these ships died.

3. What was the triangular trade?

_____

_____

SLAVERY IN THE AMERICAS; CONSEQUENCES OF THE SLAVE TRADE (Pages 569–570)
What was life like for the slaves?

Life on the plantations was harsh as well. People were sold to the highest bidder. They worked from dawn to dusk in the fields. They lived in small huts and had little food and clothing. Africans kept alive their traditional music and beliefs to try to maintain their spirits. Sometimes they rebelled. From North America to Brazil, from 1522 to the 1800s, there were small-scale slave revolts.

The Atlantic slave trade had a huge impact on both Africa and the Americas. In Africa many cultures lost generations of members. Africans began fighting Africans over the control of the slave trade.

The Africans' labor helped build the Americas. They brought skills and culture too. Many of the nations of the Americas have mixed race populations.

4. How did Africans change the Americas?

_____

_____

Name _____ Class _____ Date _____

As you read this section, write notes to answer questions about the causes and consequences of the enslavement of Africans.

How did each of the following contribute to the development of the Atlantic slave trade?	
1. European colonization of the Americas	2. Portuguese settlement of Brazil
3. African rulers	4. African merchants

What were the consequences of the Atlantic slave trade for each of the following?	
5. African societies	6. Enslaved Africans
7. American colonies	8. Present-day American cultures

Guided Reading Workbook

Section 4

The Columbian Exchange and Global Trade

Terms and Names

Columbian Exchange Global transfer of foods, plants, and animals during the colonization of the Americas

capitalism Economic system based on private ownership and the investment of wealth for profit

joint-stock company Company in which people pooled their wealth for a common purpose

mercantilism Economic policy of increasing wealth and power by obtaining large amounts of gold and silver and selling more goods than are bought

favorable balance of trade Condition resulting from selling more goods than are bought

---

Before You Read

In the last section, you read about the slave trade.

In this section, you will learn about other kinds of trade.

As You Read

Use a chart to take notes on the Columbian Exchange.

THE COLUMBIAN EXCHANGE
(Pages 571–573)
What was the Columbian Exchange?

There was constant movement of people and products from Europe and Africa to the Americas. The large-scale transfer of foods, plants, and animals was called the **Columbian Exchange.**
Important foods such as corn and potatoes were taken from the Americas to Europe, Africa, and Asia.

Some foods moved from the Old World to the New. Bananas, black-eyed peas, and yams were taken from Africa to the Americas. Cattle, pigs, and horses had never been seen in the Americas until the Europeans brought them. Deadly illnesses

also moved to the Americas. They killed a large part of the Native American population.

1. What did the Columbian Exchange take from the Americas, and what did it bring?

_____

_____

GLOBAL TRADE (Pages 573–574)
How did business change?

The settling of the Americas and the growth of trade started an economic revolution. This revolution led to new business practices still followed today.

One was the rise of an economic system called **capitalism.** It is based on private ownership of property and the right of a business to earn a profit on money it has invested.

Another new business idea was the **joint-stock company.** In this type of company, many investors pool their money to start a business and share in the profits.

2. What is capitalism?

_____

_____

THE GROWTH OF MERCANTILISM
(Pages 574–575)
Why were colonies important in mercantilism?

During the Commercial Revolution, European governments began to follow an idea called **mercantilism.** According to this theory, a country's power depended on its wealth. Getting more gold and silver increased a country's wealth. So did selling more goods than it bought. Selling more than it bought would result in a **favorable balance of trade.** Colonies played an important role because they provided goods that could be sold in trade.

The American colonies changed European society. Merchants grew wealthy and powerful. Towns and cities grew larger. Still, most people lived in the countryside, farmed for a living, and were poor.

3. Why were colonies important to European mercantilism?

_____

_____

As you read this section, note some cause-and-effect relationships relating to the European colonization of the Americas.

Causes	Event/Trend	Effects
	1. Columbian Exchange	
	2. Global trade	
	3. Inflation	
	4. Formation of joint-stock companies	
	5. Growth of mercantilism	

Section 1

Spain's Empire and European Absolutism

Terms and Names

Philip II Spanish king who took control of Portugal but failed in his invasion of England

absolute monarch King or queen with complete control

divine right Idea that a ruler receives the right to rule from God

Before You Read

In the last chapter, you read about Europe's new relationship to the Americas.

In this section, you will learn about changes occurring in Europe in the 1500s and 1600s.

As You Read

Use a chart to list the conditions that allowed European monarchs to gain power.

A POWERFUL SPANISH EMPIRE
(Pages 589–591)
How did Spain's power increase and then decrease?

Charles V of Spain ruled the Holy Roman Empire and other European countries. In 1556, he left the throne and split his holdings. His brother Ferdinand received Austria and the Holy Roman Empire. His son, **Philip II,** got Spain and its colonies.

Philip II then took control of Portugal when the king of Portugal, his uncle, died without an heir. Philip also got its global territories in Africa, India, and the East Indies. When he tried to invade England in 1588, though, he failed. The defeat made Spain weaker. However, Spain still seemed strong because of the wealth— gold and silver—that flowed in from its colonies in the Americas.

1. Who was Philip II?

_____

_____

GOLDEN AGE OF SPANISH ART AND LITERATURE (Pages 591–592)
How did works from the golden age of Spanish art and literature reflect the values and attitudes of the period?

Spain's great wealth allowed monarchs and nobles to become patrons of artists. Two of the greatest artists of the 16th and 17th century were El Greco and Diego Velásquez. El Greco's work reflected the faith of Spain during this period. The paintings of Velásquez reflected the pride of the Spanish monarchy.

In literature, Miguel de Cervantes wrote *Don Quixote de la Mancha*, which ushered in the birth of the modern European novel.

Guided Reading Workbook

The novel tells the story of a Spanish nobleman who reads too many books about heroic knights.

2. Who were some of the artists and writers of Spain's golden age?

_____

_____

THE SPANISH EMPIRE WEAKENS
(Pages 592–593)
What weakened the Spanish Empire?

Spain's new wealth led to some serious problems. The prices of goods constantly rose. Unfair taxes kept the poor from building up any wealth of their own. As prices rose, Spaniards bought more goods from other lands. To finance their wars, Spanish kings had to borrow money from banks in foreign countries. The silver from the colonies began to flow to Spain's enemies.

In the middle of these troubles, Spain lost land. Seven provinces of the Spanish Netherlands rose in protest against high taxes and attempts to crush Protestantism in the Netherlands. These seven provinces were Protestant, whereas Spain was strongly Catholic. In 1579, they declared their independence from Spain and became the United Provinces of the Netherlands. The ten southern provinces (present-day Belgium) were Catholic and remained under Spanish control.

3. Why did Spain lose its power?

_____

_____

THE INDEPENDENT DUTCH PROSPER **(Pages** 593–594)
Why did the Dutch prosper?

The United Provinces of the Netherlands was different from other European states of the time. It was a republic, not a kingdom. Each province had a leader elected by the people.

The Dutch also practiced religious tolerance, letting people worship as they wished. Dutch merchants established a trading empire. They had the largest fleet of merchant ships in the world. They were also the most important bankers in Europe.

4. Give two reasons for the success of the Dutch in trading.

_____

_____

ABSOLUTISM IN EUROPE
(Pages 594–595)
What is absolutism?

Though he lost his Dutch possessions, Philip continued to hold tight control over Spain. He wanted to control the lives of his people. Philip and others who ruled in the same way were called **absolute monarchs.** They believed in holding all power. They also believed in **divine right.** This is the idea that a ruler receives the right to rule from God.

Widespread unrest in Europe in the 17th century led to an increase in absolute rule, or **absolutism,** and its restrictions. Absolute rulers used their increased power to impose order. They wanted to free themselves from the limitations imposed by the nobility and government bodies.

5. What did absolute monarchs believe?

_____

_____

As you read about the Spanish Empire, briefly note the causes or effects (depending on which is missing) of each event or situation.

Causes	Effects
1. The gold and silver coming from its vast empire made Spain incredibly wealthy.	
2.	Spain suffered from severe inflation.
3.	The Spanish economy declined and at times Spain was bankrupt.
4. Philip raised taxes in the Netherlands and tried to crush Protestantism.	
5.	The Dutch became wealthy from trade and banking.
6.	European monarchs became increasingly more powerful.

Absolute Monarchs in Europe

The Reign of Louis XIV

Terms and Names

Edict of Nantes Order that gave Huguenots the right to live in peace in Catholic France

Cardinal Richelieu Chief minister of France who reduced the power of the nobles

skepticism Belief that nothing could be known for certain

Louis XIV French king who was an absolute ruler

intendant Official of the French government

Jean Baptiste Colbert Chief Minister of Finance under Louis XIV

War of the Spanish Succession War fought by other European nations against France and Spain when those two states tried to unite their thrones

Before You Read

In the last section, you were introduced to the idea of absolutism.

In this section, you will read about absolute power in France.

As You Read

Use a time line to list the major events of Louis XIV's reign.

RELIGIOUS WARS AND POWER STRUGGLES; WRITERS TURN TOWARD SKEPTICISM
(Pages 596–598)
What changes were occurring in France?

France was torn by eight religious wars between Catholics and Protestants from 1562 to 1598.

In 1589, a Protestant prince, Henry of Navarre, became King Henry IV. In 1593, he changed religions. He became a Catholic to please the majority of his people. In 1598, he issued an order called the **Edict of Nantes.** It gave Huguenots—French Protestants—the right to live in peace and have their own churches in some cities.

Henry rebuilt the French economy and brought peace to the land. He was followed by his son, Louis XIII, a weak

king. However, Louis had a very capable chief minister, **Cardinal Richelieu.** Richelieu ruled the land for Louis and increased the power of the crown.

The cardinal ordered the Huguenots not to build walls around their cities. He also said nobles had to destroy their castles. As a result, Protestants and nobles could not hide within walls to defy the king's power. Richelieu used people from the middle class—not nobles—to work in his government. That also reduced the power of the nobles.

French thinkers had reacted to the religious wars with horror. They developed a new philosophy called **skepticism.** Nothing could be known for certain, they argued. Doubting old ideas was the first step to learning the truth, they said.

Guided Reading Workbook

1. How did the monarchy get stronger in France?

_____

_____

LOUIS XIV COMES TO POWER
(**Pages** 598–599)
How did Louis XIV rule?

In 1643, **Louis XIV** became king at the age of about five. Cardinal Mazarin, who succeeded Richelieu as minister, ruled for Louis until he was 22. Louis became a powerful ruler, who had total control of France. He was determined to never let nobles challenge him.

He kept the nobles out of his government. He gave more power to government officials called **intendants** and made sure that they answered only to him. He also worked hard to increase the wealth of France. His chief minister of finance, **Jean Baptiste Colbert,** tried to build French industry. Colbert wanted to persuade French people to buy French-made goods and not those from other countries. He urged people to settle in the new French colony of Canada in North America. The fur trade there brought wealth to France.

2. How did Louis make sure he kept his power?

_____

_____

THE SUN KING'S GRAND STYLE; LOUIS FIGHTS DISASTROUS WARS
(**Pages** 599–602)
What changes did Louis make?

Louis enjoyed a life of luxury at his court. He built a huge and beautiful palace at Versailles near Paris. He also made sure that nobles had to depend on his favor to advance in society.

Louis made France the most powerful nation in Europe. France had a larger population and a bigger army than any other country. However, Louis made some mistakes that later proved costly. After winning some wars against neighboring countries, he became bolder and tried to seize more land. Other nations allied to stop France in the late 1680s. The high cost of these wars combined with poor harvests to produce problems at home in France.

The final war fought in Louis's time was fought over succession to the throne of Spain and lasted from 1700 to 1713. In this **War of the Spanish Succession,** France and Spain attempted to set up united thrones. The rest of Europe felt threatened and joined in war against them. Both France and Spain were forced to give up some of their American and European colonies to England. England was the new rising power.

3. How did Louis XIV bring disaster to France?

_____

_____

As you read about the French monarchy, write notes to answer the questions.

Wars between the Huguenots and Catholics create chaos in France.	
1. How did Henry of Navarre end the crisis and restore order?	
2. How did Cardinal Richelieu strengthen the French monarchy?	
3. What effect did the religious wars have on French intellectuals?	

Louis XIV became the most powerful monarch of his time.	
4. What steps did Jean Baptiste Colbert take to turn France into an economic power?	
5. In what ways did Louis XIV support the arts?	
6. Why did Louis fail in his attempts to expand the French Empire?	
7. What was the legacy of Louis XIV?	

Central European Monarchs Clash

Terms and Names

Thirty Years' War Conflict over religion, territory, and power among European ruling families

Maria Theresa Empress of Austria whose main enemy was Prussia

Frederick the Great Leader of Prussia who sought to increase his territory

Seven Years' War Conflict from 1756 to 1763 in which the forces of Britain and Prussia battled those of Austria, France, Russia, and other countries

---

Before You Read

In the last section, you read how absolute power grew in France.

In this section, you will learn about absolutism in Austria and Prussia.

As You Read

Use a chart to compare Maria Theresa with Frederick the Great.

THE THIRTY YEARS' WAR
(Pages 603–604)
What caused the Thirty Years' War?

Germany had suffered from religious wars that ended in 1555. Rulers of each German state agreed that they would decide whether their lands would be Catholic or Protestant. Relations between sides became tense over the next decades. Then in 1618, a new war broke out and lasted for 30 terrible years. It was called the **Thirty Years' War.**

During the first half of the war, Catholic forces led by Ferdinand, the Holy Roman Emperor, won. However, Germany suffered because he allowed his large army to loot towns. Then the Protestant king of Sweden, Gustavus Adolphus, won several battles against him.

In the last years of the war, France helped the Protestants. Although France was a Catholic nation, Richelieu feared the growing power of the Hapsburg family, which was headed by Frederick.

The Thirty Years' War ended in 1648 with the Peace of Westphalia. It had been a disaster for Germany. About 4 million people had died, and the economy was in ruins. It took Germany two centuries to recover.

The peace treaty weakened the power of Austria and Spain. But it made France stronger. The French gained German territory. The treaty also made German princes independent of the Holy Roman Emperor. It ended religious wars in Europe. Lastly, the treaty introduced a new way of negotiating peace—a method still used today. All states involved in the fighting meet to settle the problems of a war and decide the terms of peace.

---

1. What were three results of the Thirty Years' War?

_____

_____

_____

_____

STATES FORM IN CENTRAL EUROPE (Page 605)
Who ruled Austria?

The formation of strong states took place slowly in central Europe. The economies there were less developed than in western Europe. Most people were still peasants. This region had not built an economy based on cities and commercialism. Nobles enjoyed great influence. This helped them keep the serfs on the land and prevent the rise of strong rulers. Still, two important states arose.

The Hapsburg family ruled Austria, Hungary, and Bohemia. Their empire linked many different peoples—Czechs, Hungarians, Italians, Croatians, and Germans. **Maria Theresa,** the daughter of Charles VI, was empress of Austria in the mid–1700s. She managed to increase her power and reduce that of the nobles. She was opposed by the kings of Prussia, a new powerful state in northern Germany.

2. Who were the Hapsburgs?

_____

_____

_____

_____

PRUSSIA CHALLENGES AUSTRIA
(**Pages** 606–607)
What was Prussia?

Like Austria, Prussia rose to power in the late 1600s. Like the Hapsburgs of Austria, Prussia's ruling family, the Hohenzollerns, also had ambitions.

Prussia was a strong state that gave much power to its large, well-trained army. In 1740, **Frederick the Great** of Prussia invaded one of Maria Theresa's lands. Austria fought hard to keep the territory, but lost. Still, in fighting the War of the Austrian Succession, Maria Theresa managed to keep the rest of her empire intact.

The two sides fought again, beginning in 1756. In the **Seven Years' War,** Austria abandoned Britain, its old ally, for France and Russia. Prussia joined with Britain. The Prussians and British won. In that victory, Britain gained economic domination of India.

3. What effect did fighting between Austria and Prussia have on Britain?

_____

_____

_____

_____

As you read about the absolute monarchs that ruled in Central Europe, fill out the chart by writing notes in the appropriate spaces.

The Thirty Years' War	
1. Note two causes of the war.	
2. Note four consequences of the war and the Peace of Westphalia.	

Central Europe	
3. Note two differences between the economies of western and central Europe.	
4. Note two reasons why central European empires were weak.	

Prussia and Austria	
5. Note three steps the Hapsburgs took to become more powerful.	
6. Note three steps the Hohenzollerns took to build up their state.	

Section 4

Absolute Rulers of Russia

Terms and Names

Ivan the Terrible Ruler who added lands to Russia, gave it a code of laws, and also used his secret police to execute "traitors"

boyar Russian noble who owned land

Peter the Great Important leader of Russia who started westernization

westernization Use of western Europe as a model of change

Before You Read

In the last section, you read how Austria and Prussia became strong states.

In this section, you will learn how Russia developed into a powerful state.

As You Read

Use a cluster diagram to list the important events of Peter the Great's reign.

THE FIRST CZAR (Pages 608–609)
Who was Ivan the Terrible?

Ivan III had begun centralizing the Russian government. His son, Vasily, continued the work of adding territory to the growing Russian state. Ivan's grandson, Ivan IV, was called **Ivan the Terrible.** He came to the throne in 1533, when he was three years old.

At first, landowning nobles, known as **boyars,** tried to control Ivan. Eventually, he ruled successfully on his own. He added lands to Russia and gave the country a code of laws. After his wife, Anastasia, died, however, his rule turned harsh. He used secret police to hunt down enemies and kill them. Ivan even murdered his oldest son.

A few years after he died, Russian nobles met to name a new ruler. They chose Michael Romanov, the grandnephew of Ivan the Terrible's wife.

He began the Romanov dynasty, which ruled Russia for about 300 years.

1. What good and bad did Ivan the Terrible do?

_____

_____

_____

PETER THE GREAT COMES TO POWER (Page 609)
Who was Peter the Great?

The Romanovs restored order to Russia. In the late 1600s, Peter I came to power. He was called **Peter the Great** because he was one of Russia's greatest reformers. He began an intense program of trying to modernize Russia. He also continued the trend of increasing the czar's power.

When Peter came to power, Russia was still a land of boyars and serfs. Serfdom lasted much longer in Russia than it did in western Europe. It continued into the mid–1800s.

When a Russian landowner sold a piece of land, he sold the serfs with it. Landowners could give away serfs as presents or to pay debts. It was also against the law for serfs to run away from their owners.

Most boyars knew little of western Europe. But Peter admired the nations of western Europe. He traveled in Europe to learn about new technology and ways of working. It was the first time a czar traveled in the West.

2. Why did Peter the Great visit Europe?

_____

_____

_____

_____

PETER RULES ABSOLUTELY
(Pages 610–611)
What changes did Peter the Great make?

Peter the Great wanted Russia to be the equal of the countries of western Europe.

He wanted Russia to be strong both in its military and in its trade.

To meet these goals, Peter changed Russia. His first steps were to increase his powers, so he could force people to make the changes he wanted. He put the Russian Orthodox Church under his control. He reduced the power of nobles. He built up the army and made it better trained.

Peter also changed Russia through **westernization.** He took several steps to make Russia more western. He brought in potatoes as a new food, began Russia's first newspaper, gave more social status to women, and told the nobles to adopt Western clothes. He promoted education.

Peter also knew Russia needed a seaport that would make it easier to travel to the west. He fought a long war with Sweden to gain land along the shores of the Baltic Sea. There he built a grand new capital city, St. Petersburg. By the time of Peter's death in 1725, Russia was an important power in Europe.

3. How did Peter the Great increase his power?

_____

_____

_____

_____

As you read this section, complete the chart by explaining how Peter the
Great solved each problem he encountered in his efforts to westernize
Russia.

Problems	Solutions
1. Russian people did not believe that change was necessary.	
2. The Russian Orthodox Church was too strong.	
3. The great landowners had too much power.	
4. The Russian army was untrained and its tactics and weapons were outdated.	
5. Russian society had to change to compete with the modern states of Europe.	
6. To promote education and growth, Russia needed a seaport for travel to the West.	
7. The port needed to be built.	
8. The new city needed to be settled.	

Section 5

Parliament Limits the English Monarchy

Terms and Names

Charles I King of England who was executed

English Civil War War fought from 1642 to 1649 between the Royalists, or Cavaliers, and the Puritan supporters of Parliament

Oliver Cromwell Leader of the Puritans

Restoration Period after the monarchy was restored in England

habeas corpus Law giving prisoners the right to obtain a document saying that the prisoner cannot go to jail without being brought before a judge

Glorious Revolution Bloodless overthrow of King James II

constitutional monarchy Government in which laws limit the monarch's power

cabinet A group of government ministers that was a link between the monarch and Parliament

Before You Read

In the last section, you saw how power was becoming more absolute in Russia.

In this section, you will see how the power of the monarch was challenged and weakened in England.

As You Read

Use a chart to list the causes of the English monarchs' conflicts with Parliament.

MONARCHS DEFY PARLIAMENT
(Page 614)
Why was there tension between the monarchy and Parliament?

When Queen Elizabeth I died, her cousin James, king of Scotland, became king of England. The reign of James I began a long series of struggles between king and Parliament. They fought over money. James's religious policies also angered the Puritans in Parliament.

During the reign of his son, **Charles I,** there was continued conflict between king and Parliament. Parliament forced Charles to sign the Petition of Right in 1628. By signing, Charles agreed that the king had to answer to Parliament. But he then dissolved Parliament and tried to raise money without it.

1. How did Charles I make Parliament angry?

_____

_____

Original content © Houghton Mifflin Harcourt Publishing Company. Additions and changes to the original content are the responsibility of the instructor.

Guided Reading Workbook

ENGLISH CIVIL WAR (Pages 615–616)
Who fought the English Civil War?

When Charles tried to force Presbyterian Scots to follow the Anglican Church, Scotland threatened to invade England. Charles needed money to fight. When Charles called a new Parliament to get money, it quickly passed laws to limit his power.

Soon England was fighting a civil war. Charles and his Royalists were opposed by the supporters of Parliament. Many of Parliament's supporters were Puritans.

The **English Civil War** lasted from 1642 to 1649. Under the leadership of **Oliver Cromwell,** the forces of the Puritans won. They tried and executed Charles for treason against Parliament. This was the first time a king had faced a public trial and execution. Cromwell became a military dictator, ruling until 1658. He crushed a rebellion in Ireland and tried to reform society at home.

2. What happened as a result of the English Civil War?

_____

_____

RESTORATION AND REVOLUTION
(Page 616)
What was the Restoration?

Soon after Cromwell's death, the government collapsed. Parliament asked Charles's older son to restore the monarchy. Charles II's rule beginning in 1660 is called the **Restoration.**

Charles II's reign was calm. Parliament passed an important guarantee of freedom called **habeas corpus.** It gave every prisoner the right to get an order to be brought before a judge. The judge would then decide whether the prisoner should be tried or set free. This kept monarchs from putting people in jail just for opposing

them. It also meant that people would not stay in jail forever without a trial.

After Charles II's death in 1685, his brother became King James II. His pro-Catholic policies angered the English. They feared that he would restore Catholicism. In 1688, seven members of Parliament contacted James's older daughter, Mary, and her husband, William of Orange, prince of the Netherlands. Both were Protestants. The members of Parliament wanted William and Mary to replace James II on the throne. James was forced to flee to France. When that took place, the bloodless revolution was called the **Glorious Revolution.**

3. Why did the Glorious Revolution take place?

_____

_____

LIMITS ON MONARCH'S POWER
(Page 617)
How was the power of the monarchy decreased in England?

William and Mary agreed to rule according to the laws made by Parliament. That is, Parliament became their partner in governing. England was now a **constitutional monarchy,** where laws limited the ruler's power.

William and Mary also agreed to accept the Bill of Rights. It guaranteed the people and Parliament certain rights.

By the 1700s, it was clear that the government of England would come to a standstill if the monarch disagreed with Parliament or vice versa. This led to the development of the **cabinet.** This group of government ministers became the first link between the monarch and Parliament.

4. What three changes gave Parliament more power in England?

_____

_____

As you read this section, take notes to fill in the diagram describing
relations between Parliament and each English ruler listed.

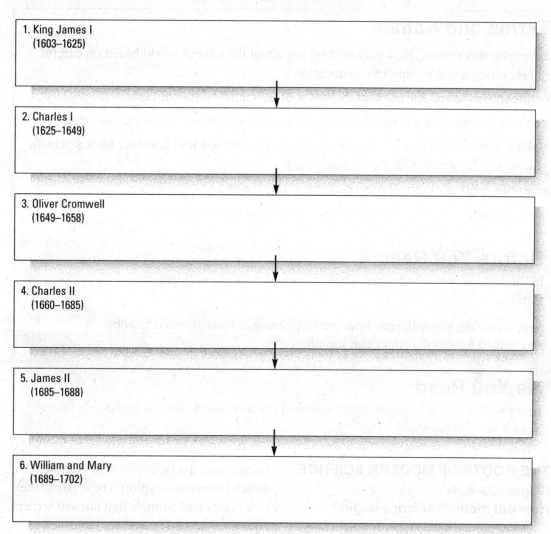

1. King James I
   (1603–1625)

2. Charles I
   (1625–1649)

3. Oliver Cromwell
   (1649–1658)

4. Charles II
   (1660–1685)

5. James II
   (1685–1688)

6. William and Mary
   (1689–1702)

Enlightenment and Revolution

Section 1

The Scientific Revolution

Terms and Names

Scientific Revolution New way of thinking about the natural world based on careful observation and a willingness to question

heliocentric theory Theory that the sun is at the center of the universe

geocentric theory View which held that the earth was the center of the universe

Galileo Galilei Scientist who was forced by the Catholic Church to take back scientific ideas that disagreed with the church's view

scientific method Logical procedure for gathering and testing ideas

Isaac Newton Scientist who discovered laws of motion and gravity

Before You Read

In the last chapter, you learned about wars and political changes in Europe.

In this section, you will read how the Enlightenment transformed Europe and helped lead to the American Revolution.

As You Read

Use a web diagram to record the events and circumstances that led to the Scientific Revolution.

THE ROOTS OF MODERN SCIENCE
(Pages 623–624)
How did modern science begin?

During the Middle Ages, few scholars questioned beliefs that had been long held. Europeans based their ideas on what ancient Greeks and Romans believed or on the Bible. People still thought that the earth was the center of the universe. They believed that the sun, moon, other planets, and stars moved around it.

In the mid-1500s, attitudes began to change. Scholars started what is called the **Scientific Revolution.** It was a new way of thinking about the natural world. It was based on careful observation and the willingness to question old beliefs. European voyages of exploration helped to bring about the Scientific Revolution. When Europeans explored new lands, they saw plants and animals that ancient writers had never seen. These discoveries led to new courses of study in the universities of Europe.

1. What was the Scientific Revolution?

_____

_____

A REVOLUTIONARY MODEL OF THE UNIVERSE (Pages 624–625)
How did new ideas change accepted thinking in astronomy?

The first challenge to accepted thinking in science came in astronomy. In the early 1500s, Nicolaus Copernicus, a Polish astronomer, studied the stars and planets.

He developed a **heliocentric theory.** Heliocentric meant sun-centered. It said that Earth, like all the other planets, revolved around the sun. Copernicus did not publish his findings until just before his death. He had been afraid that his ideas would be attacked because they went against the **geocentric theory.** This theory held that the earth was at the center of the universe. In the early 1600s, Johannes Kepler used mathematics to prove that Copernicus's basic idea was correct.

An Italian scientist—**Galileo Galilei**—made several discoveries that also undercut ancient ideas. He made one of the first telescopes and used it to study the planets. He found that Jupiter had moons, the sun had spots, and Earth's moon was rough. Some of his ideas about the earth, the sun, and the planets went against the teaching of the Catholic Church. Church authorities forced Galileo to take back his statements. Still, his ideas spread.

2. What old belief about the universe did the new discoveries destroy?

_____

_____

THE SCIENTIFIC METHOD
(**Pages** 625–626)
Why was the scientific method an important development?

Interest in science led to a new approach, the **scientific method.** With this method, scientists ask a question based on something they have seen in the physical world. They form a hypothesis, or an attempt to answer the question. Then they test the hypothesis by making experiments or checking other facts. Finally, they change the hypothesis if needed.

The English writer Francis Bacon helped create this new approach to knowledge. He said scientists should base their thinking on what they can observe

and test. The French mathematician René Descartes also influenced the use of the scientific method. His thinking was based on logic and mathematics.

3. What thinkers helped advance the use of the scientific method?

_____

_____

NEWTON EXPLAINS THE LAW OF GRAVITY; THE SCIENTIFIC REVOLUTION SPREADS
(**Pages** 626–628)
What scientific discoveries were made?

In the mid-1600s, the English scientist **Isaac Newton** described the law of gravity. Using mathematics, Newton showed that the same force ruled both the motion of planets and the action of bodies on the earth.

Other scientists made new tools to study the world around them. One invented a microscope. Others invented tools for understanding weather.

Doctors also made advances. One made drawings that showed the different parts of the human body. Another learned how the heart pumped blood through the body. In the late 1700s, Edward Jenner first used the process called vaccination to prevent disease. By giving a person the germs from a cattle disease called cowpox, he helped that person avoid getting the more serious human disease of smallpox.

Scientists made progress in chemistry as well. One questioned the old idea that things were made of only four elements—earth, air, fire, and water. He and other scientists separated oxygen from air.

4. How did the science of medicine change?

_____

_____

As you read about the revolution in scientific thinking, take notes to
answer the questions.

How did the following help pave the way for the Scientific Revolution?		
1. The Renaissance		
2. Age of European exploration		

What did each scientist discover about the universe?		
3. Nicolaus Copernicus		
4. Johannes Kepler		
5. Galileo Galilei		
6. Isaac Newton		

What important developments took place in the following areas?		
7. Scientific instruments		
8. Medicine		
9. Chemistry		

Enlightenment and Revolution

Section 2

The Enlightenment in Europe

Terms and Names

Enlightenment Age of Reason

social contract According to Thomas Hobbes, an agreement people make with government

John Locke Philosopher who wrote about government

philosophes Social critics in France

Voltaire Writer who fought for tolerance, reason, freedom of religious belief, and freedom of speech

Montesquieu French writer concerned with government and political liberty

Rousseau Enlightenment thinker who championed freedom

Mary Wollstonecraft Author who wrote about women's rights

Before You Read

In the last section, you read how the Scientific Revolution began in Europe.

In this section, you will learn how the Enlightenment began in Europe.

As You Read

Use an outline to organize the summaries' main ideas and details.

TWO VIEWS ON GOVERNMENT
(Pages 629–630)
What **were the views of Hobbes and Locke?**

The **Enlightenment** was an intellectual movement. Enlightenment thinkers tried to apply reason and the scientific method to laws that shaped human actions. They hoped to build a society founded on ideas of the Scientific Revolution. Two English writers—Thomas Hobbes and John Locke—were important to this movement. They came to very different conclusions about government and human nature.

Hobbes wrote that there would be a war of "every man against every man" if there were no government. To avoid this war, Hobbes said, people formed a **social**

contract. It was an agreement between people and their government. People gave up their rights to the government so they could live in a safe and orderly way. The best government, he said, is that of a strong king who can force all people to obey.

John Locke believed that people have three natural rights. They are life, liberty, and property. The purpose of government is to protect these rights. When it fails to do so, he said, people have a right to overthrow the government.

1. How were Hobbes's and Locke's views different?

_____

_____

THE PHILOSOPHES ADVOCATE REASON (Pages 630–632)

Who were the philosophes?

French thinkers called **philosophes** had five main beliefs: (1) thinkers can find the truth by using reason; (2) what is natural is good and reasonable, and human actions are shaped by natural laws; (3) acting according to nature can bring happiness; (4) by taking a scientific view, people and society can make progress and advance to a better life; and (5) by using reason, people can gain freedom.

The most brilliant of the philosophes was the writer **Voltaire.** He fought for tolerance, reason, freedom of religious belief, and freedom of speech. Baron de **Montesquieu** wrote about separation of powers—dividing power among the separate branches of government. The third great philosophe was Jean Jacques **Rousseau.** He wrote in favor of human freedom. He wanted a society in which all people were equal. Cesare Beccaria was an Italian philosphe. He spoke out against abuses of justice.

2. Name the types of freedoms that Enlightenment thinkers championed.

_____

_____

_____

WOMEN AND THE ENLIGHTENMENT; LEGACY OF THE ENLIGHTENMENT (Pages 633–634)

What were Enlightenment views about individuals?

Many Enlightenment thinkers held traditional views about women's place in society. They wanted equal rights for all men but paid no attention to the fact that women did not have such rights. Some women protested this unfair situation. "If all men are born free," stated British writer **Mary Wollstonecraft,** "how is it that all women are born slaves?".

Enlightenment ideas strongly influenced the American and French revolutions. Enlightenment thinkers also helped spread the idea of progress. By using reason, they said, it is possible to make society better. Enlightenment thinkers helped make the world less religious and more worldly. They also stressed the importance of the individual.

3. Explain the influence of Enlightenment ideas.

_____

_____

_____

Name _____ Class _____ Date _____

As you read this section, fill in the diagram by describing the beliefs of Enlightenment thinkers and writers.

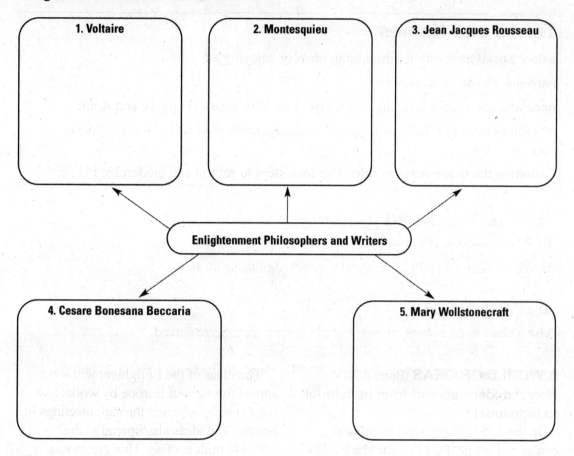

Section 3

The Enlightenment Spreads

Terms and Names

salon Social gathering for discussing ideas or enjoying art

baroque Grand, ornate style

neoclassical Simple style that borrowed ideas from classical Greece and Rome

enlightened despot Ruler who supported Enlightenment ideas but did not give up power

Catherine the Great Russian ruler who took steps to reform and modernize Russia

Before You Read

In the last section, you read how Enlightenment ideas began.

In this section, you will learn about the spread of these ideas.

As You Read

Use a chart to take notes on how Enlightenment ideas were spread.

A WORLD OF IDEAS (Page 636)
How did ideas spread from individual to individual?

In the 1700s, Paris was the cultural center of Europe. People came there from other countries to hear the new ideas of the Enlightenment. Writers and artists held social gatherings called **salons.** A woman named Marie-Thérèse Geoffrin became famous for hosting these discussions.

Geoffrin also supplied the money for one of the major projects of the Enlightenment. With her funds, Denis Diderot and other thinkers wrote and published a huge set of books called the *Encyclopedia*. Their aim was to gather all that was known about the world. The French government and officials in the Catholic Church did not like many of the ideas that were published in the *Encyclopedia*. They banned the books at first. Later, however, they changed their minds.

The ideas of the Enlightenment were spread throughout Europe by works like the *Encyclopedia* and through meetings in homes. The ideas also spread to the growing middle class. This group was becoming wealthy but had less social status than nobles. They also had very little political power. Ideas about equality sounded good to them.

1. Why were salons important?

_____

_____

_____

NEW ARTISTIC STYLES (Page 637)
How did art and literature change?

The arts—painting, architecture, music, and literature—moved in new directions in the late 1700s. They used Enlightenment ideas of order and reason.

Guided Reading Workbook

Earlier European painting had been very grand and highly decorated. It was a style known as **baroque.** Now styles began to change. A new simpler, yet elegant, style of painting and architecture developed. This style borrowed ideas and themes from Classical Greece and Rome. That is the reason it was called **neoclassical.**

In music, the style of the period is called classical. Three important composers of the time were Franz Joseph Haydn, Wolfgang Amadeus Mozart, and Ludwig von Beethoven. They composed music that was elegant and original. New musical forms were developed, including the sonata and the symphony.

In literature, the novel became popular. This new form presented long stories with twisting plots. It explored the thoughts and feelings of characters. A number of European authors, including women, began writing novels. These books were popular with the middle class. They liked entertaining stories in everyday language.

2. What new styles and forms appeared in art, music, and literature?

_____

_____

_____

ENLIGHTENMENT AND MONARCHY (Pages 638–639)
Who were the enlightened despots?

Some Enlightenment thinkers believed that the best form of government was a monarchy. In it, a ruler respected people's rights. These thinkers tried to influence rulers to rule fairly. Rulers who followed Enlightenment ideas in part but were unwilling to give up much power were called **enlightened despots.**

Frederick the Great of Prussia was an enlightened despot. He gave his people religious freedom and improved schooling. He also reformed the justice system. However, he did nothing to end serfdom, which made peasants slaves to the wealthy landowners. Joseph II of Austria did end serfdom. Once he died, though, the nobles who owned the lands were able to undo this reform.

Catherine the Great of Russia was another of the rulers influenced by Enlightenment ideas. She tried to reform Russia's laws but met resistance. She had hoped to end serfdom. But a bloody peasants' revolt persuaded her to change her mind. Instead, she gave the nobles even more power over serfs. Catherine did manage to gain new land for Russia. Russia, Prussia, and Austria agreed to divide Poland among themselves. As a result, Poland disappeared as a separate nation for almost 150 years.

3. In what way was Frederick the Great typical of an enlightened despot?

_____

_____

_____

As you read about art, literature, and politics in the Age of Reason, explain
how each of the following people reflected Enlightenment ideas.

The Arts	
1. Denis Diderot	
2. Franz Joseph Haydn	
3. Wolfgang Amadeus Mozart	
4. Ludwig van Beethoven	
5. Samuel Richardson	

Government	
6. Frederick the Great	
7. Joseph II	
8. Catherine the Great	

Section 4

The American Revolution

Terms and Names

Declaration of Independence Document declaring American independence from Britain

Thomas Jefferson Author of the Declaration of Independence

checks and balances System in which each branch of government checks, or limits, the power of the other two branches

federal system System of government in which power is divided between the national and state governments

Bill of Rights First ten amendments to the U.S. Constitution; protections of basic rights for individuals

Before You Read

In the last section, you read about the spread of Enlightenment ideas in Europe.

In this section, you will learn how Enlightenment ideas influenced the American Revolution.

As You Read

Use a chart to list the problems American colonists faced in shaping their republic and solutions they found.

BRITAIN AND ITS AMERICAN COLONIES (Page 640)
How were the colonies governed?

The British colonies in North America grew in population and wealth during the 1700s. Population went from about 250,000 in 1700 to 2,150,000 in 1770. Economically, they prospered on trade with the nations of Europe. The 13 colonies also had a kind of self-government. People in the colonies began to see themselves less and less as British subjects. Still, Parliament passed laws that governed the colonies. One set of laws banned trade with any nation other than Britain.

1. How did the colonists' image of themselves clash with their status as colonists?

_____

_____

AMERICANS WIN INDEPENDENCE (Pages 641–643)
What caused Britain and America to grow apart?

The high cost of the French and Indian War led Parliament to tax the colonists. The colonists became very angry. They had never before paid taxes directly to the British government. They said that the taxes violated their rights.

Since Parliament had no members from the colonies, they said, Parliament had no right to tax them.

The colonists met the first tax, passed in 1765, with a boycott of British goods. Their refusal to buy British products was very effective. It forced Parliament to repeal the law.

Over the next decade, the colonists and Britain grew further apart. Some colonists wanted to push the colonies to independence. They took actions that caused Britain to act harshly. Eventually, the conflict led to war. Representatives of the colonies met in a congress and formed an army. In July 1776, they announced that they were independent of Britain. They issued the **Declaration of Independence.** It was based on Enlightenment ideas. **Thomas Jefferson** wrote it.

From 1775 to 1781, the colonies and the British fought a war in North America. The colonists had a poorly equipped army, and Britain was one of the most powerful nations in the world. However, in the end, the colonies won their independence.

The British people grew tired of the cost of the war and pushed Parliament to agree to a peace. The Americans were also helped greatly by aid from France. In 1783, the two sides signed a treaty. In it, Britain recognized the independent United States of America.

2. Name some of the steps that led to the American Revolution.

_____

_____

_____

_____

AMERICANS CREATE A REPUBLIC
(Pages 644–645)
What are some fundamental ideas in the U.S. Constitution?

The 13 states formed a new government under the Article of Confederation. This government was very weak. States held all the power and the central government had little. This proved unworkable. In 1787, American leaders met again. They wrote a new framework of government.

The Constitution of the United States drew on many Enlightenment ideas. It used Montesquieu's idea of separation of powers into three branches of government. Through a system of **checks and balances,** each branch was able to prevent other branches from abusing their power. The Constitution also set up a **federal system.** Under this system, power was divided between national and state governments.

The Constitution also used Locke's idea of putting power in the hands of the people. It used Voltaire's ideas to protect the right to free speech and freedom of religion. It used Beccaria's ideas about a fair system of justice.

Many of these rights were ensured in a set of additions to the Constitution called the **Bill of Rights.** The inclusion of a bill of rights helped win approval for the Constitution.

3. Explain how the Constitution divides power.

_____

_____

_____

_____

Guided Reading Workbook

As you read this section, note some causes and effects relating to the American Revolution and the establishment of the United States as a republic.

Causes	Events	Effects
	1. British Parliament passes Stamp Act.	
	2. British close Boston harbor and station troops in city.	
	3. Second Continental Congress votes to form an army under command of George Washington.	
	4. France enters the war in 1778.	
	5. By approving the Articles of Confederation, states create a weak national government.	

Section 1

The French Revolution Begins

Terms and Names

Old Regime System of feudalism

estate Social class of people

Louis XVI Weak king who came to French throne in 1774

Marie Antoinette Unpopular queen; wife of Louis XVI

Estates-General Assembly of representatives from all three estates

National Assembly French congress established by representatives of the Third Estate

Tennis Court Oath Promise made by Third Estate representatives to draw up a new constitution

Great Fear Wave of panic

Before You Read

In the last chapter, you read about the Enlightenment and the American Revolution.

In this section, you will learn about the beginning of the French Revolution.

As You Read

Use a chart to take notes on the causes and effects of the early stages of the French Revolution.

THE OLD ORDER (Pages 651–652)
How was French society unequal?

In the 1700s, France was the leading country of Europe. It was the center of the new ideas of the Enlightenment. However, beneath the surface there were major problems. Soon the nation would be torn by a violent revolution.

One problem was that people were not treated equally in French society. A political and social system called the **Old Regime** remained in place. The French were divided into three classes, or **estates.** The First Estate consisted of the Roman Catholic clergy. The Second Estate was made up of nobles. Only about 2 percent of the people belonged to these two

estates. Yet they owned 20 percent of the land. They had easy lives.

Everybody else belonged to the Third Estate. This huge group included the bourgeoisie—merchants and skilled workers—city workers, and peasants.

Members of the Third Estate were angry. They had few rights. They paid up to half of their income in taxes, while the rich paid almost none.

1. What were the three classes of French society?

_____

_____

THE FORCES OF CHANGE
(**Pages** 652–653)
Why were the French ready for the revolution?

Three factors led to revolution. First, the Enlightenment spread the idea that everyone should be equal. The powerless people in the Third Estate liked that. Second, the French economy was failing. High taxes kept profits low, and food supplies were short. The government owed money. Third, King **Louis XVI** was a weak leader. His wife, **Marie Antoinette,** was unpopular. She was from Austria, France's long-time enemy, and was noted for her extravagant spending.

In the 1780s, France was deep in debt. Louis tried to tax the nobles. Instead, they forced the king to call a meeting of the **Estates-General,** an assembly of delegates of the three estates.

2. What three factors led to revolution?

_____

_____

_____

DAWN OF THE REVOLUTION
(**Pages** 654–655)
How did the Revolution begin?

The meeting of the Estates-General began in May 1789 with arguments over how to count votes. In the past, each estate had cast one vote. The Third Estate now wanted each delegate to have a vote. The king and the other estates did not agree to the plan because the Third Estate was larger and would have more votes.

The Third Estate then broke with the others and met separately. In June 1789, its delegates voted to rename themselves the **National Assembly.** They claimed to represent all the people. This was the beginning of representative government for France.

At one point, the members of the Third Estate found themselves locked out of their meeting. They broke down a door leading to a tennis court. Then they promised to stay there until they made a new constitution. This promise was called the **Tennis Court Oath.**

Louis tried to make peace. He ordered the clergy and nobles to join the National Assembly. However, trouble erupted. Rumors flew that foreign soldiers were going to attack French citizens. On July 14, an angry crowd captured the Bastille, a Paris prison. The mob wanted to get gunpowder for their weapons in order to defend the city.

3. Why did the National Assembly form?

_____

_____

A GREAT FEAR SWEEPS FRANCE
(**Page** 655)
What was the Great Fear?

A wave of violence called the **Great Fear** swept the country. Peasants broke into and burned nobles' houses. They tore up documents that had forced them to pay fees to the nobles. Late in 1789, a mob of women marched from Paris to the king's palace at Versailles. They were angry about high bread prices and demanded that the king come to Paris. They hoped he would end hunger in the city. The king and queen left Versailles, never to return.

4. What happened during the Great Fear?

_____

_____

As you read about the dawn of revolution in France, write notes to answer questions about the causes of the French Revolution.

How did each of the following contribute to the revolutionary mood in France?	
1. The three estates	2. Enlightenment ideas
3. Economic crisis	4. Weak leadership

How did each of the following events lead to the French Revolution?	
5. Meeting of the Estates-General	6. Establishment of the National Assembly
7. Tennis Court Oath	8. Storming of the Bastille

Section 2

Revolution Brings Reform and Terror

Terms and Names

Legislative Assembly Assembly that replaced the National Assembly in 1791

émigrés Nobles and others who left France during the peasant uprisings and who hoped to come back to restore the old system

sans-culottes Radical group of Parisian wage-earners

Jacobin Member of the Jacobin Club, a radical political organization

guillotine Machine for beheading people

Maximilien Robespierre Revolutionary leader who tried to wipe out every trace of France's past monarchy and nobility

Reign of Terror Period of Robespierre's rule

Before You Read

In the last section, you read how the French Revolution began.

In this section, you will learn what course it took and where it led.

As You Read

Use a flow chart to identify the major events that followed the creation of the Constitution of 1791.

THE ASSEMBLY REFORMS FRANCE (Pages 656–657)
What **reforms resulted from the revolution?**

In August 1789, the National Assembly took steps to change France. It made a revolutionary statement called the Declaration of the Rights of Man. One new law ended all the special rights that members of the First and Second Estates had enjoyed. Another law gave all French men equal rights. Though women did not get these rights, it was a bold step. Other laws gave the state power over the Catholic Church.

The new laws about the church divided people who had supported the Revolution.

Catholic peasants remained loyal to the church. They were angry that the church would be part of the state. Thereafter, many of them opposed the Revolution's reforms.

For months, the assembly worked on plans for a new government. During this time, Louis was fearful for his safety. One night, he and his family tried to escape the country. They were caught, brought back to Paris, and placed under guard. This escape attempt made the king and queen more unpopular. It also increased the power of his enemies.

1. What new laws came into being?

_____

_____

DIVISIONS DEVELOP (Pages 657–658)
What groups called for different kinds of changes?

In the fall of 1791, the assembly drew up a new constitution. It took away most of the king's power. The assembly then turned over its power to a new assembly, the **Legislative Assembly.**

This new assembly soon divided into groups. Radicals wanted sweeping changes in the way government was run. Moderates wanted some changes in government, but not as many as the radicals. Conservatives upheld the idea of a limited monarchy and wanted few changes in government.

There were groups outside the Legislative Assembly who wanted to influence the government, too. One group wanted an end to revolutionary changes. This group included the **émigrés,** nobles and others who had fled France during the uprisings. Another group wanted even greater changes. This group included the **sans-culottes.** These wage-earners and small shopkeepers wanted a greater voice in government.

2. In what ways did the émigrés and sans-culottes have opposite goals?

_____

_____

WAR AND EXECUTION
(Pages 658–660)
What caused the French people to take extreme measures?

At the same time, France faced serious trouble on its borders. Kings in other countries feared that revolution would spread to their lands. They wanted to use force to restore control of France to Louis XVI. Soon foreign soldiers were marching toward Paris. Many people thought that the king and queen were ready to help the enemy. Angry French citizens imprisoned them. Many nobles were killed in other mob actions.

The government took strong steps to meet the danger from foreign troops. It took away all the king's powers. In 1792, the National Convention—another new government—was formed. **Jacobins,** members of a radical political club, soon took control of this new government. They declared Louis a common citizen. He was then tried for treason and convicted. Like many others, the king was beheaded by a machine called the **guillotine.** The National Convention also ordered thousands of French people into the army.

3. What happened to the king?

_____

_____

THE TERROR GRIPS FRANCE; END OF THE TERROR (Pages 660–661)
What was the Reign of Terror?

Maximilien Robespierre became leader of France. He headed the Committee of Public Safety. It tried and put to death "enemies of the Revolution." Thousands were killed. Robespierre's rule, which began in 1793, was called the **Reign of Terror.** It ended in July 1794, when Robespierre himself was put to death.

The French people were tired of the killing and the unrest. They wanted a return to order. Moderate leaders drafted a new, less revolutionary plan of government.

4. Where did the Reign of Terror lead?

_____

_____

As you read about the events of the French Revolution, answer the
questions about the time line.

1789 Aug.	**National Assembly adopts Declaration of the Rights of Man.** →	1. What are some rights this document guarantees French citizens?
1790	**National Assembly reforms status of church.** →	2. What caused the peasants to oppose many of these reforms?
1791 Sept.	**National Assembly hands power to Legislative Assembly.** →	3. What political factions made up the Legislative Assembly?
1792 April	**Legislative Assembly declares war on Austria.** →	4. What did European monarchs fear from France?
Aug.	**Parisians invade Tuileries and imprison royal family.**	
Sept.	**Parisian mobs massacre more than 1,000 prisoners.** →	5. What effects did the September Massacres have on the government?
1793 Jan.	**Ex-king Louis XVI is executed.**	
July	**Robespierre leads Committee of Public Safety; Reign of Terror begins.** →	6. What was the stated aim of Robespierre and his supporters?
1794 July	**Robespierre is executed; Reign of Terror ends.** →	7. What were some consequences of the Reign of Terror?
1795	**National Convention adopts new constitution.**	

Napoleon Forges an Empire

Terms and Names

Napoleon Bonaparte Military leader who seized power in France

coup d'état A sudden takeover of a government

plebiscite Vote by the people

lycée Government-run public school

concordat Agreement

Napoleonic Code Complete set of laws set up by Napoleon that eliminated many injustices

Battle of Trafalgar British defeat of Napoleon's forces at sea

Before You Read

In the last section, you read about the Revolution's extremes, including the Reign of Terror.

In this section, you will learn how Napoleon grabbed power and brought order to France.

As You Read

Use a time line to take notes on the events that led to Napoleon's crowning as emperor of France.

NAPOLEON SEIZES POWER
(Pages 663–664)
How did Napoleon rise to power?

Napoleon Bonaparte was born in 1769 on the Mediterranean island of Corsica. When he was nine years old, his parents sent him to military school. In 1785, he finished school and became an artillery officer. When the revolution broke out, Napoleon joined the army of the new government.

In 1795, Napoleon led soldiers against French royalists who were attacking the National Convention. For this, he was thought of as the savior of the French republic.

By 1799, the unsettled French government had lost the people's support.

In a bold move, Napoleon used troops to seize control of the government. This was a **coup d'état,** or a sudden takeover of power. Napoleon then assumed dictatorial powers.

1. How did Napoleon get control of the government?

_____

_____

NAPOLEON RULES FRANCE
(Pages 664–665)
How did Napoleon use the Revolution's ideas in his government?

At first, Napoleon pretended to be the rightfully elected leader of France.

In 1800, a **plebiscite,** or vote of the people, was held to approve a new constitution. The people voted for it overwhelmingly, and Napoleon took power as first consul.

Napoleon made several changes that were meant to build on the Revolution's good ideas:

1. He made tax collection more fair and orderly. As a result, the government could count on a steady supply of money.

2. He removed dishonest government workers.

3. He started **lycées**—new public schools for ordinary citizens.

4. He gave the church back some of its power. He signed a **concordat,** or agreement, with the pope. This gave him the support of the organized church.

5. He wrote a new set of laws, called the **Napoleonic Code,** which gave all French citizens the same rights. However, the new laws took away many individual rights won during the Revolution. For example, they limited free speech and restored slavery in French colonies.

2. What changes did Napoleon make?

_____

_____

_____

_____

NAPOLEON CREATES AN EMPIRE
(**Pages** 665–667)
What **goals did Napoleon have beyond France's borders?**

Napoleon had hoped to make his empire larger in both Europe and the New World. In 1801, he had sent soldiers to retake the island of present-day Haiti. Slaves in that colony had seized power during a civil war. But his troops failed. Napoleon then gave up on his New World plans. In 1803, he sold the largest part of France's North American land—the huge Louisiana Territory—to the United States.

Napoleon had been stopped in the Americas. So he then moved to add to his power in Europe. In 1804, he made himself emperor of France. He took control of the Austrian Netherlands, parts of Italy, and Switzerland. Napoleon's only loss during this time was to the British navy in the **Battle of Trafalgar.** This loss kept him from conquering Britain.

3. Where did Napoleon succeed in adding lands, and where did he fail?

_____

_____

_____

_____

_____

As you read about Napoleon, note the goals and results of some of his actions.

Actions	Goal(s)	Result(s)
1. Establishment of national bank and efficient tax-collection system		
2. Enacting Napoleonic Code of law		
3. Sending troops to Saint Domingue		
4. Selling Louisiana Territory to the United States		
5. Waging Battle of Trafalgar		

Section 4

Napoleon's Empire Collapses

Terms and Names

blockade Forced closing of ports

Continental System Napoleon's policy of preventing trade and communication between Great Britain and other European nations

guerrilla Spanish peasant fighter

Peninsular War War that Napoleon fought in Spain

scorched-earth policy Policy of burning fields and slaughtering livestock so that enemy troops would find nothing to eat

Waterloo Battle in Belgium that was Napoleon's final defeat

Hundred Days Napoleon's last bid for power, which ended at Waterloo

---

Before You Read

In the last section, you read how Napoleon built his power.

In this section, you learn why he lost it.

As You Read

Use a chart to take notes on mistakes Napoleon made and the impact they had on the French Empire.

NAPOLEON'S COSTLY MISTAKES
(**Pages** 668–670)
What mistakes did Napoleon make abroad?

Napoleon's own personality posed a threat to his empire. His love of power pushed him to expand his empire. His efforts to extend French rule led to his empire's collapse.

Napoleon made three costly mistakes. His first mistake was caused by his desire to crush Britain. He wanted to hurt the British economy. So in 1806 he ordered a **blockade.** This was an effort to stop all trade between Britain and the other European nations. Napoleon called this policy the **Continental System.** It was supposed to make continental Europe more self-sufficient.

The effort failed because some Europeans secretly brought in British goods. At the same time, the British put their own blockade around Europe. Because the British navy was so strong, it worked well. Soon the French economy, along with others on the European continent, weakened.

Napoleon's second mistake was to make his brother king of Spain in 1808. The Spanish people were loyal to their own king. With help from Britain, bands of peasant fighters called **guerrillas** fought Napoleon for five years. Napoleon lost 300,000 troops during this **Peninsular War.** (The war gets its name from the Iberian Peninsula on which Spain is located.)

Guided Reading Workbook

Napoleon's third mistake was perhaps his worst. In 1812, he tried to conquer Russia, far to the east. He entered Russia with more than 400,000 soldiers. As the Russians retreated, however, they followed a **scorched-earth policy.** They burned their fields and killed their livestock so Napoleon's armies could not eat what they left behind.

Although the French got as far as Moscow, winter was coming. Napoleon was forced to order his soldiers to head back. On the way home, bitter cold, hunger, and Russian attacks killed thousands. Thousands more deserted. By the time Napoleon's army left Russian territory, only 10,000 of his soldiers were able to fight.

1. What happened to Napoleon in Russia?

_____

_____

_____

_____

_____

NAPOLEON'S DOWNFALL
(Pages 670–671)
What **other defeats did Napoleon suffer?**

Other leaders saw that Napoleon was now weaker. Britain, Russia, Prussia,

Sweden, and Austria joined forces and attacked France. Napoleon was defeated at the Battle of Leipzig, in Germany, in 1813. In 1814, Napoleon gave up his throne and was exiled, or sent away, to the tiny island of Elba off the Italian coast.

Louis XVIII took the throne in Paris. But he quickly became unpopular. The peasants feared the new king would undo the land reforms of the Revolution.

News of Louis XVIII's trouble was all Napoleon needed to try to regain his empire. In March 1815, he escaped from Elba and boldly returned to France. He took power and raised another army.

The rest of the European powers raised armies to fight against Napoleon. Led by the Duke of Wellington, they defeated Napoleon in his final battle near a Belgian town called **Waterloo.** This defeat ended Napoleon's last attempt at power, which was called the **Hundred Days.** He was then sent to the far-off island of St. Helena in the southern Atlantic Ocean. He died there in 1821.

2. What was Napoleon's last attempt at power, and where did it end?

_____

_____

_____

_____

_____

As you read about Napoleon's downfall, write notes in the chart to explain
how each action contributed to his final defeat.

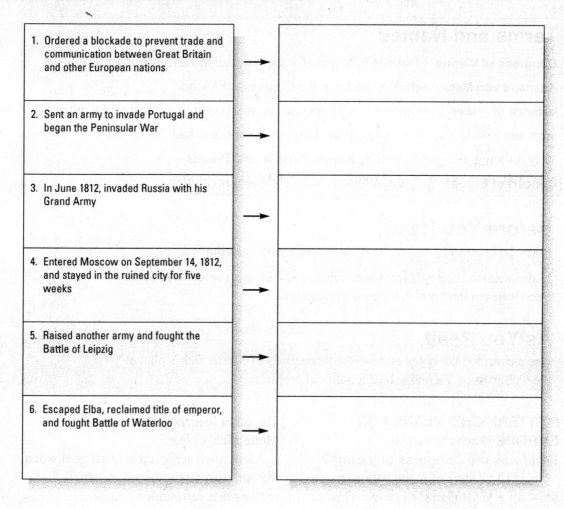

1. Ordered a blockade to prevent trade and communication between Great Britain and other European nations	
2. Sent an army to invade Portugal and began the Peninsular War	
3. In June 1812, invaded Russia with his Grand Army	
4. Entered Moscow on September 14, 1812, and stayed in the ruined city for five weeks	
5. Raised another army and fought the Battle of Leipzig	
6. Escaped Elba, reclaimed title of emperor, and fought Battle of Waterloo	

Section 5

The Congress of Vienna

Terms and Names

Congress of Vienna Meetings in Vienna for the purpose of restoring order to Europe

Klemens von Metternich Key leader at the Congress of Vienna

balance of power Condition in which no one country becomes a threat to the other

legitimacy Bringing back to power the kings that Napoleon had driven out

Holy Alliance League formed by Russia, Austria, and Prussia

Concert of Europe Series of alliances to help prevent revolution

Before You Read

In the last section, you saw how Napoleon's empire collapsed.

In this section, you will learn how the rest of Europe reacted to both the French Revolution and Napoleon's rise and fall.

As You Read

Use a chart to take notes on how the three goals of Metternich's plan at the Congress of Vienna solved a political problem.

METTERNICH'S PLANS FOR EUROPE (Pages 672–673)

What was the Congress of Vienna?

In 1814, leaders of many nations met to draw up a peace plan for Europe. This series of meetings was called the **Congress of Vienna.** The most important person at the Congress of Vienna was the foreign minister of Austria, **Klemens von Metternich.** He shaped the peace conditions that were finally accepted.

Metternich had three goals at the congress. First, he wanted to make sure that the French would not attack another country again. Second, he wanted a **balance of power** in which no one nation was strong enough to threaten other nations. Third, he wanted **legitimacy.** This meant restoring monarchs to the thrones they had before Napoleon's conquests.

The other leaders agreed with Metternich's ideas.

Metternich achieved his first goal when the congress strengthened the small nations that surrounded France. Meanwhile, France was not punished too severely. It remained independent and kept some overseas possessions. This helped achieve Metternich's second goal to create a balance of power.

The congress also worked to fulfill Metternich's third goal. Many rulers were returned to power in states throughout Europe, including France.

The Congress of Vienna created very successful peace agreements. None of the great powers fought against one another for 40 years. Some did not fight in a war for the rest of the century.

1. What three goals did Metternich have?

_____

_____

_____

_____

POLITICAL CHANGES BEYOND VIENNA (Pages 673–675)
How did European leaders respond to the effects of the French Revolution?

Many European rulers were nervous about the effects of the French Revolution. In 1815, Czar Alexander of Russia, Emperor Francis I of Austria, and King Frederick William III of Prussia formed the **Holy Alliance.** Other alliances created by Metternich were called the **Concert of Europe.** The idea of these alliances was for nations to help one another if revolution came.

Across Europe, conservatives held control of European governments. Conservatives were people who opposed the ideals of the French Revolution. They also usually supported the rights and powers of royalty. They did not encourage individual liberties. They did not want any calls for equal rights.

But many other people still believed in the ideals of the French Revolution. They thought that all people should be equal and share in power. Later they would again fight for these rights.

People in the Americas also felt the desire for freedom. Spanish colonies in the Americas revolted against the restored Spanish king. Many colonies won independence from Spain. National feeling grew in Europe, too. Soon people in areas such as Italy, Germany, and Greece would rebel and form new nations. The French Revolution had changed the politics of Europe and beyond.

2. What happened to ideas about freedom and independence?

_____

_____

_____

_____

As you read about the meeting of the Congress of Vienna, fill in the
diagram below.

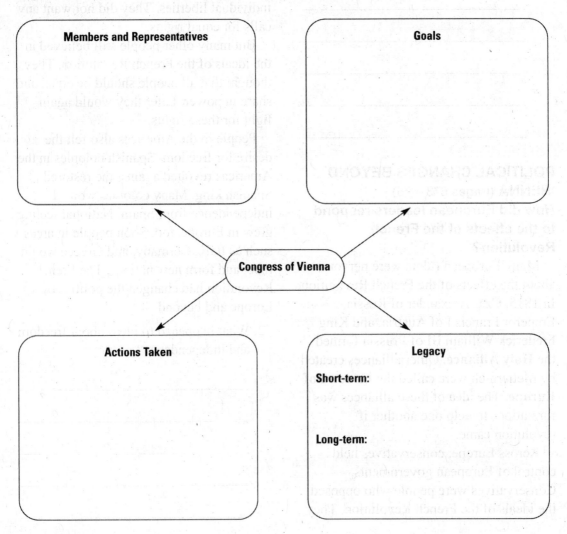

Members and Representatives

Goals

Congress of Vienna

Actions Taken

Legacy

Short-term:

Long-term:

Nationalist Revolutions Sweep the West

Latin American Peoples Win Independence

Terms and Names

peninsulares Latin Americans born in Spain

creoles Spaniards born in Latin America

mulattos Africans or people of mixed European and African ancestry

Simón Bolívar Leader of Venezuelan independence movement

José de San Martín Leader who helped win independence for Chile and Argentina

Miguel Hidalgo Priest who began the revolt against Spanish rule in Mexico

José Morelos Leader of the Mexican revolt after Hidalgo was defeated

Before You Read

In the last section, you read about revolution and the Congress of Vienna.

In this section, you will learn how Latin American countries got their independence.

As You Read

Use a chart to identify details about Latin American independence movements.

COLONIAL SOCIETY DIVIDED
(Pages 681–682)
What classes existed in Latin American society?

In Latin America, society was divided into six classes of people. *Peninsulares*—those born in Spain—were at the top. Next were **creoles,** or Spaniards who had been born in Latin America. Below them were mestizos. Mestizos had mixed European and Indian ancestry. Next were **mulattos,** with mixed European and African ancestry, and then Africans. At the bottom were Indians.

1. Which groups of society were of European ancestry?

_____

_____

REVOLUTIONS IN THE AMERICAS
(Page 682)
Where in Latin America was independence first declared?

In the early 1800s, colonial peoples in Latin America fought for independence. The French colony of Saint Domingue was the first Latin American colony to fight for independence.

Guided Reading Workbook

Almost all of the people who lived in the French colony were slaves of African origin. In 1791, about 100,000 of them rose in revolt. Toussaint L'Ouverture, a former slave, became their leader. In 1802 Napoleon sent troops to the island to end the rebellion. They failed. In 1804, the colony declared its independence as Haiti.

2. How did Haiti become independent?

_____

_____

CREOLES LEAD INDEPENDENCE
(Pages 682–684)
Why did Creoles want independence?

Creoles felt that they were not treated fairly. This bad feeling boiled over when Napoleon overthrew the king of Spain and named his own brother as king. Creoles in Latin America had no loyalty to the new king. They revolted. Even after the old king was restored, they did not give up their fight for freedom.

Two leaders pushed much of South America to independence. **Simón Bolívar** was a writer, fighter, and political thinker. He survived defeats and exile to help win independence for Venezuela in 1821. **José de San Martín** helped win independence for Argentina in 1816 and Chile in 1818. Bolívar led their combined armies to a great victory in 1824. This victory gained independence for all the Spanish colonies.

3. Which two great leaders led the fights for independence in Venezuela, Chile, and Argentina?

_____

_____

MEXICO ENDS SPANISH RULE; BRAZIL'S ROYAL LIBERATOR
(Pages 685–686)
How did Mexico and Brazil achieve independence?

In Mexico, mestizos and Indians led the fight for independence. In 1810, **Miguel Hidalgo,** a village priest, called for a revolt against Spanish rule. Creoles united with the Spanish government to put down this revolt by the lower classes.

Hidalgo lost, but Padre **José María Morelos** took over leadership of the rebels. Fighting continued until 1815, when the creoles won.

After a revolution in Spain put a new government in power, the creoles joined with the other groups fighting for independence. In 1821, Mexico won its independence. In 1823, the region of Central America separated itself from Mexico.

In Brazil, 8,000 creoles signed a paper asking the son of Portugal's king to rule an independent Brazil. He agreed. Brazil became free that year through a bloodless revolt.

4. How were the drives for independence in Mexico and Brazil different?

_____

_____

As you read this section, fill out the chart below to help you better
understand why and how Latin Americans fought colonial rule.

Independence for Haiti

Reasons	Strategy
1. Why did slaves in the French colony of Saint-Domingue revolt?	2. What events led up to General Dessalines's declaration of independence for Haiti?

South American Wars of Independence

Reasons	Strategy
3. How did events in Europe lead to revolution in the Spanish colonies?	4. What tactics did José de San Martín and Simón Bolívar use to defeat Spanish forces in South America?

End of Spanish Rule in Mexico

Reasons	Strategy
5. What is the significance of the *grito de Dolores*?	6. What role did Indians, mestizos, and Creoles play in Mexico's independence from Spain?

Guided Reading Workbook

Europe Faces Revolutions

Terms and Names

conservative People who supported the monarchy

liberal People who wanted to give more power to elected legislatures

radical People who wanted to end the rule by kings and give full voting rights to all people

nationalism Belief that a person's loyalty belongs to the nation itself instead of to the nation's ruler

nation-state Country with its own independent government

the Balkans Region including all or part of present-day Greece, Albania, Bulgaria, Romania, Turkey, and former Yugoslavia

Louis-Napoleon Winner of the presidential election in France in 1848; later emperor

Alexander II Ruler of Russia who freed the serfs

Before You Read

In the last section, you read about Latin American independence movements.

In this section, you will learn about revolutions in Europe.

As You Read

Use a web diagram to identify major revolutions in Europe.

CLASH OF PHILOSOPHIES; NATIONALISM DEVELOPS
(Pages 687–689)
What forces and peoples struggled for power?

There was a power struggle in Europe in the first half of the 1800s. Three forces were involved. **Conservatives** wanted to continue to support the kings who had ruled these lands for many centuries. These were nobles and other people who owned large amounts of property. **Liberals** wanted to give more power to elected legislatures. They were typically middle-class merchants and business people. **Radicals** wanted the end of rule by kings and full voting rights for all.

At the same time, another movement arose in Europe—**nationalism.** This was the belief that a person's loyalty should go not to the country's ruler but to the nation itself. When the nation also had its own independent government, it became a **nation-state.** Nationalists thought that people with a common language and culture were a nation. And they had the right to their own government. These ideas grew out of the French Revolution.

1. What different goals did conservatives, liberals, and radicals have?

_____

Guided Reading Workbook

NATIONALISTS CHALLENGE CONSERVATIVE POWER
(**Pages** 689–690)
What changes were occurring in Western Europe?

The first people to win self-rule during this period were the Greeks. Greece had been part of the Ottoman Empire for centuries. The Ottomans controlled most of **the Balkans.** That region includes most of modern Greece, Albania, Bulgaria, Romania, Turkey, and the former Yugoslavia. In 1821, the Greeks revolted against Turkish rule. The Greeks won their independence by 1830.

Other revolts broke out in other parts of Europe. In 1830, the Belgians declared their independence from rule by the Dutch. Nationalists began a long struggle to unify all of Italy. The Poles revolted against Russian rule. Conservatives managed to put down these rebellions. However, new ones broke out again in 1848 among Hungarians and Czechs. Once again, they were put down forcibly.

2. What groups challenged conservative rule?

_____

RADICALS CHANGE FRANCE
(**Page** 690)
Why did French radicals lose?

Events differed in France. Riots in 1830 forced the king to flee, and a new king was put in his place. Another revolt broke out in 1848. The king was overthrown and a republic established. However, the radicals who had won began arguing. They differed over how much France should be changed. Some wanted only political changes. Others wanted social and economic changes that would help the poor.

When these forces began to fight in the streets, the French gave up on the radical program. They introduced a new government. It had a legislature and a strong president. The new president was **Louis-Napoleon,** Napoleon Bonaparte's nephew. He later named himself emperor of France. He built railroads and helped industry. The economy got better and more people had jobs.

3. What did Louis-Napoleon accomplish for France?

_____

REFORM IN RUSSIA (**Pages** 690–691)
How did Alexander II change Russia?

In the early 1800s, Russia still did not have an industrial economy. The biggest problem was that serfdom still existed there. Peasants were bound to the nobles whose land they worked. Russia's rulers were reluctant to free the serfs, though. They feared they would lose the support of the nobles.

A new ruler of Russia, **Alexander II,** decided to free the serfs. Though it seemed bold, Alexander's move went only part way. Nobles kept half their land and were paid for the other half that went to the peasants. The former serfs were not given the land. They had to pay for it. This debt kept them still tied to the land. The czar's efforts to make changes ended when he was assassinated in 1881. Alexander III, the new czar, brought back tight control over the country. He also moved to make the economy more industrial.

4. What major reform was made in Russia at this time?

_____

As you read about uprisings in Europe, make notes in the chart to explain
the outcomes of each action listed.

1. French citizens' armies win their revolution for liberty and equality. →	
2. Greeks revolt against the Ottoman Turks. →	
3. Nationalist groups in Budapest, Prague, and Vienna demand independence and self-government. →	
4. Charles X tries to set up an absolute monarchy in France. →	
5. Paris mobs overthrow monarchy of Louis-Philippe. →	
6. Louis-Napoleon Bonaparte is elected president of France and later assumes the title of Emperor Napoleon III. →	
7. In the Crimean War, Czar Nicholas I threatens to take over part of the Ottoman Empire. →	
8. Alexander II issues the Edict of Emancipation. →	

Nationalist Revolutions Sweep the West

Nationalism
Case Study: Italy and Germany

Terms and Names

Russification A policy of forcing Russian culture on ethnic groups in the Russian Empire

Camillo di Cavour Prime minister who unified northern Italy

Giuseppe Garibaldi Leader of the Red Shirts who won control over parts of southern Italy

Otto von Bismarck Leader who worked to expand Prussia

Junker Wealthy German landholders

realpolitik Tough, practical politics

kaiser Emperor

Before You Read

In the last section, you read about revolutions and reform in western Europe.

In this section, you will learn about nationalism.

As You Read

Use a time line to list major events in the unification of Italy and of Germany.

NATIONALISM: A FORCE FOR UNITY OR DISUNITY (Pages 692–693)
What is nationalism?

Nationalists thought that many factors linked people to one another. First was nationality, or a common ethnic ancestry. Shared language, culture, history, and religion were also seen as ties that connected people. People sharing these traits were thought to have the right to a land they could call their own. Groups with their own government were called nation-states.

Leaders began to see that this feeling could be a powerful force for uniting a people. The French Revolution was a prime example of this. However, nationalism could also be a force to rip apart empires. This happened in three empires in Europe.

1. What shared characteristics can unite people and create a strong national feeling?

_____

_____

NATIONALISM SHAKES AGING EMPIRES (Page 693)
Why did nationalism divide empires?

Feelings of nationalism threatened to break apart three aging empires. The Austrian Empire was forced to split in two.

Guided Reading Workbook

One part was Austria, the other was Hungary. In Russia, harsh rule and a policy called **Russification** that forced other peoples to adopt Russian ways helped produce a revolution in 1917. This revolution overthrew the czar. Like the other two, the Ottoman Empire broke apart around the time of World War I.

2. What three empires were torn apart by nationalism?

_____

_____

CAVOUR UNITES ITALY (Page 694)
How did nationalism unite Italy?

Italians used national feeling to build a nation, not destroy an empire. Large parts of Italy were ruled by the kings of Austria and Spain. Nationalists tried to unite the nation in 1848. But the revolt was beaten down. Hopes rested with the Italian king of the state of Piedmont-Sardinia. His chief minister was Count **Camillo di Cavour.** Cavour worked to expand the king's control over other areas of the north.

Meanwhile, **Giuseppe Garibaldi** led an army of patriots that won control of southern areas. Garibaldi put the areas he conquered under control of the Italian king. In 1866, the area around Venice was added to the king's control. By 1870, the king completed the uniting of Italy.

3. Who helped unify Italy?

_____

BISMARCK UNITES GERMANY;
A SHIFT IN POWER (Page 695)
How was Germany united?

Germany had also been divided into many different states for many centuries. Since 1815, 39 states had joined in a league called the German Confederation. Prussia and Austria-Hungary controlled this group. Over time, Prussia rose to become more powerful. Leading this move was prime minister **Otto von Bismarck.** He was supported by wealthy landowners called **Junkers.** Bismarck was a master of **realpolitik**—tough power politics.

Bismarck worked to create a new **confederation** of German states. Prussia controlled it. To win the loyalty of German areas in the south, he purposefully angered a weak France so that it would declare war on Prussia. Prussia won the Franco-Prussian War in 1871. The war with France gave the southern German states a nationalistic feeling. They joined the other states in naming the king of Prussia as emperor, or **kaiser,** of a strong united Germany.

These events changed the balance of power in Europe. Germany and Britain were the strongest powers, followed by France. Austria, Russia, and Italy were all even weaker.

4. What was the result of the defeat of France and the uniting of Germany?

_____

_____

Name _____ Class _____ Date _____

As you read this section, take notes to answer questions about nationalism as a force for disunity and unity.

How did nationalism lead to the breakup of these empires?		
1. Austro-Hungarian	2. Russian	3. Ottoman

How did each of the following help unify Italy?		
4. Camillo di Cavour	5. Giuseppe Garibaldi	6. King Victor Emmanuel

How did each of the following lead to German unification?		
7. Policy of realpolitik	8. Seven Weeks' War	9. Franco-Prussian War

Guided Reading Workbook

Nationalist Revolutions Sweep the West

Section 4

Revolutions in the Arts

Terms and Names

romanticism Movement in art and ideas that focused on nature and the thoughts and feelings of individuals

realism Movement in art that tried to show life as it really was

impressionism Style of art using light and light-filled colors to produce an "impression"

Before You Read

In the last section, you read how political borders changed in Europe.

In this section, you will learn about changes in the arts in Europe.

As You Read

Use a chart to note details about movements in the arts.

THE ROMANTIC MOVEMENT
(Pages 698–699)
What is romanticism?

In the early 1800s, the Enlightenment gradually gave way to another movement, called **romanticism.** This movement in art and ideas focused on nature and on the thoughts and feelings of individuals. Gone was the idea that reason and order were good things. Romantic thinkers valued feeling, not reason, and nature, not society. Romantic thinkers held idealized views of the past as simpler, better times. They valued the common people. As a result, they enjoyed folk stories, songs, and traditions. They also supported calls for democracy. However, not all romantic artists and thinkers supported all of these ideas.

Romantic writers had different themes. During the first half of the 19th century, the Grimm brothers collected German folk tales. They also created a German dictionary and worked on German grammar. These works celebrated being

German long before there was a united German nation. Other writers wrote about strong individuals. Some wrote about beauty and nature.

Germany produced one of the greatest early Romantic writers. Johann Wolfgang von Goethe wrote *The Sorrows of Young Werther*. It was a story about a young man who kills himself after he falls in love with a married woman.

British Romantic poets William Wordsworth and Samuel Taylor Coleridge honored nature as the source of truth and beauty. A type of horror story called a Gothic novel became popular. Novels such as Mary Shelley's *Frankenstein* were tales about good and evil.

Romanticism was important in music as well. Composers wrote music to appeal to the hearts and souls of listeners. Ludwig van Beethoven, a German, was the foremost of these composers. Romanticism made music a popular art form.

Guided Reading Workbook

1. What did Romantic thinkers and artists value?

_____

_____

_____

_____

2. For what purposes did writers use realism?

_____

_____

_____

_____

THE SHIFT TO REALISM IN THE ARTS (Pages 700–701)
What is realism?

In the middle 1800s, the grim realities of industrial life made the dreams of romanticism seem silly. A new movement arose—**realism.** Artists and writers tried to show life as it really was. They used their art to protest unfair social conditions. French writer Emile Zola's books revealed harsh working conditions for the poor. They led to new laws aimed at helping those people. In England, Charles Dickens wrote many novels that showed how poor people suffered in the new industrial economy.

A new device, the camera, was developed in this period. Photographers used cameras to capture realistic images on film.

IMPRESSIONISTS REACT AGAINST REALISM (Page 701)
What is impressionism?

In the 1860s, Parisian painters reacted against the realistic style. This new art style—**impressionism**—used light and light-filled colors to produce an impression of a subject or moment in time. Impressionist artists like Claude Monet and Pierre-Auguste Renoir glorified the delights of the life of the rising middle class in their paintings. Composers created music that set a mood by using different music structures, instruments, or patterns.

3. What was the focus of impressionist art and music?

_____

_____

As you read this section, take notes to answer questions about the artistic and intellectual movements of the 1800s.

Nationalism ushers in a romantic movement in arts and ideas.

1. How did the ideas of romanticism contrast with Enlightenment ideas?	2. How were the ideas of romanticism reflected in literature?
3. How was romanticism reflected in art?	4. How did romanticism affect the music of the time?

Realism in art and literature replaces romantic idealism.

5. What trends or events led to a shift from romanticism to realism?	6. How did photography exemplify the art of the new industrial age?
7. What were some themes common to realist novels?	8. What did realist novelists hope to accomplish with their exposés?